# Skier's Guide to
# CALIFORNIA

Volume 1: Northern California and Lake Tahoe

# Other books on California that you'll enjoy from Gulf Publishing Company:

*Birder's Guide to Northern California*
by LoLo and Jim Westrich

*California Herbal Remedies*
by LoLo Westrich

*Camper's Guide to California Parks, Lakes, Forests, and Beaches, Volume 1: Northern California*
by Mickey Little

*Camper's Guide to California Parks, Lakes, Forests, and Beaches, Volume 2: Southern California*
by Mickey Little

*Diving and Snorkeling Guide to Northern California*
by Steve Rosenberg

*Diving and Snorkeling Guide to Southern California*
by Dale and Kim Sheckler

*Guide to Shipwreck Diving: Southern California*
by Darren Douglass

*Mariner's Atlas: Southern California*
by ChartCrafters, Inc.

*Skier's Guide to California: Volume 2: Central Sierras and Southern California*
by Nadine Nardi Davidson

# Skier's Guide to CALIFORNIA

## Volume 1: Northern California and Lake Tahoe

❄

### Nadine Nardi Davidson

**Gulf Publishing Company**
Houston, Texas

> *To my husband, Dr. Harold Davidson,
> for taking me to all these places.*

## Skier's Guide to California
## Volume 1: Northern California and Lake Tahoe

Copyright © 1991 by Nadine Nardi Davidson. All rights reserved. Printed in the United States of America. This book, or parts thereof, may not be reproduced in any form without permission of the author and the publisher.

Cover photo: Backcountry skiing in Lake Tahoe, © Larry Proser.

**Library of Congress Cataloging-in-Publication Data**

Davidson, Nadine Nardi.
  Skiers's guide to California/Nadine Nardi Davidson.
     p.     cm.
  Includes index.
  Contents: v. 1. Northern California and Lake Tahoe
  **ISBN 0-87201-795-8**
  1. Skis and skiing—California—Guide-books.  2. Skis and skiing—Nevada—Guide-books.  3. California—Description and travel—1981- —Guide-books.  4. Nevada—Description and travel—1981- —Guide-books.  I. Title.
GV854.5.C2D38   1991
796.93'09794—dc20                                         90-39838
                                                             CIP

# Contents

Guide to the Trail Maps .................................................... vii
Acknowledgments ........................................................... viii
Preface ........................................................................... ix
How to Use This Guide ..................................................... x
Ski Tips ........................................................................... xii

### Part I: Northern California

1. Cedar Pass ................................................................. 3
2. Mt. Shasta Ski Park .................................................... 11
3. Lassen Park Ski Area .................................................. 22
4. Stover Mountain ......................................................... 31
5. Coppervale ................................................................. 35
6. Plumas Eureka Ski Bowl ............................................. 42

Color Trail Maps ............................................................. 51

### Part II: Lake Tahoe Area

7. Sugar Bowl ................................................................. 77
8. Donner Ski Ranch ....................................................... 87
9. Soda Springs .............................................................. 94
10. Boreal ....................................................................... 99
11. Tahoe Donner ........................................................... 107
12. Northstar-at-Tahoe .................................................... 117
13. Diamond Peak .......................................................... 130
14. Mount Rose .............................................................. 143
15. Squaw Valley ............................................................ 151
16. Alpine Meadows ....................................................... 171
17. Granlibakken ............................................................ 181
18. Homewood ................................................................ 186

| | |
|---|---|
| 19. Heavenly Valley | 196 |
| 20. Sierra Ski Ranch | 214 |
| 21. Kirkwood | 223 |
| Glossary of Ski Terms | 234 |
| Index | 237 |

Courtesy of Diamond Peak.

# Guide to the Trail Maps

| | |
|---|---|
| Alpine Meadows | 68 |
| Boreal | 62 |
| Cedar Pass | 6 |
| Coppervale | * |
| Diamond Peak | 60 |
| Donner Ski Ranch | 54 |
| Granlibakken | * |
| Heavenly Valley | 70-71 |
| Homewood | 74 |
| Kirkwood | 73 |
| Lassen Park Ski Area | 64 |
| Mount Rose | 65 |
| Mt. Shasta Ski Park | 55 |
| Northstar-at-Tahoe | 56 |
| Plumas Eureka Ski Bowl | 43 |
| Sierra Ski Ranch | 72 |
| Soda Springs | 53 |
| Squaw Valley | 66 |
| Stover Mountain | * |
| Sugar Bowl | 52 |
| Tahoe Donner | 63 |

\* *Not available*

# Acknowledgments

❄

I wish to thank Stacy Herbert and Dr. Elena Lorenz for their research assistance, and Joan Prestine, Sandy Hatch, Dr. Claire Panosian, Lillian Ross, and Terry Dunnahoo for their helpful suggestions.

I am grateful to the following individuals for their cooperation and assistance: Dan Nourse, Alpine Meadows; Earle Davis, Boreal/Soda Springs Ski Areas; Don Lancaster and Wilma Andrews, Cedar Pass Ski Corporation; Bob Sorvaag, Coppervale; Lee Weber, Diamond Peak; Sheila Walsh, Donner Ski Ranch; Christy Keeney, Granlibakken; Tim Newhart, Diana Arington, and John Hulcrun, Heavenly Valley; Mark Lowenstern and Roberto Taddeo, Homewood; Jack Wolf and Jan Vandermade, Kirkwood; Darren Houston, Lassen Park Ski Area; Todd Marjoris, Mount Rose; Tim Larive and Sandy Schwartz, Mt. Shasta; Julie Maurer and Mike Wolterbeek, Northstar-at-Tahoe; Philip Intorf, Plumas Ski Club; Kathy Pavich and Judi Harkins, Sierra Ski Ranch; Bill Jensen and Suellen McGeorge, Squaw Valley; Barbara Montandon and Ted Pilgrum, Stover Mountain Ski Club; Jeff Gedrose and Lori Bery, Sugar Bowl; Don Frye, Tahoe Donner; and Tom Hiscox, Lake Tahoe Visitors Authority.

# Preface

With more than 40 ski areas and nearly 50,000 acres of skiable terrain, California and Nevada offer some of the best skiing in the world. Straddling California and Nevada, the Lake Tahoe basin alone offers 15 downhill and more than 10 cross-country ski areas, with some of the most stunning scenery in the world. In fact, no matter where you are in California or Nevada, you're no more than a three- or four-hour drive away from a ski area.

Volume 1 of the *Skier's Guide to California* covers the ski areas found in Northern California and the Lake Tahoe Area. Volume 2 of the series covers the ski areas in the Central Sierras and Southern California.

The ski areas detailed in these volumes range from small, homey facilities to the largest ski area in the nation; from posh resorts with exciting night life and state-of-the-art equipment to casual, western-style resorts where the night life consists of dogsled rides on moonlit nights. There are ski areas for every pocketbook; some where children ski free, some where they cater to senior citizens, and even one, Badger Pass (Volume 2), that grants a sympathy discount to 40-year-olds.

These books are designed to help the reader discover all the variety that California and Nevada offer in cross-country skiing, snowmobiling, tobogganing, sledding, tubing, and winter mountaineering.

*Nadine Nardi Davidson*
Los Angeles, California

# How To Use This Guide

A paragraph or two at the beginning of each chapter introduces the reader to each ski area. The *Location* section explains how to get to each facility by car, commercial air service, train, and bus.

The *Terrain* section highlights a sampling of runs at each resort and tells skiers where they can find beginner, intermediate, and advanced terrain. The trail maps use round circles to indicate the easiest runs on the mountain, squares to indicate more difficult terrain, and diamonds to indicate the most difficult terrain. Double diamonds are used to identify runs for experts only, or to indicate that the run may require special skills.

In general, ski areas rate their runs in comparison to other runs on the same mountain and not according to a standardized formula. Thus, a run that is assigned a black diamond at one ski area might be considered intermediate at another.

Information included in the *Facilities* section reviews special rates or programs not listed in the boxed chart, *Facilities at a Glance*. Mountain statistics and rate information in the boxed facilities charts are based on information supplied by each ski area. Some data, particularly figures on average annual snowfall, are not uniformly calculated and are based on best estimates. Although rates are current at the time of this writing, they are subject to change at any time without notice. On the average, lift ticket and ski school rates tend to go up about $2 per year.

The *Special Events* are included to give readers an idea of the types of special events each area offers. These events vary from year to year. For updates on special events, readers are advised to check with the ski area.

*Winter Activities* contains information on nearby cross-country trails, snowmobiling, snow play, sleigh rides, ice skating, dogsledding, and mountaineering. The availability of these activities depends on snow conditions, and readers are advised to check current conditions before heading for the mountains.

Information on *Winter Activities, Shopping,* and *Après-Ski* can change quickly, as retail establishments can go in and out of business routinely in mountain communities.

*Restaurants* and *Accommodations* are not intended to be complete, but were included for the reader's convenience. Attempts were made, where possible, to include restaurants and lodges in each of three categories; that is, expensive ($$$), moderate ($$), and inexpensive ($). Some properties are included because of their proximity to the ski area, and their inclusion does not necessarily attest to their quality. In some cases, such as in national forests and other areas with little commercial development, the only dining and lodging facilities available may be quite basic and not meet AAA standards. Such motels and lodges have been listed for the convenience of travelers who wish to stay near the ski area.

Restaurant price ratings are based on the approximate average cost of a dinner entrée. Restaurants where the average cost of entrées is under $7.50 have been assigned one dollar sign ($). Restaurants with entrées under $17.50 receive two dollar signs ($$), and three dollar signs ($$$) have been assigned to restaurants with an average entrée cost of more than $17.50.

Hotel prices have been divided into three categories as well. One dollar sign ($) indicates inexpensive, with some rooms under $55 per night. Two dollar signs ($$) indicate moderate—some rooms under $135 per night. Three dollar signs ($$$) indicate expensive—rooms are more than $135 per night, based on weekend rates for a double room.

Dollar ratings for condominiums are based on the lowest price for a 1-bedroom unit. One dollar sign ($) has been assigned to properties with 1-bedroom units under $100, two dollar signs ($$) for properties offering 1-bedroom units under $150, and three dollar signs ($$$) to those starting above $150. Properties where the smallest unit has 2 bedrooms are assigned ($) for units under $135, ($$) for those under $200, and ($$$) for 2-bedroom units over $200.

As this book goes to press, listings are current, but are subject to change without notice.

# Ski Tips

❄

Some ski areas in California and Nevada are more suited than others for certain ability levels, budgets, or tastes. These ski tips are designed to help you quickly find an area that fits your needs, although we recommend that you consider all the ski areas in this book before making your final decision.

**Best bets for:**

**Advanced Skiers**
- Kirkwood
- Squaw Valley
- Sugar Bowl

**Après-ski Activities**
- Heavenly Valley
- Squaw Valley

**Beginners**
- Boreal
- Lassen Park Ski Area
- Tahoe Donner

**Budget Minded**
- Cedar Pass
- Coppervale
- Donner Ski Ranch
- Granlibakken
- Plumas Eureka Ski Bowl
- Stover Mountain

**Children Under 7**
- Northstar-at-Tahoe
- Squaw Valley
- Tahoe Donner

**Children 7-12**
- Kirkwood
- Northstar-at-Tahoe
- Squaw Valley

**Families, All Ages**
- Diamond Peak
- Kirkwood
- Northstar-at-Tahoe

**Intermediate Skiers**
- Alpine Meadows
- Heavenly Valley
- Kirkwood
- Mt. Shasta Ski Park

**Luxury Seekers**
- Squaw Valley

**Night Skiers**
- Boreal
- Donner Ski Ranch
- Mt. Shasta Ski Park

**Physically Challenged Skiers**
- Alpine Meadows
- Diamond Peak
- Kirkwood
- Mount Rose

**Racing**
- Alpine Meadows
- Sierra Ski Ranch
- Soda Springs
- Squaw Valley

**Scenic Areas**
  Diamond Peak, North Shore, Lake Tahoe
  Heavenly Valley, South Shore, Lake Tahoe
  Homewood, West Shore, Lake Tahoe
  Lassen Park Ski Area, Lassen National Park

**Seniors**
  Alpine Meadows
  Boreal
  Diamond Peak

**Singles**
  Sierra Ski Ranch
  Squaw Valley

**Snowboarders**
  Boreal
  Donner Ski Ranch
  Homewood
  Mt. Shasta Ski Park

**Youth and Student Groups**
  Mt. Shasta Ski Park
  Sierra Ski Ranch

# Part I

## ❄

# Northern California

# Cedar Pass

❄

*502 Short Street
Alturas, CA 96101
Information: (916) 233-2113
Snowphone: (916) 233-3323*

### Driving distances

| | |
|---|---|
| Alturas | 17 mi |
| Chico | 231 mi |
| Eureka | 314 mi |
| Klamath Falls | 101 mi |
| Medford | 177 mi |
| Red Bluff | 195 mi |
| Redding | 162 mi |
| Reno | 186 mi |
| Sacramento | 318 mi |
| Susanville | 125 mi |

*For road conditions, call
(916) 233-5761*

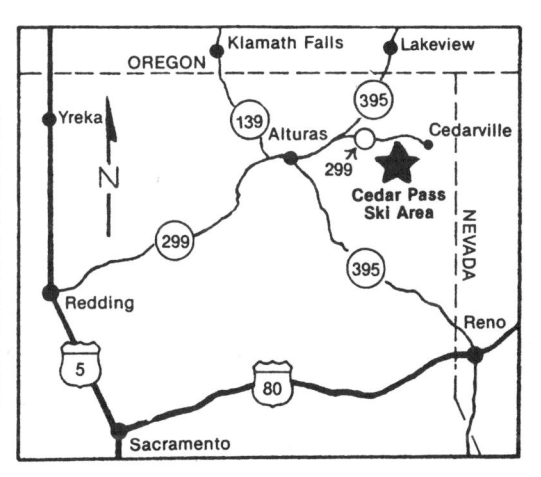

Isolated in the remote northeast corner of California, Cedar Pass is a small weekend and holiday ski area that reflects a quiet, neighborly character. In a county that bills itself as "the place where the West still lives," it's an area where ranch hands work and look like cowboys and where the deer and antelope still play. And with only 2.3 residents per square mile, traffic and lift lines are as foreign as an English saddle. Although the runs are short, a dedicated skier can log as many as 30 runs a day amid the tranquility and grace of white firs and golden eagles.

Operated and maintained by volunteers, Cedar Pass is the epitome of a local, friendly ski area and offers beginner to advanced skiing terrain at modest prices.

## LOCATION

Cedar Pass is in Modoc County off SH 299 between US 395 and Cedarville, 20 miles west of Alturas, California, and 186 miles north of Reno, Nevada.

## FACILITIES AT A GLANCE

*Season:* Mid-November–Late March or Easter.
*Hours:* 10 a.m.– 4 p.m. Saturdays, Sundays, and holidays.
*Night Skiing:* None.
*Area:* 100 acres with 7 runs.
  Beginner: 20%
  Intermediate: 50%
  Advanced: 30%
*Base Elevation:* 6,000 ft
*Summit Elevation:* 6,400 ft
*Vertical Drop:* 400 ft
*Longest Run:* 1,600 ft
*Snowmaking:* None.
*Snowboarding:* Permitted. No chair lift access.
*Avg. Annual Snowfall:* 40 in.
*Lift Capacity:* 125 per hr.

*Lifts:* 2 surface lifts (1 Rope Tow and 1 T-Bar)

| Name | Length | Vertical Rise |
| --- | --- | --- |
| Rope Tow | 350 ft | 150 ft |
| T-Bar | 1,400 ft | 400 ft |

*Lift Passes:*

|  | All Day | Afternoon |
| --- | --- | --- |
|  | 10 a.m.–4 p.m. | 1 p.m.–4 p.m. |
| Adults | $12 | $9 |
| Children 6–18 | $10 | $7 |
| Children 5 and under | FREE | FREE |

*Season Passes:* When puchased prior to December 8—$108 adult, $90 youth (6–18). When purchased after December 9—$120 adult, $100 youth (6–18). Children 5 and under ski free. Family pass rates available.

*Food & Drink:* A food bar at the base lodge sells beverages, hot dogs, and other snacks.

*Parking & Transportation:* Parking is free at the base. No RV overnight parking.

*Ski Rentals:*   None.

*Ski School:*   By appointment only. Contact Don Lancaster, (916) 233-2819.

*Races & Clinics:*   None.

*Day Care:*   None at Cedar Pass. Child Care Resource and Referral in Alturas will refer babysitters and day-care facilities available for drop-ins, (916) 233-5437.

*Camper Facilities:*   Brass Rail Campground, 6 miles west of the ski area on US 395, has 53 RV sites. Rates are $9.56 per night or $12.42 with hookups. Showers, laundry, heated pool, spa on premises, (916) 233-5322. The Sunrise Motel & Trailer Park in Cedarville, 1/2 mile east of Cedar Pass, has 14 RV sites with hookups available for $10 each. Laundry, restrooms, showers, and dump on site, (916) 279-2161.

*Medical:*   First aid by ski patrol. Modoc Medical Center is 20 miles west in Alturas.

Access from Lakeview, Oregon, is via US 395 south to SH 299, and then east 11 miles to the ski area. From Klamath Falls, Oregon, take SH 139 south 81 miles. Turn left on SH 299 at Canby and go 19 miles to Alturas. At Alturas, turn north on US 395 and go 6 miles to SH 299 east. From I-5 and Redding, head northeast on SH 299 for 145 miles to Alturas, then north on US 395 to SH 299. From Reno and US 395, turn east on SH 299, 6 miles after Alturas.

The closest airport to Cedar Pass is at Klamath Falls, Oregon, with direct flights from San Francisco, San Jose, Redding, Portland, Seattle, Eugene, and Spokane, and connections from other cities. The closest major airport is at Reno, with direct service from many U.S. cities. United Express and American Eagle offer direct air service into Redding Airport from Sacramento, San Francisco, and San Jose.

Amtrak's "Coast Starlight" from Sacramento, with connections from other California cities, stops in Klamath Falls. The "California Zephyr" stops in Reno/Sparks daily. Four-wheel-drive and cars equipped for skiers are available in Medford and Klamath Falls with 3-day notice.

Greyhound stops in Alturas on the way from Reno.

## TERRAIN

All runs at Cedar Pass can be accessed by the T-Bar and most are groomed to offer a choice of terrain. All 7 trails are steepest off the top, gradually rolling

6   Skier's Guide to California

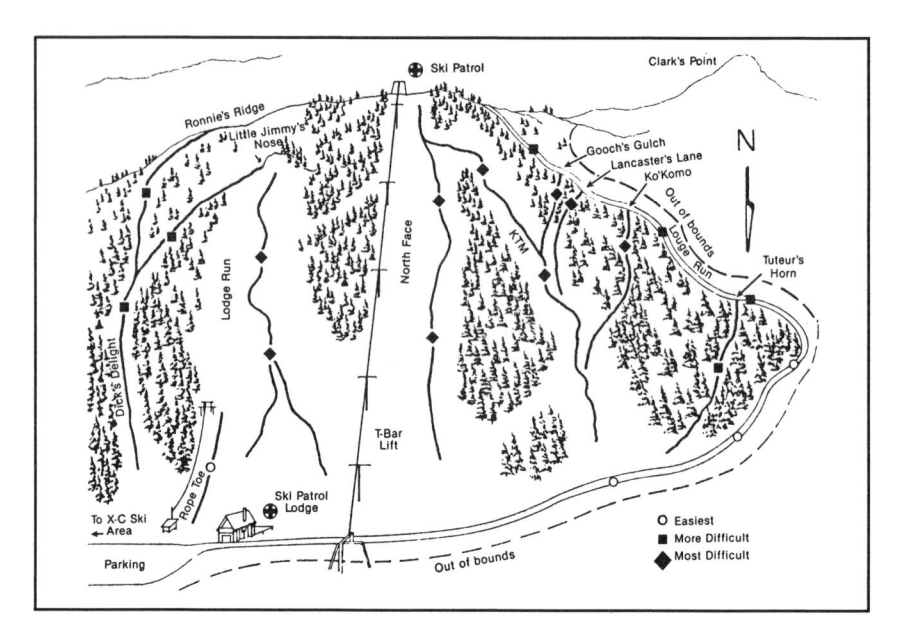

*Cedar Pass*                    Courtesy of Cedar Pass Ski Corporation.

out to more intermediate pitches midway down the mountain. To the right off the T-Bar, the ungroomed *KTM* is a challenging powder run that narrows into a chute. Another advanced run, *North Face*, along the T-Bar, is generally groomed smooth along one side and littered with moguls on the other, giving skiers a choice of terrain. The adjacent *Lodge Run* banks off a ridge with slopes at different angles and one side steeper than the other.

On the far left, the fall line is most intense on *Ronnie's Ridge* and *Little Jimmy's Nose*, but both turn into a long, straight cruising run on *Dick's Delight*. *Louge Run* is the easiest way down from the top and also the longest route. At the summit, it's intermediate but, after a sharp right turn toward the bottom, it lightens into beginner terrain. Four paths through the trees, *Gooch's Gulch*, *Landcaster's Lane*, *Ko-Komo*, and *Tuteur's Horn*, are slightly steeper shortcuts to the base.

The beginner area at the bottom of the hill has its own rope tow. Beginners using the T-Bar for the first time will want to avoid the face and ski the gentler perimeters.

## SPECIAL EVENTS

- *Valentine's Day Skifest*—February. Downhill and cross-country races for all ages.

## WINTER ACTIVITIES

### Cross-Country

Ungroomed and unmarked trails of varying difficulty are located around Cedar Pass ski area. Access to the area via the T-Bar is $3. Children under 5 are free. No lessons or ski rentals on site. Cross-country equipment rentals are available at the Sports Hut in Alturas.

### Snowmobiling

Snowmobiling is permitted south of Cedar Pass at *Bear Flats*, and 40 miles north at *Ft. Bidwell*. No rentals on site.

### Tobogganing, Tubing, and Snow Play

A hill at the top of SH 299, 1 mile west of Cedar Pass, is used for tubing and sledding. No equipment rental on site.

### Ice Skating

The *Alkali Lakes*, 2 miles east of Cedar Pass off SH 299, are frozen in winter and used for ice skating. No services on site. The outdoor *Alturas Ice Rink*, West C and Fourth St., Alturas, is available for public use when weather conditions permit. No rentals or lessons on site. No fee.

### Ice Fishing

Ice fishing is permitted on nearby lakes, but not streams. A license and permit are required.

## OTHER ACTIVITIES

**Bowling:** Modoc Lanes, Alturas.
**Cinema:** The Niles Theater, Alturas.

## SHOPPING

The closest groceries are located west on SH 299 in Cedarville at the *Cedarville Grocery* on Main, and at the *California Market* on 1st St. *Surprise Valley Drug* is also on Main in Cedarville.

Most of the shops in the vicinity of Cedar Pass are located 20 miles southwest in Alturas. Groceries and liquor are available at *Better Buy Market, California Market,* and *Walt's Grocery. B&W Alturas Pharmacy* and *Enderlin's Modoc Pharmacy* carry sundries and drugs. Gift items are featured at the *What Not Craft Shop,* 330 N. Main St. The *Wooden Duck,* 127 Main St., carries an assortment of gourmet coffees, teas, baskets, and gifts. Antique hunters can check out *Yesterday's Memories* at 907 N. Main. *Calico Cow* and *Ardies Classie Lassie,* also on Main St., carry women's apparel.

## APRÈS-SKI

The lounge at the *Brass Rail* in Alturas is a popular gathering spot. *Benny's,* also in Alturas, with a pool table and jukebox, is another local hangout. Skiers headed east from Cedar Pass can dance away any leftover energy until 2 a.m. at the *Alkali Saloon* in Cedarville.

## RESTAURANTS

**Beacon Restaurant   $$**                                      *(916) 233-2623*
2nd and Main St. in Alturas. Known for broasted chicken, the Beacon Restaurant also serves barbecued ribs, steak, and pork chops. Open from 6 a.m. to 10 p.m.

**Brass Rail Basque Restaurant   $$**                           *(916) 233-2906*
US 395, 6 miles from Cedar Pass. Family-style dining on selections that vary daily from chili to steak to ravioli to scallops. Open from 5:30 p.m. to 10:30 or 11 p.m. Closed Mondays.

**California Pines Lodge   $$**                                 *(916) 233-4672*
Centerville Road, 9 miles south of Alturas. Dinner selections feature prime rib and fish, including lobster tails. Open for breakfast, lunch, and dinner from 8 a.m. to 8:30 p.m. Friday, Saturday, and Monday, and 8 a.m. to 5 p.m. on Sunday. Closed Tuesday through Thursday.

**Country Hearth   $$**                                         *(916) 279-2280*
547 Main St., Cedarville. The Country Hearth restaurant and bakery features chicken-fried steak and shrimp as well as nightly specials, including Mexican fare on Tuesdays and pizza on Fridays. Open from 6 a.m. to 8:30 or 9 p.m.

**Ft. Bidwell Hotel Restaurant   $$**                           *(916) 279-6199*
Main and Garrison, Ft. Bidwell, 25 miles north of Cedar Pass. The Ft. Bidwell combines American and Italian cuisine with entrées of calamari, pasta, chicken, NY steak, and red snapper. Beer and wine. Open for dinner daily from 5 p.m. to 9 p.m., and for Sunday breakfast.

**Historic Niles Hotel and Saloon**  $$ *(916) 233-4761/3261*
304 S. Main St., Alturas. Serves cornish game hen, halibut, NY steak, top sirloin, prime rib, lobster, and shrimp. Open Wednesday through Sunday, 5:30 p.m. to 9:30 p.m., and until 10 p.m. on weekends. The saloon is open from 11 a.m. to 2 a.m. daily. Occasional live entertainment.

**King Wah's**  $$ *(916) 233-4657*
404 W. 12th St., Alturas. Chinese and American cuisine includes chow mein, chicken, and sweet-and-sour spareribs. Open daily from 11 a.m. to 10 p.m.

**Pasta & Pizza**  $$ *(916) 233-5600*
220 S. Main St., Alturas. Menu offerings include pizza, linguini, chicken parmigiana, scallopini, lasagna, tortellini, and ravioli. Beer and wine. Open daily from 11 a.m. to 11 p.m.

**The Alamo**  $ *(916) 233-3094*
County Road 54, Alturas. Mexican menu choices include tacos, burritos, chile rellenos, enchiladas, tostadas, tamales, and quesadillas. Open from 4 p.m. to 9 p.m. Fridays and Saturdays, and 11 a.m. to 7 p.m. on Sundays.

**Eleventh Frame Restaurant**  $ *(916) 233-5569*
119 S. Main St., Alturas. Located at the Modoc Lanes bowling alley, the restaurant offers entrées of steak, veal cutlets, ham, chicken, and liver. Open from 9 a.m. to 7 p.m. Monday through Thursday and to 8 p.m. on weekends. Bar open until 2 a.m. daily.

**Ila's Restaurant**  $ *(916) 279-2157*
S. Main St., Cedarville. Casual restaurant featuring pork chops, turkey, shrimp, and steak. Open for breakfast, lunch, and dinner from 6 a.m. to 9 p.m.

**Stage Stop Pizza**  $ *(916) 233-3121*
203 S. Main St., Alturas. In addition to pizza, shrimp, chicken, scallops, ravioli, and submarine sandwiches are offered from 3 p.m. to 10 p.m. Monday through Friday, and 11 a.m. to 11 p.m. Saturday, 10 p.m. on Sunday.

**Wagon Wheel Cafe**  $ *(916) 233-5166*
308 W. 12th St., Alturas. A mix of southwestern and downhome entrées include fried chicken, enchiladas, meatloaf, barbecued chicken, stuffed bell peppers, and fish. Beer and wine. Open from 6 a.m. to 9 p.m. Monday through Saturday, and 7 a.m. to 9 p.m. Sunday.

## ACCOMMODATIONS

**California Pines Lodge**  $$ *(916) 233-4672*
Centerville Road, 9 miles southwest of Alturas. Rooms with double and queen-size beds have TV, phones, and daily towel service. Open Friday through Monday only. Restaurant and bar on premises.

**Best Western Trailside Inn**  $ *(916) 233-4111*
343 N. Main St., Alturas. Thirty-nine units with king-size, queen-size, and double beds, TV, phones, and daily maid service. Four rooms with kitchenettes.

**Drifters' Inn**  $ *(916) 233-2438*
SH 299 and US 395 (Lakeview Hwy), Alturas. Nineteen rooms, two with kitchens, have 1, 2, or 3 beds, TV, phones, in-room coffee, and showers or bath/shower combinations. Maid service.

**Dunes Motel**  $ *(916) 233-3545*
511 N. Main St., Alturas. Forty-nine attractive rooms with king-size, 1 or 2 queen-size, or double beds with TV, phones, and daily maid service. 24-hr restaurant. Senior discounts.

**Essex Motel**  $ *(916) 233-2821*
1216 N. Main St., Alturas. Thirteen units have double, queen, or king-size beds with private baths, TV, phones and in-room coffee. Some kitchenettes. Maid service.

**Ft. Bidwell Hotel**  $ *(916) 279-6199*
Main and Garrison, Ft. Bidwell, 25 miles north of Cedar Pass. Originally built in 1906, the Ft. Bidwell is an historic hotel with double and single beds with private baths. No TV or phones in rooms. TV in lobby. Maid service. Breakfast is included in the rate.

**Hacienda Motel**  $ *(916) 233-3459*
At the junction of US 395 and SH 299. Twenty rooms and suites with double, king, and queen-size beds, TV, phones, and maid service.

# Mt. Shasta Ski Park

*104 Siskiyou Ave.*
*Mt. Shasta, CA 96067*
*Information: (916) 926-8610*
*Snowphone: (916) 926-8686*

### Driving distances

| | |
|---|---|
| Alturas | 202 mi |
| Chico | 133 mi |
| Eureka | 209 mi |
| Klamath Falls | 89 mi |
| Medford | 106 mi |
| Mt. Shasta | 12 mi |
| Redding | 64 mi |
| Reno | 235 mi |
| Sacramento | 233 mi |
| San Francisco | 282 mi |
| San Jose | 310 mi |

*For road conditions, call (916) 842-2716*

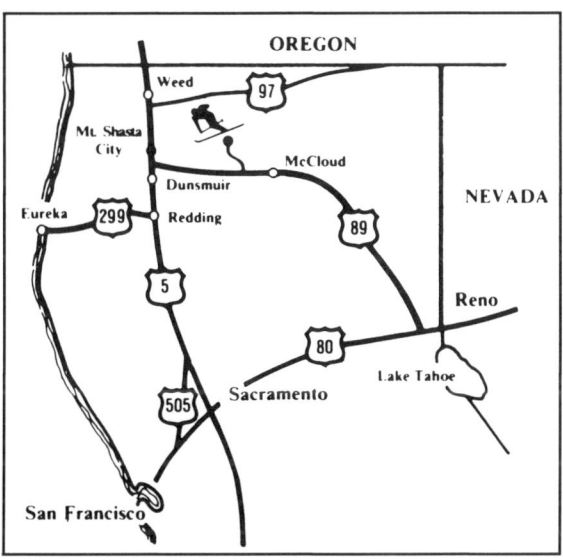

Siskiyou County in northern California is dense with volcanic forests, craggy peaks, and wild rivers. At 14,162 ft, the imposing Mt. Shasta towers above all, including the nearby city and lake, which is the largest man-made lake in California.

Mt. Shasta Ski Park sits on the southeast flank of the mountain, its 150 acres, kindling aspirations for further development. The raw material for additional slopes on the mountain is abundant. Future expansion plans call for three additional chair lifts, a tripling of the skiable acreage, and an increase in vertical footage to 2,300 ft. But, as growth is not a simple issue in a community that prides itself on environmental concerns, the fate of further development of the Mt. Shasta Ski Park or of a proposed adjacent ski area remains unresolved.

In the meantime, the ski area draws skiers from northern California to its easily accessible slopes for both day and night skiing. And, with economical lodging in town and free lift passes for children under 8, the mountain offers families an affordable opportunity for winter activity in an unpretentious environment.

## LOCATION

Mt. Shasta Ski Park is off SH 89 in Siskiyou County, 12 miles east of I-5 and the city of Mt. Shasta.

From the north or south, exit I-5 at SH 89 and head east 6 miles to Ski Park Hwy. Turn left, or north, 4 miles to the ski area.

United Express and American Eagle offer direct air service into Redding Airport from Sacramento, San Francisco, San Jose, and Klamath Falls, Oregon, with connecting flights from other cities. Additional air service from San Francisco is available 133 miles southeast in Chico. United Airlines and USAir also fly directly into Medford, Oregon, 106 miles north of Mt. Shasta, from Los Angeles, San Diego, San Francisco, and Portland, Oregon.

With advance notice, 4-wheel-drive cars are available from Avis at the Redding, Medford, and Chico airports. Also upon request, National Car Rental at the Redding Airport offers ski racks for an additional charge.

ABS (Airport Bus Service) transports passengers from the Redding Airport to Mt. Shasta for $80 per van one way. The vehicle accommodates up to 6 people, (916) 222-5456.

Amtrak's "Coast Starlight" from Sacramento, with connections from other California cities, stops in Dunsmuir, 7 miles south of Mt. Shasta City. There are no car rental agencies at the Amtrak stop in Dunsmuir.

Greyhound has daily service into Mt. Shasta from several California cities.

## TERRAIN

The terrain at Mt. Shasta Ski Park is graded into separate sections of difficulty. The beginner slopes are grouped together off Marmot Ridge, while most of the intermediate and advanced slopes are cut from the higher, perpendicular Douglas Butte. The runs on Douglas Butte also fall neatly into two sides, with the intermediate runs on one side and the most difficult runs on the other. Thus, skiers can head confidently for their favorite terrain.

Groomed less frequently than the other advanced runs, the *West Face*, under the Douglas Lift, presents the biggest moguls and greatest degree of difficulty. The smoother *North Saddle* remains a favorite cruiser for both advanced and intermediate skiers. Another favorite is the longest run via *North Saddle* to *Spotted Owl* and *Horseshoe Bend*.

Beginners can ski from top to bottom uninterrupted by more difficult terrain by taking the Marmot Lift to *Telemark* and then *Blue Grass* to *Winter Way*.

For those who seek the enchantment of skiing through the trees, opportunities are everywhere on the mountain, but not advisable in poor visibility.

A *half-pipe* for snowboarders is located on the lower part of *Coyote Road*.

## FACILITIES

Mt. Shasta Ski Park offers discounts almost daily. On Tuesdays, all lift tickets are $12. Skiers get two passes for the price of one when they ski on Wednesday nights. On Thursdays, a free lesson is included in the price of the lift ticket and, on Fridays, ski, boot, and pole rentals are $5.

### FACILITIES AT A GLANCE

| | |
|---|---|
| *Season:* | Mid-November–Late April. |
| *Hours:* | 9 a.m.–4 p.m. Sunday–Tuesday. |
| | 9 a.m.–9 p.m. Wednesday–Saturday. |
| *Night Skiing:* | On 7 runs, Wednesday–Saturday. |
| *Area:* | 300 acres with 22 runs. |
| | Beginner: 20% |
| | Intermediate: 60% |
| | Advanced: 20% |
| *Base Elevation:* | 5,500 ft |
| *Summit Elevation:* | 6,600 ft |
| *Vertical Drop:* | 1,100 ft |
| *Longest Run:* | 1.2 miles. |
| *Snowmaking:* | On 30 acres. |
| *Snowboarding:* | Permitted. |
| *Avg. Annual Snowfall:* | 106 in. |
| *Lift Capacity:* | 3,950 per hr. |
| *Lifts:* | 2 triple chair lifts and 1 surface tow |

| Name | Length | Vertical Rise |
|---|---|---|
| Douglas Lift | 3,200 ft | 1,112 ft |
| Marmot Lift | 3,600 ft | 688 ft |
| Ski School Lift | NA | 50 ft |

*(continued)*

*(continued from previous page)*

| Lift Passes: | All Day | Afternoon/Night* |
|---|---|---|
| | 9 a.m.–4 p.m. | 12:30 p.m.–4:00 p.m. |
| Adults | $23 | $16 |
| Children 8–12 | $16 | $11 |
| Children under 8 | $3 | $3 |
| Seniors 62+ | $16 | $11 |

*Night skiing 4 p.m.–10 p.m. Wed–Sun.

| Multiday Rates: | Day use or night use. | |
|---|---|---|
| | Adult | Child/Senior |
| 2 consecutive days | $42 | $28 |
| 3 consecutive days | $60 | $40 |

| Season Passes: | Adult | Child/Senior |
|---|---|---|
| Ski any day | $460 | $320 |
| Ski midweek | $300 | $200 |
| Ski night only | $150*/$200 | $110*/$150 |
| Ski after February 15 | $250 | $175 |

*When purchased by December 15.

*Group Rates:* Available by prior arrangement for 15+ persons.

*Food & Drink:* A cafeteria, full bar, and 15,000-sq-ft heated patio are located in the Panther Creek Lodge. Breakfast and lunch are served daily; dinner when open for night skiing. Vending machines and a lunch room are located in the adjacent Red Fir Lodge.

*Parking & Transportation:* The upper and lower parking lots hold 800 cars and limited buses. RV parking permitted overnight. No hookups.

*Ski Rentals:* Base lodge shop open 8 a.m.–4:30 p.m., and 8 a.m.–10 p.m. for night skiing. Includes skis, boots, poles.
    All day: Adult $16. Child $12.
    Half day: Adult $13. Child $10.
    Ski pants: $7.
    Snowboards: $25 all day. $15 half day.
      $27 high-performance board.
      $23 half-day high performance.

*Ski School:* Phone (916) 926-8617
    *Method:* ATM.

*Ski School:* (continued)
   *Ski School Director:*   Janine Gerdes.
   *Class Lessons:*   10 a.m., 11:30 a.m., 1:30 p.m., and 3 p.m.
     $18   (1 1/2 hr)
     $25   (3 hr)
   *Learn-to-Ski Package:*   Wednesday through Friday. Includes 1 1/2-hr class lesson, lift ticket and rental equipment.
     $35 adult. $30 child 8–10/senior. $12.50 child under 8.
   *"Pup's" Package:*   Ages 4–7 years, 10 a.m.–3 p.m.
     $25   1 1/2 hr lesson, lift ticket, and equipment.
     $40   3-hr lesson, lift ticket, equipment, and lunch.
     $55   All day, including lunch.
   *Private Lessons:*   $30 per hr.
   *Snowboard Lessons:*   $15 1 1/2-hr class lesson.
                         $24 1 1/2-hr private lesson.

*Races & Clinics:*
   *Coin-operated Timer:*   Slalom course on North Saddle, weekends, for 50¢ a run. Electronic timing.
   *Clinics:*   10 a.m.–11:30 a.m./1:30 p.m.–3 p.m. Includes giant slalom or slalom techniques for groups of 3 or more. $20 1 1/2-hr session. $25 two sessions. $70 two consecutive days.
   *Private Race Training:*   $30 per hr. $50 2 hrs. $20 for an additional person. Two person maximum. Thursday night races sponsored by local ski shop.

*Day Care:*   Day care for ages 2–12 available at Mt. Shasta Montessori & Day Care in Mt. Shasta from 7 a.m. to 5 p.m. $2.20 per hr includes insurance and snacks, but not lunch, (916) 926-2331.

*Camper Facilities:*   RV sites and showers are $12 at Chateau Shasta Mobile Home and RV Park at 704 Old Stage Road in Mt. Shasta. At the Mt. Shasta KOA at 900 N. Mt. Shasta Blvd., cabins, tents, or RV sites are $12 to $16.50 with full hookups. Bathrooms, game room, laundry, and store on site, (916) 936-4029 or (800) 736-3617. Lake Siskiyou Campground, W.A. Barr Road in Mt. Shasta, is open for winter camping, (916) 926-2618.

*Medical:*   First aid by ski patrol. Closest hospital is Mercy Medical Center in Mt. Shasta, 12 miles west. Helicopter evacuation available.

*Other:*   Ski check on weekends for $1.

## SPECIAL EVENTS

- *Junior Race Camp*—December. 5-day training camp for all ages.
- *Santa Claus Appearance*—Christmas week.
- *California Snowboard Series*—January. Half-pipe, moguls, and slalom races.
- *Coyote Classic*—January. Slalom and giant slalom races.
- *Shasta Alpine/Telemark Race*—January and March.
- *Special Olympics Skiathon*—February.
- *Alpenfest Winter Carnival*—February. Para-skiing demonstration, fireworks, triathlon (downhill, cross-country, and running), snow sculpture, slalom races, USSA freestyle contest, Bavarian music, air shows, torchlight parade.
- *Junior Bobcat Championships*—February. Races for ages 4 to 18.
- *Sweetheart Day at the Park*—February. Couples race for prizes.
- *Shasta Schuss*—February. Races for trophy.
- *Rotary Skiathon*—March. Money-raiser for the Special Olympics.
- *Shasta Snowboard Challenge*—March.
- *Easter Bunny Appearance*—Easter week.

## WINTER ACTIVITIES

### Cross-Country

The closest cross-country area is located just west of SH 89 and Ski Park Hwy. The ungroomed trails are the site of the Nordic segment of the Winter Triathlon.

*Castle Lake Cross-Country Ski Area* is 11 miles west of the town of Mt. Shasta, off W.A. Barr Road. The 30-odd miles of packed and groomed trails are 15% beginner, 45% intermediate, and 40% advanced. The longest trail, Trinity, is a 7-mile advanced trail. Trail passes are $10 adult and $9 for ages 8–12 or 65–75. Children under 8 and seniors over 75 are free. Group lessons and junior ski lessons begin at 10 a.m. and 1 p.m. daily. Rates are from $10 to $20. Private lessons are $30 an hour. Skis, boots, and poles are $9.50 a day. Facilities include a warming hut with food and beverages, equipment rentals and accessories, restrooms, and parking lot for 80 cars. Multi-day rates and night skiing available.

Additional advanced trails are located at *Scott Camp Creek*, off the road to Castle Lake. Ski packages with lodging in Mt. Shasta or at Scott Camp Chalet are also available, (916) 926-3443.

*Mt. Shasta Cross-Country* is located on Everett Memorial Hwy, in the Shasta-Trinity National Forest, 10 miles east of I-5 and 20 miles from Mt. Shasta Ski Park. The 2,000 acres here include 3 miles of marked beginner and intermediate trails and unmarked terrain for advanced skiers. Parking at the junction of Everett Memorial Hwy and Lower Sand Flat Road is limited to 2 or 3 cars. The beginner trail is level and runs 1.3 miles to Sand Flat.

Farther up the road, at the junction with Upper Sand Flat Road, there is parking for 15 or 20 cars. The trail is 1/2 mile to Sand Flat. The mile-long Overlook Loop Trail connects to Lower Sand Flat Trail and provides views of the city of Mt. Shasta.

A larger parking lot that holds 50 or 60 cars is located on Everett Memorial Hwy at Bunny Flat, about 12 miles east from I-5. The 3/4 mile trail from Bunny Flat is intermediate, with gentle, open terrain that connects to the Sand Flat trails.

From the Bunny Flat trailhead to the peak, it takes experienced skiers about 10 hours via Avalanche Gulch or Cascade Gulch, and about two hours to ski back down. Skiers should be aware of avalanche hazards in these areas.

The Forest Service posts bulletins at the Sand Flat and Bunny Flat junctions with information on trails and emergency procedures. Restrooms are available at Bunny Flat. There are no lessons or equipment rentals on site, but rentals are offered nearby at the House of Ski, 1208 Everett Hwy, (916) 926-2359. For additional information on Mt. Shasta cross-country, contact the Mt. Shasta Ranger District, (619) 926-4511.

## Snowmobiling

Two nearby areas for snowmobiling are located at *Pilgrim Creek Road* at McCloud and *Medicine Lake/Harris Springs Road* off SH 89 just east of Bartle. Snowmobiling is permitted opposite the Mt. Shasta cross-country area, south of Everett Memorial Hwy and adjacent to *Bunny Flat*. No rentals or lessons available on site. *The Deer Mt. Snowmobile Park* is located on the north side of Mt. Shasta peak, via US 97, 17 miles east of Weed and 38 miles from Mt. Shasta Ski Park. A paved parking lot is 4 miles south on Deer Mt. Road. Restrooms are located at the site.

## Tobogganing, Tubing, and Snow Play

A snow-play area with parking is located at *Snowman's Hill*, at the junction of SH 89 and Ski Park Hwy, (916) 926-4511. Another area for sledding, tubing, and play is at *Bunny Flat* on Everett Memorial Hwy, 10 miles east of I-5, adjacent to the Mt. Shasta cross-country trails. Equipment rentals are not available at either site.

More than 1,000 ft of beginning to advanced luge runs are located at *Castle Lake* cross-country area. The cost is $1 for the first run, $5 for six runs, and $10 for 13 runs.

**Ice Skating**

*Castle Lake* at the end of Castle Lake Road, adjacent to the Nordic ski area, offers 10,000 sq ft of skating, a warming hut, and skate rentals. A full day of skating is $5.50 or $3.50 for half-day. Rental skates are $4. For information, call (916) 926-3443.

**Ice Fishing**

*Castle Lake*, 10 miles southwest of the city of Mt. Shasta, is a popular ice fishing spot for rainbow and brook trout. The road to the lake is usually accessible to cars in winter. It's important to check road and weather conditions as well as ice thickness before venturing out on the lake. Contact the Mt. Shasta Ranger District, (916) 926-4511.

Other lakes in the area popular for ice fishing are *Gumboat Lake* and *Mumbo Lake*.

## OTHER ACTIVITIES

**Cinema:** Palace Theater, Weed.
**Fitness and Racquetball:** Mt. Shasta Racquetball, Mt. Shasta.
**Golf:** Lake Shastina Golf Resort and Weed Golf Club, Weed.
**Museums:** Sisson Museum, Mt. Shasta.

## SHOPPING

In addition to the retail shop at Mt. Shasta Ski Park, ski equipment and snowboards are available at the *Sportman's Den*, 402 N. Mt. Shasta Blvd., the *House of Ski*, on Everett Memorial Hwy, and the *Fifth Season*, 426 N. Mt. Shasta Blvd.

Groceries and liquor are available 9 miles away in McCloud at *Mac's Liquor and Deli*, 116 N. Minnesota, and in Mt. Shasta at *Mt. Shasta Supermarket*, corner of Lama and Chestnut St. Food and spirits are also available at *Cervelli's Market & Deli*, 625 S. Mt. Shasta Blvd., *George's Liquors*, 419 Chestnut St., and *Sports & Spirits*, 300 W. Lake.

Gift items and collectibles are displayed at *Marty's Enterprises*, W. Minnesota in McCloud, and at *Gower's House of Music & Gifts* and *My Favorite Things*, both on Mt. Shasta Blvd. in Mt. Shasta. Also in Mt. Shasta, *Accents Boutique*, *Directions*, and *Fashion Crossroads*, all on Mt. Shasta Blvd., specialize in women's clothing, while *J & J Clothing Co.* features men's wear.

## APRÈS-SKI

The bar in the lodge is open through the lunch hour until 5 p.m., or 10 p.m. for night skiing. Popular gathering spots for après-ski relaxing include the lounge at *The Tree House Motor Inn* and the bar at *Mike and Tony's*. *Lalo's* is the place for Mexican-style appetizers. For dancing, *Gelli's* presents live music Thursday, Friday, and Saturday nights from 9 p.m. to 2 a.m. No cover charge. The *Gold Room* also features disco or live bands until 2 a.m. No cover charge.

## RESTAURANTS

**Bellissimo**  $$  *(916) 926-4461*
204 A W. Lake St., Mt. Shasta. Bellissimo features Oriental and American cuisine, including Thai prawns, Chinese chicken breast, rib-eye steak, pasta, and homemade cheesecake. Open for dinner on weekends.

**McCloud Guest House**  $$  *(916) 964-3160*
606 W. Colombero Dr., 9 miles east of Mt. Shasta Ski Park. This turn-of-the-century dining room retains original touches, including imported woodwork, beveled glass, and mirrors. A massive fireplace warms the foyer. Entrées include veal scallopini, coquilles St. Jacques, and roast prime rib of beef au jus, as well as chicken and seafood selections. Beer and wine. Open Thursday through Sunday.

**Michael's**  $$  *(916) 926-5288*
313 N. Mt. Shasta Blvd., Mt. Shasta. Open Tuesday through Saturday from 11 a.m. to 9 p.m., Michael's is a candlelit, romantic restaurant featuring Italian favorites such as manicotti and veal picatta. Beer and wine.

**Mike and Tony's**  $$  *(916) 926-4792*
501 S. Mt. Shasta Blvd., Mt. Shasta. American and Italian dishes include pasta, steak, and chicken. Closed Wednesdays.

**Piemont**  $$  *(916) 926-2402*
1200 S. Mt. Shasta Blvd., Mt. Shasta. Family-style Italian cuisine is the specialty of the house. Entrées include steak, as well as homemade fresh ravioli and other pastas. Closed Mondays.

**Tree House Inn Restaurant**  $$  *(916) 926-3101*
Lake St. at the central Mt. Shasta exit off I-5. The Tree House menu features steak, chicken, and seafood, including beer-batter-dipped jumbo prawns. Inclusive dinners offer a choice of soup or salad bar, rice or vegetable. Weight watchers and children's plates are also available. Open for breakfast, lunch, and dinner.

**Jerry's Restaurant**  $  *(916) 926-4818*
401 W. Lake St., Mt. Shasta. Jerry's is a family-style restaurant offering sandwiches, burgers, seafood, steaks, salads, and munchies. Open 24 hours.

**Lalo's    $**                                                    *(916) 926-5123*
520 N. Mt. Shasta Blvd., Mt. Shasta. Lalo's is open seven days a week for breakfast, lunch, and dinner. It offers Mexican and American food including steak, seafood, and combination dinners with tacos, enchiladas, and chili rellenos. Salad bar. Children's and weight-watcher's menu. Pleasant room with tables and booths.

**Marilyn's Family Restaurant    $**                                *(916) 926-9918*
1136 S. Mt. Shasta Blvd., Mt. Shasta. Marilyn's bills itself as the home of the 10¢ cup of coffee. American and Italian cooking are featured as well as great pies. Beer and wine.

**Perko's Koffee Kup    $**                                         *(916) 926-6404*
112 Morgan Way in the Mt. Shasta Shopping Center. Perko's is a family-style restaurant open for breakfast, lunch, and dinner. Dinner selections include charbroiled steak, seafood, chicken, and fresh pasta. Ask for doggie bag. Junior and senior menus.

## ACCOMMODATIONS

The closest accommodations to the Ski Park are located 9 miles east in McCloud and 12 miles west in Mt. Shasta.

**Best Western Tree House Motor Inn    $$**                          *(916) 926-3101*
*Nationwide, (800) 528-1234*
Lake St. at the Central Mt. Shasta exit off I-5, 12 miles from the ski area. The premier lodge in town, the Tree House has 95 comfortable rooms. Most rooms and suites have 1 king-size or 1 or 2 queen-size beds, a sitting area, phone, TV, vanity with double sinks, and combination shower and bath. Facilities include a restaurant, coffee shop, indoor swimming pool, conference room, and large, rustic lounge with fireplace.

**Lake Shastina Golf Resort    $$**                                  *(916) 938-3201*
5925 Country Club Dr., Weed, 27 miles from Mt. Shasta Ski Park. One-bedroom condominiums and 2-, 3-, and 4-bedroom homes on golf course or lake. Condominium units each have a bedroom and a hide-a-bed in the living room. Units have decks, TV, phones, kitchenettes, and daily maid service. Winter rates include free golf on 18-hole course designed by Robert Trent Jones, Jr. Other facilities include a golf shop, two tennis courts, restaurant, and lounge open for lunch daily and dinner on Friday and Saturday. Ski packages available.

**McCloud Guest House    $$**                                        *(916) 964-3160*
606 West Colombero Dr., McCloud. Built in 1907, this restored country home was once the residence of a lumber company president. Former guests included President Herbert Hoover, actress Jean Harlow and various members of the Hearst family. The 5 spacious rooms are individually decorated in turn-of-the-century style and have queen-size beds and private baths, some with clawfoot tubs. A large parlor with a pool table is located on the second floor, with the

restaurant on the first floor. Breakfast is included in the rate. The guest house is open Thursday through Sunday.

**Mt. Shasta House   $$**   *(916) 926-5089*
113 S. A St., Mt. Shasta. A small bed-and-breakfast house on a residential street. Five cozy rooms sleep from 2 to 4 and have TV and phones. Two rooms have private baths. Fireplace in lounge. Breakfast included.

**Alpine Lodge Motel   $**   *(916) 926-3145*
908 S. Mt. Shasta Blvd. Twenty rooms and suites, some with electric fireplaces and kitchens. In-room coffee, TV, and phones. Spa on premises. Restaurant and lounge adjacent.

**Das Alpenhaus   $**   *(916) 926-4617*
504 S. Mt. Shasta Blvd. The motel has 18 small rooms, with TV, some with kitchenettes. Showers in the bathrooms. In-room coffee provided. No phones. Modest and clean. Ski packages available.

**Evergreen Motel   $**   *(916) 926-2143*
1312 Mt. Shasta Blvd., Mt. Shasta. Twenty rooms with queen-size beds, some rooms with kitchens, all have TV and phones. Spa on premises.

**Finlandia Motel   $**   *(916) 926-5596*
1612 S. Mt. Shasta Blvd. Motel with 13 rooms with mountain views, kitchens, and TV. No phone in rooms.

**Mt. Shasta Ranch   $**   *(916) 926-5089*
1008 W. A. Barr Road, Mt. Shasta. The Mt. Shasta Ranch is a congenial bed-and-breakfast a few minutes' drive from the center of town. Four comfortable bedrooms in the main house each have a private bath. Behind the main house, 5 bedrooms share bathrooms and a kitchen, an arrangement favored by couples and friends traveling together. A separate two-bedroom cottage, heated by a wood-burning stove, includes a small kitchen, living area, TV, and bathroom. No phone. For an additional charge, guests can share tables for a typical breakfast of sweet rolls, bagels, quiche with chili sauce, juice, and coffee. A piano, TV, and fireplace add a homey touch to the comfortable den.

**Stoney Brook Inn   $**   *(916) 964-2300*
309 W. Colombero, McCloud. A restored bed-and-breakfast with 17 rooms, some with kitchens. Suites have bedrooms with private baths, sitting areas, TV, and kitchens.

**Swiss Holiday Lodge   $**   *(916) 926-3446*
2400 S. Mt. Shasta Blvd., south of Mt. Shasta. Rooms with king-size, queen-size, and double beds all have mountain views. TV, HBO, and complimentary coffee. One-bedroom apartments each include a fireplace, full kitchen, and phone. Other facilities include a spa and community kitchen on site. Ski packages available.

# Lassen Park Ski Area

*Lassen Volcanic National Park*
*Mineral, CA 96063*
*Information: (916) 595-3376*
*Snowphone: (916) 595-4464*

### Driving distances

| | |
|---|---|
| Alturas | 172 mi |
| Chico | 68 mi |
| Eureka | 228 mi |
| Fresno | 344 mi |
| Los Angeles | 565 mi |
| Klamath Falls | 214 mi |
| Medford | 228 mi |
| Red Bluff | 49 mi |
| Redding | 79 mi |
| Reno | 148 mi |
| Sacramento | 185 mi |
| San Diego | 699 mi |
| San Francisco | 235 mi |
| San Jose | 265 mi |

*For road conditions, call*
*(916) 244-1500*

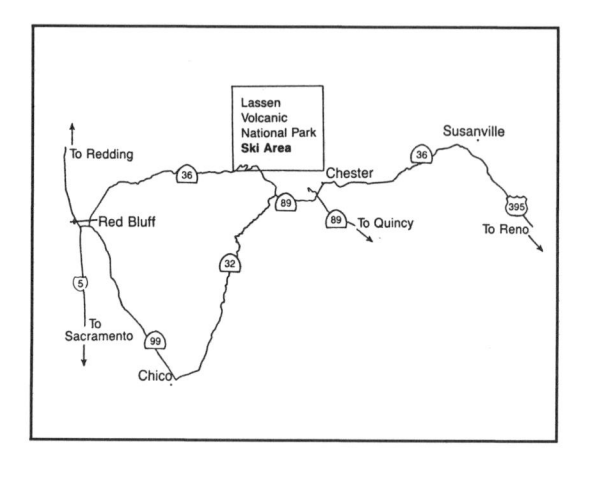

Lassen Peak has been quiet since 1919, when a series of nearly 300 lava eruptions ceased. Left behind is a legacy of beauty that is as awesome in winter as it is in summer. Nestled between snow-covered pinnacles, lush forests, and clouds of hot vapors, Lassen Park Ski Area is only a small part of the geothermal wonderland that is Lassen Volcanic National Park.

The skier headed to Lassen in late March has an opportunity to capture the best of two seasons. Heading east from Red Bluff on SH 36, yellow carpets of wild flowers announce the arrival of spring. Yet just a few miles further, a new storm can deposit several inches of fresh snow on the slopes of Lassen, reminding the skier that there's still time to enjoy winter's pleasures.

In fact, snowfall on Lassen Volcanic National Park usually ranges somewhere between 400 to 700 inches a year. It's not for a lack of snow that the ski area closes, but so the park can prepare for its spring and winter visitors.

Because of its location within the National Park and minimal development around it, Lassen Ski Area is likely to remain the compact day-ski area that it is presently. But while its size may be small, it's anything but ordinary to ski a volcano.

## LOCATION

Lassen Park Ski Area is on the southwest side of Lassen Volcanic National Park and the northwest corner of Tehama County where it meets Shasta County. The ski area is located on SH 89, 4 miles north of the junction with SH 36, 52 miles east of Red Bluff and I-5, and 30 miles west of Chester.

Access from the north is cut off in the winter with the closure of SH 89 at the park. From I-5 at Red Bluff, take SH 36 east 44 miles to SH 89 north. The turnoff is 4 miles after the town of Mineral. From US 395, take SH 36 west past Susanville and Chester, 63 miles to SH 89 north. From Quincy to the south, take SH 89 north 71 miles to the ski area. SH 89 and SH 36 are the same road west of Chester until SH 89 splits off to the north about 12 miles after the SH 32 turnoff. From Chico to the southwest, take SH 32 north 52 miles and turn left 16 miles, staying on SH 89 to the ski area.

Redding Airport is 75 miles northwest of Lassen Park Ski Area. United Express and American Eagle offer direct air service into Redding Airport from Sacramento, San Francisco, San Jose, and Klamath Falls, Oregon, with connecting flights from other cities. Additional air service from San Francisco is available 68 miles southwest in Chico. Cars equipped for skiers are not available at either airport, but 4-wheel-drive vehicles can be rented at the Redding Airport.

Amtrak's "Coast Starlight" from Sacramento, with connections from other California cities, stops in Chico and Redding. There are no car rental agencies at the Amtrak stop in either Redding or Chico.

Greyhound has daily service into Red Bluff, Mineral, and Chester, (800) 237-8211.

## TERRAIN

The runs at Lassen average $1/2$ mile in length and are all accessible from one triple-chair lift that deposits skiers at the summit. To the left of the lift, the *Face* presents the most challenging and moguled terrain with a 45 to 50° vertical. To the right of the lift, the black diamond trail *High Traverse* drops into *Hairy Face*, another wide, but smoother, steep.

On the far left, *Forest Run* is a favorite intermediate slope and also the longest at 3/4 mile. Its swooping contours are perfect for sweeping turns. On the right of the lift, *Northeast Passage* starts out as a novice run but is more challenging at the bottom, while *Bodine's Bliss* is a scenic trail through the firs.

Beginners learn on the areas served by the Bunny Tow and Intermediate Tow at the bottom of the mountain. For a longer run from the top, novices can find an easy way down via *Northeast Passage* midway to the *Cat Track* cutoff on the right. From the cutoff, skiers pass under the lift and around to the left to the base of the chair.

The average lift line is less than 3 minutes, and 10 to 12 minutes on the busiest holidays.

## FACILITIES

Entrance fees to Lassen Volcanic National Park are collected at the access road to Lassen Park Ski Area. The fees are $1 per vehicle, or 50¢ per bus passenger or person on foot. Frequent visitors can purchase a Golden Eagle passport for $25 that allows unlimited entry into all national parks and monuments for a year. A skier who brings a beginner to Lassen to sign up for the Learn-to-Ski package can ski for half price. Ski 9 times, 10th time is free.

## FACILITIES AT A GLANCE

| | |
|---|---|
| *Season:* | Mid-November–Late March or Easter. |
| *Hours:* | 9 a.m.–4 p.m. weekends, holidays, and Christmas and Easter vacations. |
| *Night Skiing:* | None. |
| *Area:* | 80 acres with 10 runs. |
| | Beginner: 40% |
| | Intermediate: 40% |
| | Advanced: 20% |
| *Base Elevation:* | 6,600 ft |
| *Summit Elevation:* | 7,200 ft |
| *Vertical Drop:* | 600 ft |
| *Longest Run:* | 3,960 ft |
| *Snowmaking:* | None. |
| *Snowboarding:* | Permitted. |
| *Avg. Annual Snowfall:* | 450 in. |

*Lift Capacity:* 1,800 per hr.

*Lifts:* 1 triple chair lift and 2 surface tows

| Name | Length | Vertical Rise |
| --- | --- | --- |
| Bumpass Heaven | 2,500 ft | 600 ft |
| Bunny Rope Tow | 300 ft | 30 ft |
| Stadelli Rope Tow | 400 ft | 40 ft |

*Lift Passes:*

| | All Day 9 a.m.–4 p.m. | Afternoon 12:30 p.m.–4 p.m. |
| --- | --- | --- |
| Adults | $19 | $12 |
| Rope tows only | $10 | $7 |
| Children 8-12 | $12 | $10 |
| Rope tows only | $7 | $6 |
| Children under 8 | FREE | FREE |
| Seniors 55–69 | $12 | $10 |
| Seniors 70 + | FREE | FREE |

*Season Passes:* $200 1st family member, $175 2nd family member, $150 3rd family member, $125 each additional family member. 10% off if purchased prior to November 17th; 15% discount if purchased prior to November 1. Student, senior, and handicapped passes, $150.

*Group Discounts:* $3 off lift ticket and $4 off rentals for groups of 10 or more on Fridays, or 20 or more on Saturdays or Sundays.

*Food & Drink:* Cafeteria with beer and wine at base lodge is open from 8:30 a.m. to 4 p.m.

*Parking & Transportation:* Parking is free at the base. RV overnight parking is permitted. No hookups.

*Ski Rentals:* The base rental shop is open from 8:30 a.m. to 4:30 p.m. Rentals include skis, poles, and boots.

| | Adult | Child |
| --- | --- | --- |
| All day | $15 | $11 |
| Half day | $11 | $9 |
| *Demos* all day | $21 | $16 |
| Half day | $12 | $12 |
| *Snowboards* all day | $20 | $15 |
| Half day | $15 | $15 |
| *Cross-country* all day | $11 | $8 |
| Half day | $8 | $5 |

*(continued)*

*(continued from previous page)*

*Ski School:* (916) 595-3376
  *Method:* ATM.
  *Ski School Director:* Jim McDaniel.
  *Class Lessons:* 10 a.m., 12 p.m., 2 p.m. Class size limited to 6.
    $15  (1³/₄ hr)
    $24  (3¹/₂ hr)
  *First Time Special:*  $28 adult. $23 child 8–12. Includes 1³/₄-hr lesson, use of surface tows, and rental equipment.
  *KAPT I*—(Kids Are People Too, I): Ages 4–11. 10 a.m.–3 p.m. Includes games, exercises, lunch, ski instruction, rentals, and use of surface tows.
    $32 all day, 10 a.m.–3 p.m.
    $19 half day, 1 p.m.–3 p.m. No lunch.
  *KAPT II:* The II program is suited to children who are more advanced skiers. Rates include use of the chair lift, as well as rentals, instruction, and lunch.
    $37 all day, 10 a.m.–3 p.m.
    $24 half day, 1 p.m.–3 p.m. No lunch.
  *Private Lessons:*  $25 per hr. Additional hr, $15. Each additional person, $15.
  *Snowboard Lesson:*  $25 per hr. Additional hr $15. Additional person $15.
*Races & Clinics:*  See Special Events.
*Day Care:*  None.
*Camper Facilities:*  RV overnight parking is permitted at the base lot. No hookups.
*Medical:*  First aid by ski patrol and National Park Service. Seneca Hospital is 30 miles east in Chester.
*Other:*  Outside lockers for rental. Retail shop.

## SPECIAL EVENTS

- *Free Beginner's Day*—January. Free equipment rentals, lesson, and use of surface tow.
- *Snowboard Competition*—February. Two-day slalom and half-pipe.

- *Telemark Ski Race*—March.
- *Grand Finale Downhill*—March.
- *Mogul Competition*—March.
- *Junior Carnival*—March. Games, races, and free admission for children under 12.

## WINTER ACTIVITIES

### Cross-Country

*Lassen Ski Touring Center*, adjacent to the downhill mountain on Ski Park Road, has 50 miles of ungroomed trails. Back country trails throughout the park are subject to closure due to hazardous conditions. Class lessons are $15 ($1^3/4$ hr). Private lessons are $25 and each additional person is $15. Telemark instruction is also available. A 3-hour guided tour with rentals is $28, or $21 without rentals. Reservations are required for the tour.

A cross-country trailhead is also located on the north side of Lassen Volcanic National Park on SH 89 at *Manzanita Lake*. Due to the closure of SH 89 within the park, this trailhead is not convenient to the Alpine ski area. Back country permits are required for overnight camping. Classes in snow shelters and snow survival techniques are also available for groups, (916) 595-4444.

Fifteen miles of groomed, marked trails are located at *Mineral Lodge* on SH 36, 4 miles west of the SH 89 turnoff for Lassen Park Ski Area. Trails radiate from the junction of SH 172 and SH 36; one trail leads to a warming hut. No rentals or lessons on site, (916) 595-4422.

### Snowmobiling

*Morgan Summit Snowmobile Park* is located at the junction of SH 36 and SH 89, south of Lassen Park Ski Area. 90 miles of groomed trails are maintained by the Forest Service. No rentals or lessons. Restaurant, bar, and lodge located 2 miles east in Mineral.

### Snowshoe Tours

Guided snowshoe tours into the back country are conducted by park rangers at 1:30 p.m. on Saturdays, Sundays, and holiday periods except Christmas and Thanksgiving. The tour takes in the Sulfur Works, with its steam fumaroles and bubbling mud pits. Groups can reserve a guide on other days. The tour is free and covers $1^1/2$ miles. Snowshoes are provided free of charge, (916) 595-4444.

## OTHER ACTIVITIES

**Fishing:** Lake Almanor.

## SHOPPING

The *Ski Shop* at Lassen Park Ski Area sells ski accessories, T-shirts, and sweat shirts. Ten miles west, the *General Store* at Mineral Lodge rents and sells ski equipment, sundries, and gift items. Heading east 25 miles toward Chester on SH 36, fresh-baked goodies are available at the *Cedar Chalet Bakery*, between SH 89 south and Chester Ski Road.

Two miles further east in Chester, most shops are located on Main St. (SH 36). Groceries and liquor stores include the *Olde Towne Corner Store, Chester Village Market and Deli, Ches-Mart,* and *Super Saver Market.* The *Lassen Drug Company* is an old-fashioned drugstore with a soda fountain. Visitors in search of gift items can check out *Stover Landing, Sally's Hallmark Shop,* and *David Price Jewelers* on Willow Way. Sporting goods are found at the *Ayoob Department Store*.

## APRÈS-SKI

Lassen Ski Area is primarily a day ski area devoid of après-ski life. Skiers headed east on SH 36 will find an atmospheric lounge with roaring fire and piano music at the *Timber House* in Chester. Those headed east toward I-5 will find a number of watering holes in Red Bluff.

## RESTAURANTS

**Timber House    $$$**                                            *(916) 258-2729*
SH 36 and First St. in Chester, 30 miles east of the ski area. Large tree trunks with branches twist across the ceiling, subdued lights hang inside timber rounds, and a large, curved bar cut from the center of a tree create the impression of being inside a fantasy forest, sitting around a roaring fire. Dinner selections include chicken breast cordon bleu and lobster tails, as well as prime rib, steak, and seafood. Cheese bread is a specialty of the house. Piano entertainment in the evenings. Open for breakfast, lunch, and dinner until 10 p.m.

**Knotbumper Restaurant    $$**                                   *(916) 258-2301*
274 Main, Chester. Casual deli, serving sandwiches and shrimp, salmon, NY steak, and halibut. Beer and wine. Open for lunch and dinner except Sundays, from 11 a.m. to 9 p.m.

**Red Onion**  $$ *(916) 258-3002*
433 Main St., Chester, 30 miles east of the ski area. American and continental cuisine includes steak, pork, lamb, trout, Weiner schnitzel, lobster, and duckling. Child's menu. Open for lunch and dinner.

**St. Bernards**  $$ *(916) 258-3382*
SH36, Chester, 20 miles east of the ski area. Kerosene lanterns and lace tablecloths add to the old-time atmosphere at the St. Bernard. Entrées include steak and seafood, with prime rib offered on Fridays and Saturdays. Complete dinners include home-baked breads. Open for breakfast, lunch, and dinner.

**Black Forest Restaurant**  $ *(916) 258-2941*
SH 36, 10 miles west of Chester. Family-style restaurant features both German and American home-style cooking. Open for breakfast, lunch, and dinner. Bar open until 2 a.m.

**Mineral Lodge**  $ *(916) 595-4422*
SH 36 in Mineral, 10 miles west of the ski area. Spacious dining room is open for breakfast, lunch, and dinner until 7 p.m. Menu selections include hearty portions of barbecued ribs, steaks, and pasta. The adjacent Rafter Room bar is open until people leave, usually around 9 p.m.

## ACCOMMODATIONS

With a couple of exceptions, winter lodging in the vicinity of Lassen Park Ski Area is fairly basic and can be found along SH 36 to Chester and the east shores of Lake Almanor. Additional accommodations are available in Red Bluff 48 miles west via SH 36.

**Timber House**  $$ *(916) 258-2789*
SH 36 and First St. in Chester, 30 miles east of the ski area. Sixteen moderate first-class rooms have either twin, double, queen, or king-size beds, TV, phones, and bathrooms with separate vanities. RV spaces also available. Restaurant and bar open Thursday through Monday.

**Black Forest**  $ *(916) 258-2941*
SH 36 at Mill Creek, 20 miles east of the ski area and 10 miles west of Chester. Nine rooms with private bathrooms with showers; somewhat worn furnishings. Cross-country ski rentals. Adjacent restaurant and bar open on weekends.

**Cedar Lodge**  $ *(916) 258-2904*
SH 36, 1/2 mile west of the SH 89 junction. Eleven units, 4 with kitchenettes, have either twin, 1 or 2 double, queen or king-size beds. No TV, phones, or maid service. A 2-bedroom apartment accommodates up to six.

**Dorado Inn**  $ *(916) 284-7790*
4379 SH 147, Lake Almanor, about 38 miles east of Lassen Park Ski Area. Seven to 12 units, which can be combined into 1- or 2-bedroom apartments, have full kitchens and TV. No phone.

**Lakeside Resort Motel**   $   *(916) 284-7376*
3747 E. Shore Drive (SH 147), Lake Almanor, about 38 miles from Lassen Park Ski Area. Twelve units each have a queen-size bed and sofa bed and accommodate 4 to 6 people. Units have kitchens and TV. No phones.

**McGovern's Mt. Lassen Vacation Chalets**   $   *Reservations, (415) 897-8377*
SH 36 in Mineral. Three chalets each have 3 bedrooms, living and dining areas, bathrooms, and fully equipped electric kitchens. The living areas are supplied with wood for the wood stoves and books and games for children. Guests supply own sheets and towels. No phones or TV.

**Mill Creek**   $   *(916) 595-4449*
SH 172 off SH 36 at Mill Creek, 11 miles east of entrance to Lassen Park Ski Area. Rustic cabins with private bathrooms and tubs, some with kitchens. Coffee shop and grocery store at the lodge. No TV or phones. Coffee shop hours 9 a.m. to 6 p.m.

**Mineral Lodge**   $   *(916) 595-4422*
SH 36, in Mineral. Mineral Lodge offers the closest accommodations to Lassen Park Ski Area. Sparsely furnished rooms have 1 or 2 double or twin beds with private bathrooms and showers. No TV or phones. Restaurant, bar, and general store with downhill and cross-country rentals, repair, and tune-ups.

**Seneca Motel**   $   *(916) 258-2815*
504 Cedar and Martin Way, Chester. Eleven units, 8 with kitchens, have a double or queen-size beds, TV, and daily maid service. No phones in rooms.

**St. Bernard Lodge**   $   *(926) 258-3382*
SH 36, 20 miles east of the ski area and 10 miles west of Chester. The St. Bernard Lodge has 7 turn-of-the-century rooms with knotty-pine interiors and shared bathrooms. Rooms are comfortably decorated with homey charm and are particularly ideal for couples traveling together. Restaurant and full bar downstairs.

# Stover Mountain

*P.O. Box 23*
*Chester, CA 96020*
*Information: (916) 258-3965*

| **Driving distances** | |
|---|---|
| Chico | 70 mi |
| Eureka | 247 mi |
| Red Bluff | 60 mi |
| Redding | 90 mi |
| Reno | 125 mi |
| Sacramento | 161 mi |

*For road conditions, call*
*(916) 244-1500*

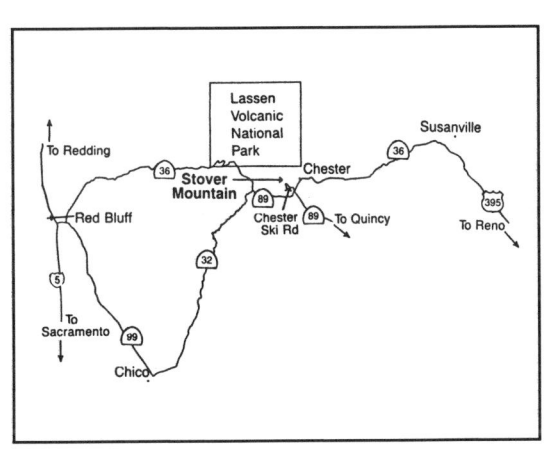

Stover Mountain is a small weekend ski facility hidden among the trees in Lassen National Forest, 30 miles east of Lassen Park Ski Area.

Privately owned and maintained by the Stover Mountain Ski Club, the facility includes two surface lifts and intermediate and advanced slopes. Although Stover is small, its slopes are challenging—there are no gentle pitches for beginners.

Because Stover is a basic ski mountain with few on-site services, skiers enjoy economical lift rates. In fact, some locals ski every weekend during the season. Even for those who aren't members of the Stover Ski Club, Stover's backyard atmosphere makes it easy for skiers to get acquainted.

## LOCATION

Stover Mountain is in Plumas County, on Chester Ski Road, 2 miles north of SH 36, 2 miles west of Chester, and 63 miles east of Red Bluff and I-5.

From Red Bluff, follow SH 36 21 miles past the junction with SH 89 and Lassen Park Ski Area, to Chester Ski Road. Chester Ski Road is not well marked, but it is on the north side of the highway opposite the Cedar Chalet Bakery. Stover Mountain is 2 miles up Chester Ski Road.

From US 395, drive west on SH 36 past the Coppervale ski area and Lake Almanor, 2 miles west of Chester. Turn right or north on Chester Ski Road.

From Quincy, south of Lake Almanor, follow SH 89 north 44 miles to the junction with SH 36. Turn right on SH 36 to Chester Ski Road. From Chico, take SH 32 north and turn east 11 miles on SH 36 to Chester Ski Road.

Redding Airport is 86 miles northwest of Stover Mountain. United Express and American Eagle offer direct air service into Redding Airport from Sacramento, San Francisco, San Jose, and Klamath Falls, Oregon, with connecting flights from other cities. Additional air service from San Francisco is available 68 miles southwest in Chico. Cars equipped for skiers are not available at either airport but 4-wheel drive vehicles can be rented at the Redding Airport.

Amtrak's "Coast Starlight" from Sacramento, with connections from other California cities, stops in Chico and Redding. There are no car rental agencies at the Amtrak stop in Redding or Chico.

Greyhound has daily service into Red Bluff, Mineral, and Chester, 4 miles east.

## TERRAIN

Stover Mountain's principal slope, served by a poma lift, is a short, intermediate hill. The slope is broad enough for wide turns and traverses or for racing. Two of the steeper runs are for experts. Beginners generally start on an adjacent slope served by a rope tow. Although somewhat gentler, the slope is still more intermediate than beginner.

## FACILITIES AT A GLANCE

*Season:* Christmas—Late March.
*Hours:* 10 a.m.–4 p.m. weekends, holidays, and weekdays during Christmas vacation.
*Night Skiing:* None.
*Area:* 65 acres with 10 runs.
Beginner: 0%
Intermediate: 80%
Advanced: 20%
*Base Elevation:* 5,200 ft

## Stover Mountain

*Summit Elevation:* 6,000 ft
*Vertical Drop:* 800 ft
*Longest Run:* 800 ft
*Snowmaking:* None.
*Snowboarding:* Permitted. Chair lift not available.
*Avg. Annual Snowfall:* 48 in.
*Lift Capacity:* 1,500 per hr.

*Lifts:* 2 surface tows (1 poma lift and 1 rope tow)

| Name | Length | Vertical Rise |
| --- | --- | --- |
| Poma Lift | 1,000 ft | 850 ft |
| Rope Tow | 250 ft | 250 ft |

| *Lift Passes:* | All Day | Afternoon |
| --- | --- | --- |
| | 10 a.m.–4 p.m. | 1 p.m.–4 p.m. |
| Adults | $10 | $7 |
| Rope tow only | $7 | $7 |
| Children | $10 | $7 |
| Rope tow only | $7 | $7 |

*Season Passes:* Membership passes are $125 for families, $60 for adults, and $40 for students and children.

*Group Discounts:* $2 off all-day lift ticket price for 20 or more people.

*Food & Drink:* A warming hut at the base has a wood-burning stove and chairs. No food or beverage service, water, or electricity.

*Parking & Transportation:* Parking is free at the base. No RV overnight parking.

*Ski Rentals:* None.

*Ski School:* None.

*Races & Clinics:* See Special Events.

*Day Care:* None.

*Camper Facilities:* None.

*Medical:* Seneca Hospital, 30 miles east in Chester.

*Other:* Outdoor toilets.

## SPECIAL EVENTS

- *Winterfest Races*—January.
- *Dogsled Races*—January. SH 36, 1.5 miles south of Stover Mountain.

## WINTER ACTIVITIES

A meadow for snowmobiling is located on SH 36, $1^1/_2$ miles south of the junction with SH 89. A hill for tobogganing and other snow-play activities is 1.5 miles south of Stover on Chester Ski Road.

For additional information on cross-country skiing and winter activities, see Lassen Park Ski Area.

## SHOPPING, APRÈS-SKI, RESTAURANTS, AND ACCOMMODATIONS

For other nearby activities, shopping, dining, and accommodations information, see Lassen Park Ski Area and Coppervale.

# Coppervale

❄

*P.O. Box 300*
*Susanville, CA 96130*
*Information: (916) 257-6181, Lassen Community College.*
*(916) 257-9965, Coppervale.*

| Driving distances | |
|---|---|
| Alturas | 126 mi |
| Chico | 87 mi |
| Red Bluff | 86 mi |
| Redding | 115 mi |
| Reno | 102 mi |
| Sacramento | 151 mi |

*For road conditions, call*
*(916) 257-5126*

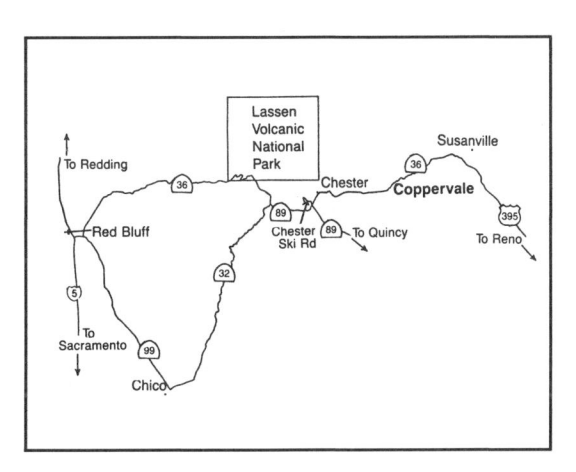

Operated by Lassen Community College since 1950, Coppervale is open to the public Tuesday and Thursday afternoons and all day on weekends and holidays.

Like Stover Mountain 21 miles east, Coppervale is reminiscent of rural, New England-style ski areas, where almost any hill with a 30° vertical has some kind of lift on it. Coppervale's old-style ski lifts and snow cats preserve a connection with the past. With primarily advanced-intermediate terrain, Coppervale also preserves some traditional challenges, including steep chutes and mogul runs. Not surprisingly, local college students often graduate from Coppervale as accomplished skiers.

## LOCATION

Coppervale is located on SH 36 in Lassen County, 86 miles east of I-5 and Red Bluff and 21 miles west of Susanville. From Red Bluff, go east on SH 36 all the way to Coppervale, 6 miles past the town of Westwood. From US 395 at Johnstonville, take SH 36 west 18 miles to the ski area. From Quincy to the south, follow SH 89 north 31 miles to SH 147 along the east shore of Lake Almanor 10 miles, and turn right on SH 36 at the town of Westwood. From Chico, take SH 32 north and turn east on SH 36. The ski area is 16 miles east of Chester. SH 44 comes down from the north through the Cascade mountain range and runs into SH 36, 11 miles east of the ski area.

Redding Airport is 107 miles northwest of Coppervale. United Express and American Eagle offer direct air service into Redding Airport from Sacramento, San Francisco, San Jose, and Klamath Falls, Oregon, with connecting flights from other cities. Additional air service from San Francisco is available 68 miles southwest in Chico. Direct service into Reno, 114 miles southeast, is available from most major cities. Cars equipped for skiers are not available at either airport, but 4-wheel-drive vehicles can be rented at the Reno or Redding airports.

Amtrak's "Coast Starlight" from Sacramento, with connections from other California cities, stops in Chico and Redding. There are no car rental agencies at the Amtrak stop in either Redding or Chico.

Greyhound has daily service into Chester, 20 miles west and Susanville, 15 miles east.

## FACILITIES AT A GLANCE

| | |
|---|---|
| *Season:* | Mid-December–late March. |
| *Hours:* | 9:30 a.m.–4 p.m., weekends, holidays, and 1 p.m.–4:30 p.m. Tuesdays and Thursdays. |
| *Night Skiing:* | None. |
| *Area:* | 65 acres, 8 runs. |
| | Beginner: 40% |
| | Intermediate: 30% |
| | Advanced: 30% |
| *Base Elevation:* | 5,250 ft |
| *Summit Elevation:* | 5,827 ft |
| *Vertical Drop:* | 600 ft |
| *Longest Run:* | 4,000 ft |
| *Snowmaking:* | None. |
| *Snowboarding:* | Permitted. |
| *Avg. Annual Snowfall:* | 175 in. |

*Lift Capacity:* 600 per hr.

*Lifts:* 2 surface lifts (1 poma & 1 T-Bar)

| Name | Length | Vertical Rise |
| --- | --- | --- |
| Poma Lift | 1,350 ft | 600 ft |
| T-Bar | 500 ft | 100 ft |

*Lift Passes:* All Day, 9:30 a.m.–4 p.m.

| | Adults | Children under 10 |
| --- | --- | --- |
| Weekends and holidays | $8 | FREE |
| Tuesdays and Thursdays | $6 | FREE |

*Food & Drink:* There are no food or beverage facilities at Coppervale. The warming hut at the base has a wood-burning stove and deck for skiers who bring their own lunch and snacks.

*Parking & Transportation:* Parking is free at the base. Overnight RV parking is permitted. No hookups.

*Ski Rentals:* None at the mountain. Equipment rentals are available in Susanville at Tinkers to Teens, (916) 257-3767.

*Ski School:* Available only through Lassen Community College physical education classes.

*Races & Clinics:* None.

*Day Care:* None.

*Camper Facilities:* None.

*Medical:* Closest hospital is Lassen Community Hospital, 15 miles east in Susanville.

## TERRAIN

Although only 75 acres, Coppervale Ski Area offers a variety of terrain for all levels of ability. Advanced skiers will find the most challenging descent to the immediate right of the poma lift where *The Face* develops into a world-class mogul field between storms. To the immediate left of the poma lift, *The Chute* is a narrow bump run with a 60° pitch. The 3/4-mile *Ridge Run* is an intermediate smoothy for easier cruising. *The Bowl* is another intermediate favorite that's wide enough for the average skier but steep enough to be interesting. Adjacent to the *Ridge Run*, another wide slope starts as an intermediate run and, halfway down, joins a slope suitable for beginners.

First-timers usually start on the shorter rope tow, which drops skiers off halfway up the mountain.

Except for *The Face* and *The Chute*, the terrain at Coppervale is groomed smooth. Given its location in sparsely populated Lassen County, there's rarely a lift line.

## WINTER ACTIVITIES

### Cross-Country

At present, there are no marked or groomed cross-country trails in the vicinity of Coppervale. The area around *Eagle Lake Summit*, off Eagle Lake Road (County Road A1) 10 miles north of Susanville, is popular for Nordic skiing. Parking is free. Parking for cross-country skiers is also available at *Willard Hill*, 6 miles west of Coppervale, and at the *Bogard Rest Stop*, 44 miles east of Susanville on SH 36. Restrooms and trash bins are located at the *Bogard Rest Stop*. No lessons, rentals, or other facilities are available.

See Lassen Park Ski Area for additional cross-country information.

### Snowmobiling

Although there are no marked snowmobile trails in the vicinity of Coppervale, snowmobiles are permitted in the Eagle Lake Ranger District almost everywhere except in the Osprey Management Area and in the campgrounds at the south end of Eagle Lake. The *Bogard Rest Stop*, 44 miles east of Susanville on SH 36, is a staging area, with restrooms and trash bins for snowmobilers. The parking area is surrounded by 360° flat terrain for snowmobiling and cross-country skiing.

See also *Morgan Hill* under Lassen Park Ski Area.

### Tobogganing, Tubing, and Snow Play

*Willard Hill*, SH 36, 6 miles east of Coppervale is a challenging hill for sledding, tobogganing, and tubing. Part of the hill has been blocked off because of prior accidents. There are no rentals or concessions on site. Parking is free on an adjacent gravel lot. *Eagle Lake Summit*, Eagle Lake Road, is also used for snow-play activities. Parking is free. *Jamesville Grade*, 30 miles southeast, off US 395 before the Jamesville Grade, is steep and only for experienced sledders. No equipment rentals or lessons are available at these sites. The area is frequently closed in winter and it's best to check first with the Lassen National Forest Ranger District in Susanville, (916) 257-2151.

**Ice Skating**

The tennis courts in Chester are used for ice skating, weather permitting.

## OTHER ACTIVITIES

**Bowling:** Sierra Bowling, Susanville.
**Cinema:** Sierra Theater, Susanville.
**Fishing:** Lake Almanor.

## SHOPPING

*Tinkers to Teens*, 15 miles east in Susanville on Main St., sells and rents both downhill and cross-country skis along with other sports equipment. A *Safeway* market is located in the Sierra Shopping Center along with a *Payless* drugstore. The Lassen Shopping Center includes a *Thrifty Drug*. *Rexall Drugs* is located in the Susanville Center.

The *Depot Gift Shop*, in Susanville's historic uptown, carries antiques and gifts. *J.C. Penney* carries clothing for men and women of all ages. The *Bootery* carries shoes for both sexes, plus women's apparel. Three miles further east in Johnstonville, *The Pardner* features western wear.

## APRÈS-SKI

The closest night life is in Susanville, 15 miles east of Coppervale. The *Black Rock Tavern* in the Hotel Mt. Lassen is a popular gathering spot, open from 3 p.m. to 2 a.m. The Tavern sports a large-screen TV and has occasional live music. The *Pioneer Bar* in Susanville offers pool and snooker tables. Open from 6 a.m. to 2 a.m., there's dancing to the jukebox, and live country music on Friday and Saturday nights. The *Northwood's Mahogany Room* and the *Galley* also have a dance floor and jukebox with occasional live bands.

## RESTAURANTS

**Aardvark Pizza**  $$  *(916) 257-7017*
450 Richmond Road, Susanville. Pizza, ravioli, calzone, and sandwiches are served daily from 10 a.m. to 9 p.m., 10:30 p.m. on Saturday. Beer and wine.

**The Galley**  $$  *(916) 825-3333*
50925 Stone Road, Susanville. The Galley's knotty-pine interior and open-beam ceilings create a jaunty, nautical atmosphere for entrées of fish, steak, prime rib,

and barbecued ribs. Jukebox and dancing. Open for breakfast, lunch, and dinner from 7 a.m. to 9 p.m.

**Northwood's Mahogany Room** $$ *(916) 257-6161*
Main and Lassen St. in the Hotel Mt. Lassen. Continental cuisine at the Mahogany Room includes chicken Kiev, chicken marsala, and chicken almondine. Lobster, steak, and prime rib are also available. Jukebox and dancing. Occasional live music.

**Burger King** $ *(916) 257-8787*
2535 Main St., Susanville. Burgers, trimmings are sold daily from 7 a.m. to 11 p.m., midnight on Saturday.

**Denny's** $ *(916) 257-6107*
2535 Main St., Susanville. Open 24 hours a day, seven days a week, Denny's menu offers typical American short-order fare including chicken, steak, fish, and hamburgers.

**McDonald's** $ *(916) 257-8132*
3000 Main St., Susanville. Specializing in fast hamburgers and trimmings, McDonald's is open from 6 a.m. to 10 p.m. daily.

**Mi Casita** $ *(916) 257-9419*
2301 Main St., Susanville. Mi Casita serves Mexican dishes such as chile verde, steak ranchero, chile rellenos, chimichangas, and compuesta. Beer, wine, and margaritas. Open from 11 a.m. to 9 p.m. Closed Sundays.

**Roundtable Pizza** $ *(916) 257-5354*
In the Lassen Shopping Center, Susanville. Open daily from 10 a.m. to 10 p.m., and 11 p.m. on Friday and Saturday.

**T & A Restaurant** $ *(916) 257-2826*
2101 Main St., Susanville. Chinese dishes include chow mein, sweet and sour pork, teriyaki steak, and chicken. Beer and wine. Open daily from 11 a.m. (noon on Saturday) to 9 p.m.

## ACCOMMODATIONS

**Best Western Trailside Inn** $ *(916) 257-4123*
2785 Main St., Susanville. Seventy first-class rooms, with king-size, queen-size or double beds, includes TV, phone, and daily maid service. Coffee shop adjacent.

**Frontier Inn Motel** $ *(916) 257-4141*
2685 Main St., Susanville. The Frontier Inn has a variety of apartments, from studios to 2-bedroom units with queen-size, king-size, or waterbeds, all with phones, TV, and daily maid service. Continental breakfast included.

**Hotel Mt. Lassen** $ *(916) 257-6609*
Main and Lassen St., Susanville. Rooms with queen-size or two double-beds have TV, phones, and daily maid service.

**River Inn Motel**  $  *(916) 257-2782*
1710 Main St., Susanville. Forty-nine units with 1 or 2 double, queen-size, or king-size beds with TV, phones, and daily maid service. Non-smoking rooms available. Restaurant and lounge across the parking lot.

**Roseberry House**  $  *(916) 257-5675*
609 North St. Small bed-and-breakfast has 4 rooms, 2 with double beds, 1 with queen-size bed and 1 with a queen-size and a single bed. All have private baths. TV in the library. Rates include full breakfast.

**Super Budget Motel**  $  *(916) 257-2782*
2975 Johnstonville Road, Susanville. Forty-nine new, spacious rooms that sleep up to 4, with 1 or 2 beds. Radio, TV, phone, and daily maid service.

For information on restaurants and lodges in the Chester area, see Lassen Park Ski Area.

# Plumas Eureka Ski Bowl

*Plumas Eureka State Park*
*310 Johnsville Road*
*Blairsden, CA 96103*
*Information: (916) 836-2317*

| Driving distances | |
|---|---|
| Alturas | 198 mi |
| Chico | 118 mi |
| Redding | 175 mi |
| Reno | 62 mi |
| Sacramento | 155 mi |
| Susanville | 98 mi |
| San Francisco | 240 mi |
| Truckee | 48 mi |

*For road conditions, call (916) 581-1400, California; (702) 793-1313, Nevada*

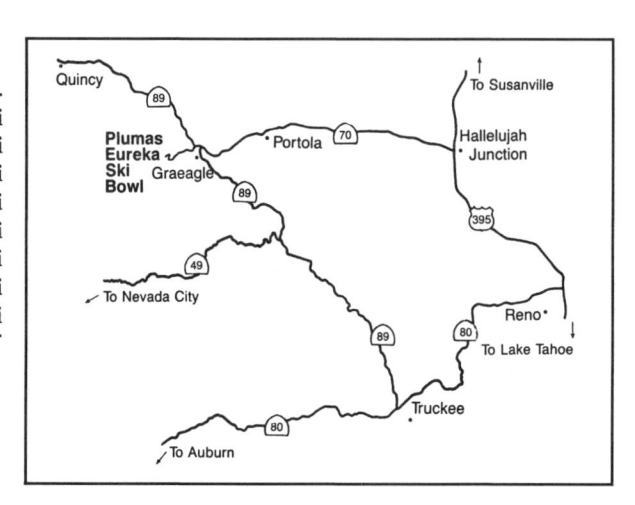

Plumas Eureka is a non-profit ski facility maintained by the Plumas Ski Club. Although the present facility was established in 1955, the skiing tradition here dates back more than a century, according to local oral history. It was about 1863 when miners strapped long boards on their feet and rode the ore bucket up Gold Mountain (now known as Eureka Peak) for a downhill plunge at high speeds.

Today, the area has a poma lift and bunny tow to pull skiers up the mountain. Open Wednesdays, weekends, and holidays, the Plumas Eureka Ski Bowl provides a rustic ski experience at modest prices.

## LOCATION

Plumas Eureka Ski Bowl is in Plumas Eureka State Park in Plumas County, 5.5 miles west of Graeagle at the junction of SH 89 and SH 70. The Ski Bowl

Plumas Eureka Ski Bowl   43

is 15 miles from Portola, 30 miles southwest of Quincy, and 62 miles west of Reno.

Access from the north is via SH 89 from Chester and Quincy. From Reno, take US 395 north 23 miles to SH 70, and west 38 miles to the ski mountain, a few miles west of Graeagle. From Truckee and North Lake Tahoe to the south, take SH 89 north 48 miles. From Auburn, Grass Valley, and Nevada City to the south, take SH 49, the Gold Country Highway, northeast to SH 89 and turn left or north 18 miles to Graeagle. Turn left on the Johnsville/Plumas Eureka State Park turnoff, 5 miles to the ski area.

Direct service into the Reno airport, 62 miles southeast, is available from most major cities. Four-wheel-drive or cars equipped for skiers are available for rent at the Reno airport.

Amtrak's "California Zephyr" stops in Truckee, as well as at Reno/Sparks. Auto rentals are available in Truckee at the AAA Auto Rental, adjacent to the

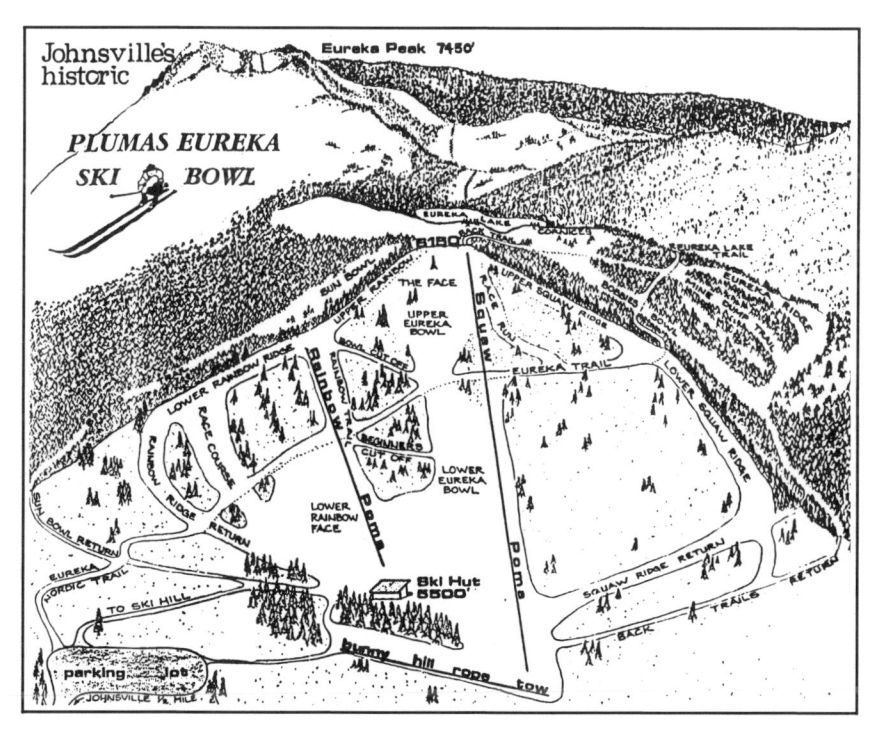

*Plumas Eureka Ski Bowl*   Courtesy of Plumas Eureka Ski Bowl, operated by Plumas Ski Club.

Amtrak station. Although there is no car rental agency at the Reno train station, rental car delivery to the station can be prearranged with some auto agencies.

Greyhound also operates service into Graeagle and Portola. The bus will also stop in Blairsden when a passenger requests.

## TERRAIN

Much of Plumas Eureka Ski Bowl is just that—an open bowl with well-groomed intermediate terrain.

The back side, however, is left ungroomed for advanced skiers who enjoy unpacked powder. Here smooth, steep runs like *Eureka Lake Trail* and *Eureka Ridge* begin off a cornice at the top and run through the trees. Another advanced run, *Bobbie's Bowl*, the longest route to the bottom, brings skiers back to the front side. The toughest challenge is on the opposite side of the mountain on *Sun Bowl*, where a serious pitch at the top lessens on the bottom half.

For intermediate skiers, *Upper Eureka Bowl* rolls broadly down the face with a gentler pitch at the bottom. *Upper Squaw Ridge* and *Upper Rainbow Ridge* are fast, groomed cruisers that sweep around opposite sides of the face.

The beginner *Bunny Hill* is served by a rope tow. Once novices have gained a little confidence, they can drop off either poma lift half way up onto *Lower Eureka Bowl* or *Lower Rainbow Face*. Both slopes provide ample space for wide radius turns.

## FACILITIES AT A GLANCE

| | |
|---|---|
| *Season:* | December 15–March 31. |
| *Hours:* | 10 a.m.–4 p.m. Wednesdays, Sundays, and holidays. |
| | 8:30 a.m.–4 p.m. Saturdays. |
| *Night Skiing:* | None. |
| *Area:* | 320 acres with 15 runs. |
| | Beginner: 15% |
| | Intermediate: 75% |
| | Advanced: 10% |
| *Base Elevation:* | 5,500 ft |
| *Summit Elevation:* | 6,150 ft |

*Vertical Drop:* 650 ft
*Longest Run:* 1 mile.
*Snowmaking:* None.
*Snowboarding:* Permitted. No chair-lift access.
*Avg. Annual Snowfall:* 220 in.
*Lift Capacity:* 1,000 per hr.

*Lifts:* 3 surface lifts (2 pomas and 1 rope tow)

| Name | Length | Vertical Rise |
| --- | --- | --- |
| Bunny Rope Tow | 700 ft | 50 ft |
| Rainbow Poma | 1,500 ft | 350 ft |
| Squaw Poma | 2,650 ft | 650 ft |

*Lift Passes:*

| | All Day | Afternoon |
| --- | --- | --- |
| | 10 a.m.–4 p.m. | 1 p.m.–4 p.m. |
| Saturdays | 8:30 a.m.–4 p.m. | 1 p.m.–4 p.m. |
| Adults | $12 | $9 |
|   Rope tow only | $5 | $5 |
| Children under 13 | $9 | $7 |
|   Rope tow only | $5 | $5 |
| Seniors 65–69 | $12 | $10 |

*Food & Drink:* Hot dogs, soup, chili, hot chocolate, and cold beverages are available at the base Ski Hut.

*Parking & Transportation:* Parking is free at the base. No RV overnight parking.

*Ski Rentals:* None.

*Ski School:* None. Lessons are conducted by the Plumas Unified School District and by the local college in class programs.

*Races & Clinics:* None.

*Day Care:* None.

*Camper Facilities:* In Blairsden, 3 miles east, the Little Bear Campground & RV Park opens mid-March. Rates are $17. No hookups in winter, (916) 836-2774.

*Medical:* First aid by ski patrol. Closest hospital is Eastern Plumas District Hospital, 15 miles east in Portola.

*Other:* Ski lockers (bring your own lock), restrooms, and open-pit fireplace located in the Ski Hut.

# WINTER ACTIVITIES

## Cross-Country

There are a wide variety of cross-country trails, ranging from flat, groomed track skiing to challenging peaks for advanced skiers with telemarking ability. Three trails are marked for Nordic skiing within *Plumas Eureka State Park*. An intermediate to advanced trail at Plumas Eureka Ski Bowl is groomed and leads through Johnsville to Eureka Lake Road. The Jamison Mine Trail branches out from the parking areas adjacent to the Museum. It runs 4.5 miles up County Road A14 from the intersection at SH 89 just north of Graeagle. The beginner-intermediate terrain is ungroomed. The Madora Lake Trail, across the road from Jamison Mine Trail, is also ungroomed, with beginner-intermediate terrain.

Unmarked and ungroomed trails are located off SH 89, south of Graeagle on Gold Lake Road and the unplowed Mohawk/Chapman Road. The terrain varies from beginner to advanced and leads to the *Lakes Basin Area*.

Ungroomed wilderness trails are located 44 miles from Plumas Eureka Ski Bowl and 14 miles west of Quincy at *Bucks Lake*. Trails vary from 3 to 8 miles each way. The Bucks Summit Trail to Spanish Peak is intermediate and advanced. Big Creek Road and Snake Lake Road are beginner trails. Overnight lodging in rustic cabins is available at *Bucks Lake Lodge*. A bar, restaurant, store, and cross-country ski rentals are also found at the lodge, (916) 283-2262. The *Lakeshore Resort* offers both lodge and cabin accommodations. Facilities include a fireplace lounge, bar, restaurant, and store, (916) 283-2333. During the high-snow season, the lodges are accessible only by cross-country skis or snowmobile.

Five miles southeast of Quincy, the intermediate-advanced Squirrel Creek Road leads from SH 89 to *Argentine Ridge*.

East of Portola, a 6 mile beginner-intermediate trail runs from SH 70 on Grizzly Road on the east side of the Smith Peak State Game Refuge to *Lake Davis*.

## Snowmobiling

*Bucks Lake Snowmobile Rentals*, Bucks Lake Road, 20 miles west of Quincy, rents snowmobiles and conducts tours in the Bucks Lake area. A snowmobile shuttle into the area is $15 for one person and $20 for two. The 1-hour Bucks Lakes Tour is $25 for one person and $35 for two. A 5-hour tour is $120 for one person and $160 for two, with $10 off for skiers staying overnight in one of the rustic cabins at Bucks Lake Lodge. Half-day and full-day tours are also available, (916) 283-2333.

The *Lakes Basin* area, south of Graeagle on Gold Lake Road, is also popular for snowmobiling.

## Tobogganing, Tubing, and Snow Play

Although there are no areas specifically designated for sledding and other snow-play activities, visitors can use any area of the Park not used for skiing. For further information, contact the Plumas Ranger District at (916) 836-2380.

## OTHER ACTIVITIES

**Fishing:** Gold Lake, 30 minutes east of Graeagle; Bucks Lake, 30 minutes southwest of Quincy. Ice fishing at Davis Lake, 20 minutes north of Portola.
**Fitness:** Quincy Racquetball and Health Center, Quincy.
**Hunting:** Seasonal permits by lottery.
**Museums:** Plumas Eureka State Park Museum, Eureka Stamp Mill & Mine, Johnsville; Railroad Museum, Portola; Plumas County Museum, Quincy.
**Racquetball:** Quincy Racquetball and Health Center, Quincy.
**Riding:** Whitehawk Ranch, Blairsden.
**Video Games:** Gumba's Pizzeria, Blairsden.

## SHOPPING

Four miles east in Blairsden, The *Blairsden Market and Deli* has a complete grocery with a produce department, meat, liquor, and deli sandwiches. Sporting goods, games, and toys are available at *Blairsden Mercantile*. *Country Elegance*, Bonta St., offers handcrafted gifts, jewelry, and ceramics. *40 Carat* features women's apparel and accessories for all occasions.

A few miles south in Graeagle, skiers can pick up groceries, including produce, dairy products, meat, beer, and wine, at the *Graeagle Store*. Souvenirs, T-shirts, sweatshirts, and Indian items, including ceramics, jewelry, giftware, and collectibles are available at *Juanita Laird's The Gift Shop*. The *Witch's Brew* carries a melange of sportswear, sweaters, gifts, film, audio book cassettes, and paperbacks. *Graeagle Boutique* specializes in women's sportswear and junior and misses sizes. Souvenirs, gifts, and sweatshirts are also found at *Graeagle Sorts 'N' Sports*.

## APRÈS-SKI

Plumas County is known more for peace and tranquility than night life, but there are a few local fun spots. The cocktail lounge at *Blairsden House*, Bonta

St. in Blairsden, is open from 11 a.m. to 1 a.m. A jukebox provides music for dancing, and there's live country-western or rock-and-roll bands every third Saturday. *Reno's Mohawk Tavern*, a rustic watering hole, is 3 miles east of the ski area in Mohawk. The *Knotty Pine Tavern* in Graeagle is a local spot for a game of pool or just talking.

## RESTAURANTS

**Alpine Moon**   $$   *(916) 832-5360*
165 E. Sierra, Portola. Standard coffee-shop menu is offered for breakfast, lunch, and dinner.

**Beckwith Tavern**   $$   *(916) 832-5084*
SH 70 and Clover Valley Road, Beckwourth. Country-style dinner house serves steak, prime rib, halibut and prawns. Children's menu. Open for dinner from 5 p.m. to 9 p.m. Closed Wednesdays and Thursdays.

**Blairsden House**   $$   *(916) 836-1300*
Bonta St., Blairsden. American cuisine, featuring steaks, seafood (including lobster and crab), fried pork chops, and chicken cordon bleu. Children and senior's menu. Open for dinner from 5 p.m. to 9 p.m. Lounge open from noon to 1 a.m., with live music every 3rd Saturday. Closed Tuesdays.

**The Log Cabin**   $$   *(916) 832-5243*
64 E. Sierra (SH 70), Portola. German specialties, including sauerbraten, Wiener schnitzel, and jagerschnitzel are served in a room warmed by Tamarack wood panneling. Dinners include soup and salad. Open for dinner from 5 p.m. to 9 p.m. Closed Tuesdays. Bar opens at 4 p.m.

**Mt. Tomba**   $$   *(916) 836-2359*
SH 70, 6 miles west of Blairsden. Mt. Tomba is a family-style restaurant serving favorite Mexican dishes as well as steak, chicken, and seafood. Open Thursday through Saturday from 5 p.m. to 9 p.m., and 3 p.m. to 8 p.m. on Sunday.

**River Pines Resort**   $$   *(916) 836-0576*
SH 89, Blairsden, 6 miles from Plumas Eureka Ski Bowl. Continental dishes include tournedos, veal scallopini, chicken Kiev, and calamari. Open for lunch and for dinner from 5 p.m. to 10 p.m. Friday, Saturday, and Sunday.

**Gumba's Pizzeria**   $   *(916) 836-1212*
350 Bonta St., Blairsden. Serving pizzas, hamburgers, spare ribs, steaks, and hot wings, Gumba's is open for lunch and dinner daily from 10 a.m. to 9 p.m. Beer and wine, video games, jukebox, and TV.

**Red Feather Cafe**   $   *(916) 832-0349*
$258^1/_2$ Commercial, Portola. The Red Feather is a coffee shop serving American fare from 11 a.m. to 7:30 p.m. Closed Sundays.

## ACCOMMODATIONS

In addition to the listings below, condominium units with 2 to 4 bedrooms can be rented through **Plumas Pines Vacation Rentals**, (916) 836-0444. Two night minimum stay. Homes with 2 to 4 bedrooms are rented for 3 nights or a week through **Hamlin Realty**, (916) 836-2525.


**Graeagle Meadows Vacation Rentals   $$**                          *(916) 836-2221*
SH 89, Graeagle. Sixty-nine 2-bedroom, 2-bath condominiums each have a TV, phone, and fireplace, and fully-equipped kitchens with washer/dryer. Maid service arranged for extra charge. Three night minimum.

**Plumas Pines Vacation Rentals and Plumas Eureka Estates $$**  *(916) 836-0444*
14 Poplar Valley Road, Blairsden. Thirty-five deluxe villas on the Plumas Eureka golf course each have 2, 3, or 4 bedrooms, fireplace, phone, TV, and fully-equipped kitchens. Some units include a spa tub. Extra charge for maid service.

**White Sulpher Springs Ranch   $$**                                *(916) 836-2387*
SH 89, Clio, 10 miles from Plumas Eureka Ski Bowl. Currently a bed-and-breakfast, the Ranch was first built in 1850 and established in 1867 as a hotel for the Truckee-Quincy stage. Many of the original furnishings have been retained. Six rooms in the main building have king-size, queen-size, or double beds and shared baths, 1 with private bath. Each room is distinctly decorated. The "Marble Room" features a collection of marble-topped antique furniture, rose wallpaper, brocade bedspread, and a velvet "fainting" couch. Guests also share a parlor, and dining room, and are provided with a full breakfast. A separate cottage sleeps up to four. No TV or phone. No daily maid service.

**River Pines Resort   $**                                          *(916) 836-0444*
SH 89, Graeagle, 6 miles from Plumas Eureka Ski Bowl. Fourteen original units, 4 with mini-kitchens, each have 1 or 2 bedrooms and TV. No phones or maid service. Thirty new deluxe units have 2 double beds or a king-size bed, TV, phones, and daily maid service. Jacuzzi on premises. Restaurant open on weekends. A Winterfest package includes breakfast for two for Thursday, Friday, or Saturday arrivals.

**Sierra Motel   $**                                                *(916) 832-4223*
380 E. Sierra, Portola, 20 miles from the ski area. Eleven of the 23 units are rented with queen-size beds, private baths, phones, TV, and maid service.

**Sleepy Pines Motel   $**                                          *(916) 832-4291*
74631 SH 70, Portola. Seventeen units, some with kitchenettes, have either queen-size or double beds, phones, TV, and maid service.

**Sunset Motel   $**                                                *(916) 832-4240*
165 W. Sierra, Portola. Six units with single and doubles beds, 3 units with kitchenettes, have TV, and maid service. No phone. One unit has a spa.

**Upper Feather Bed & Breakfast**  $ *(916) 832-0107*
256 Commercial St., Portola. Originally built in 1910, this bed-and-breakfast has 6 country-style rooms with double or twin beds, in-room wash basins, and shared bathrooms. No TV or phones. Full breakfast included in rate. Short walk to railroad station.

*Skiers of all levels enjoy Heavenly Valley's 24 lifts and 9 mountain peaks.*
Courtesy of Heavenly Valley.

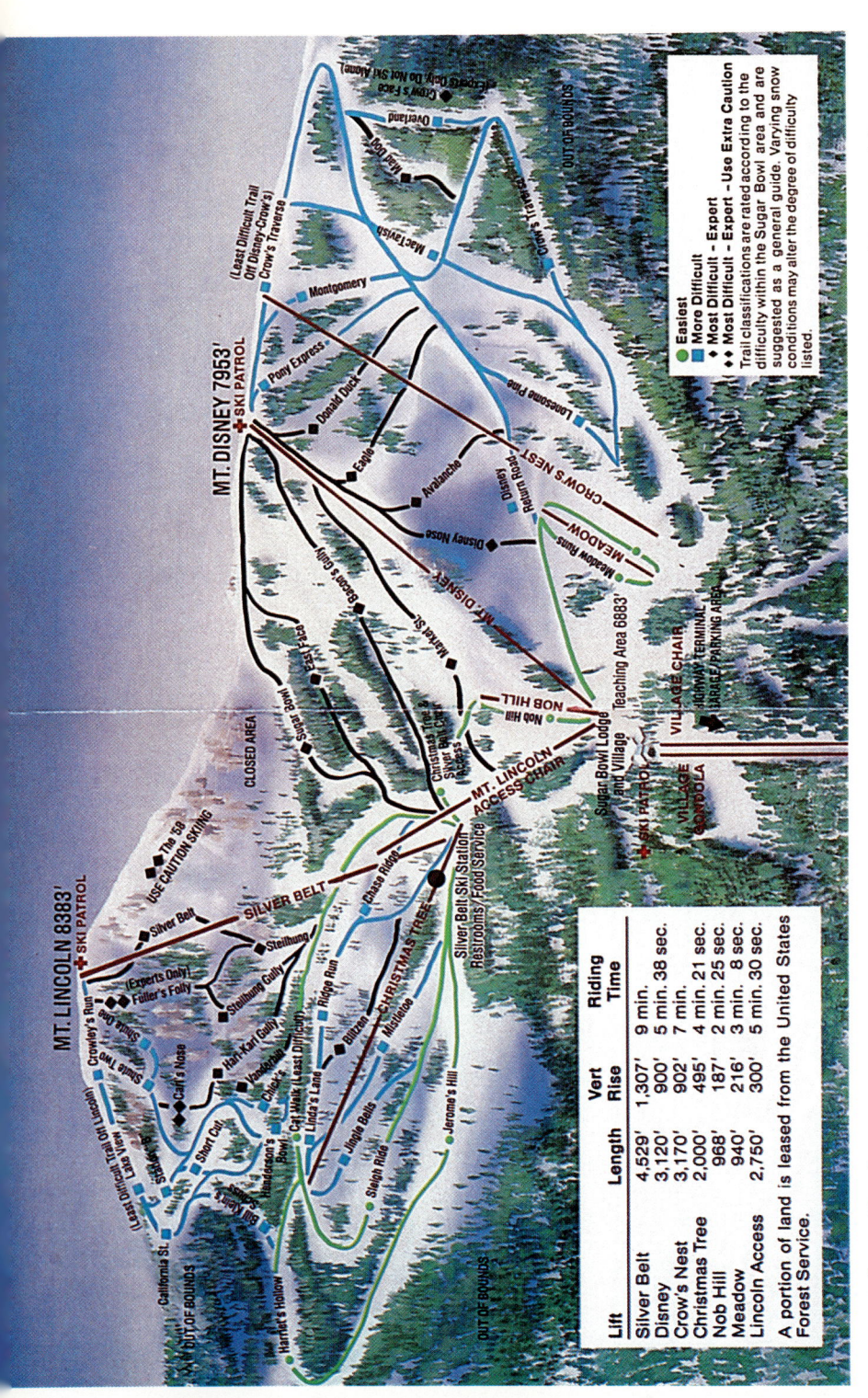

*Sugar Bowl*

## 53

● **EASIEST**
1. Creampuff
2. Sunshine
3. Alley Cat
4. Scooter

■ **MORE DIFFICULT**
5. Lodge Return
6. Bee Vee
7. Roller Coaster
8. Home Run
9. Meadow

◆ **MOST DIFFICULT**
10. Chablis
11. Roaring 20's
12. Flying 30
13. Mad Dog
14. Nose Dive
15. Gold Rush
16. Race Course

Courtesy of Boreal/Soda Springs.

*Soda Springs*

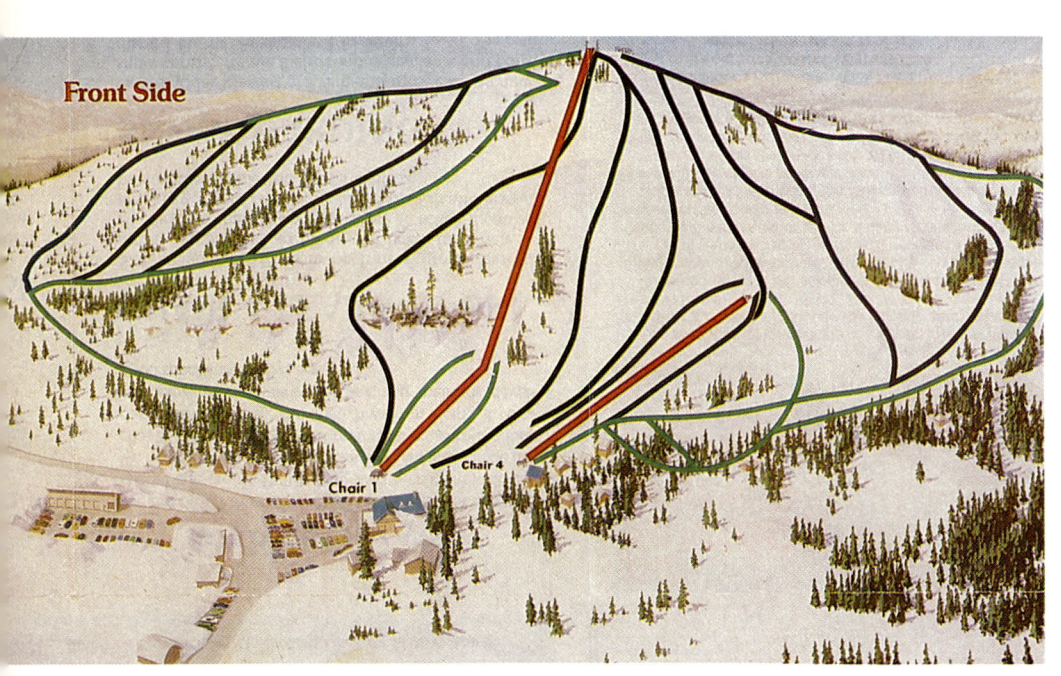

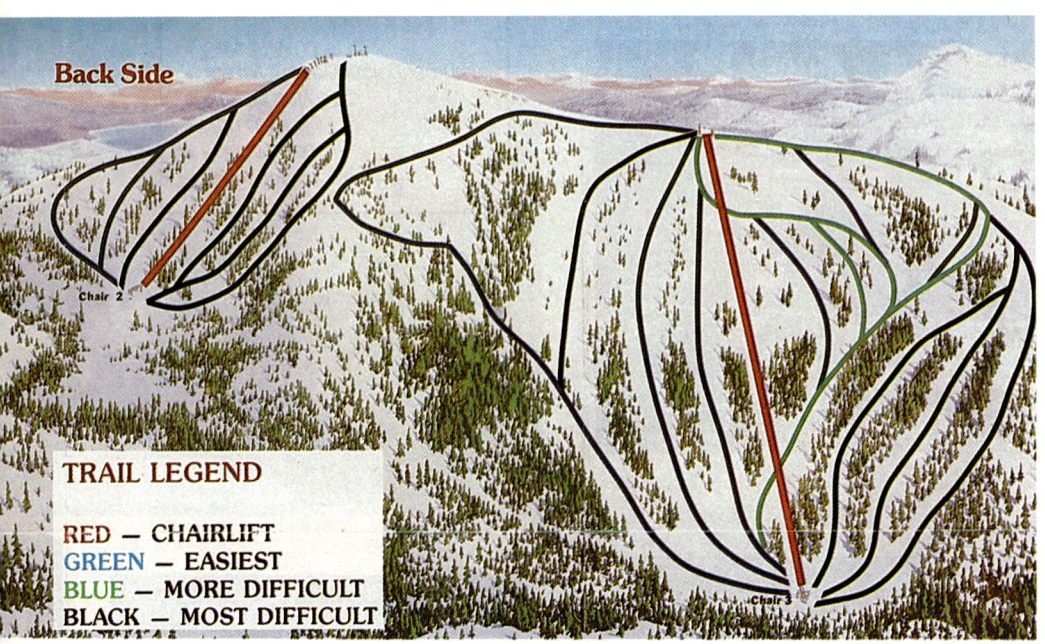

54

*Donner Ski Ranch*            Courtesy of Donner Ski Ranch.

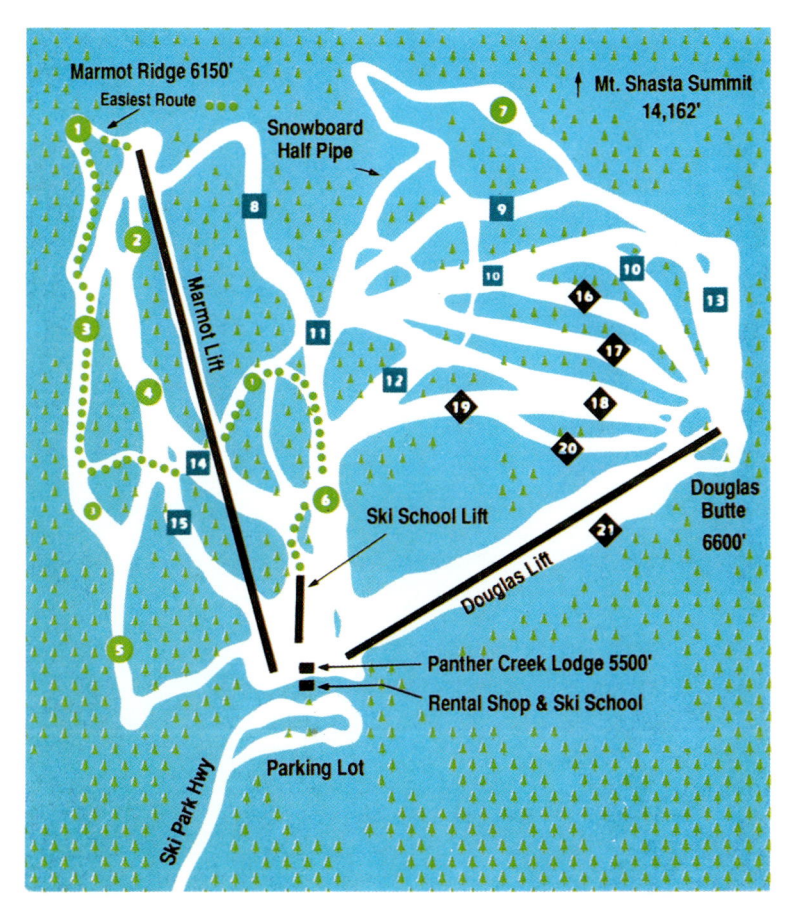

*Mount Shasta*  Courtesy of Mount Shasta Ski Park.

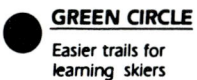

### ● GREEN CIRCLE
Easier trails for learning skiers

1. Easy Street
2. Telemark
3. Blue Grouse
4. Fresh Aire
5. Wintun Way
6. Panther Creek
7. Coyote Road

Snowboard Half Pipe off Coyote

### ■ BLUE SQUARE
Intermediate trails for all-around skiers

8. Silvertip
9. Spotted Owl
10. Highland Glide
11. Horse Shoe Bend
12. Horizon
13. North Saddle
14. Snowshoe
15. Challenge

### ◆ BLACK DIAMOND
Most difficult trails for skilled skiers

16. Halley's Comet
17. Red Tail
18. Black Fox
19. Flying Squirrel
20. Rocky Ridge
21. West Face

56

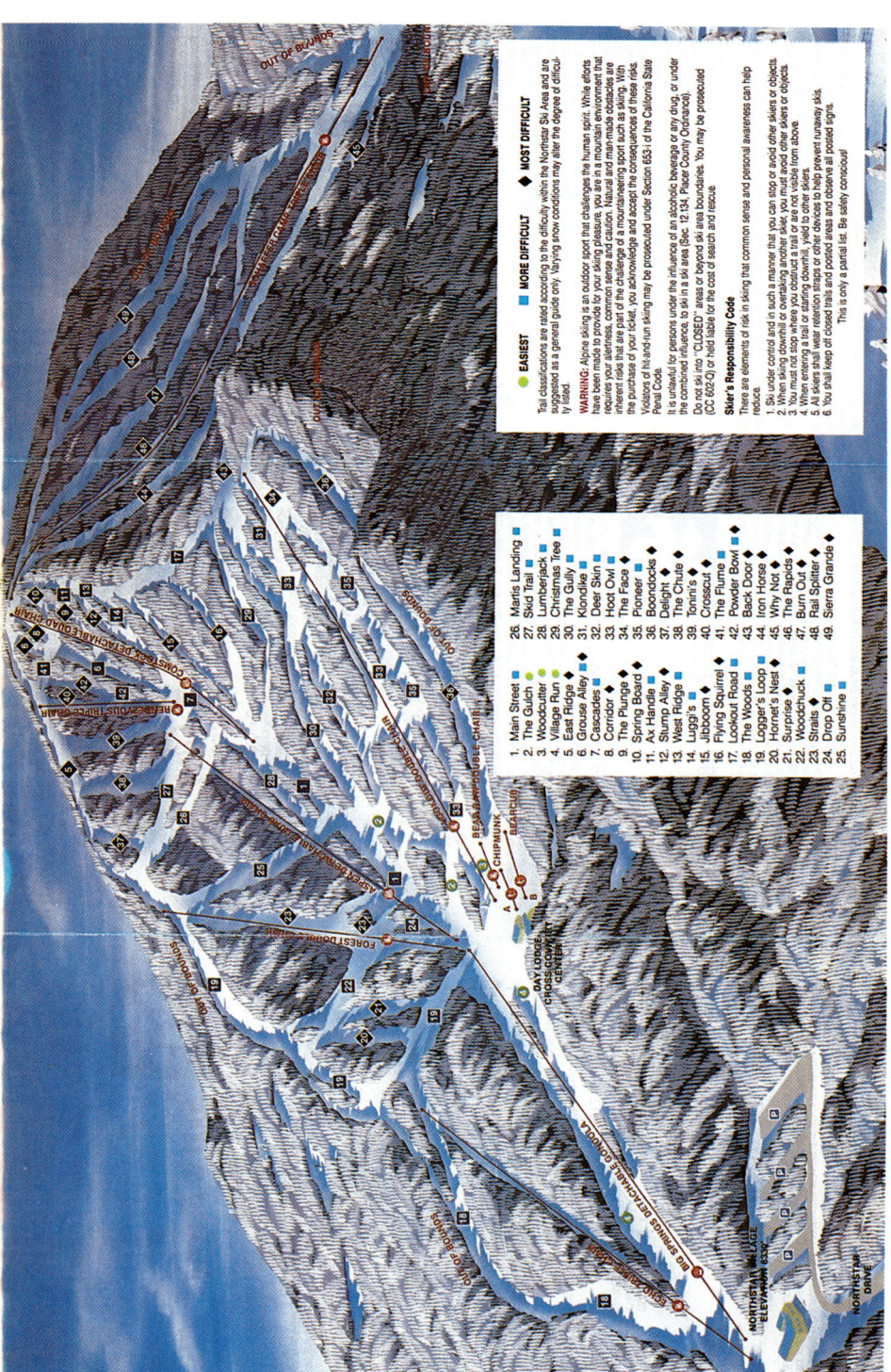

*Northstar-at-Tahoe.* Courtesy of Northstar-at-Tahoe.

*Northstar-at-Tahoe offers 230 on-site accommodations ranging from hotel-type units to condominiums and homes. Courtesy of Northstar-at-Tahoe.*

*Kids have a great time learning to ski at Kirkwood—they're often better skiers than their parents!* Courtesy of John Kelly/Kirkwood.

*After a day on the slopes, it's time for some après-ski fun at Northstar-at-Tahoe.* Courtesy of John Kelly/Northstar-at-Tahoe.

*For those in search of speed, Mt. Shasta Ski Park offers racing clinics, as well as private race training. Courtesy of Kevin Lahey and Mt. Shasta Ski Park.*

*Diamond Peak*

Courtesy of Diamond Peak.

61

*Breathtaking views of Lake Tahoe are everywhere at Diamond Peak.*

Courtesy of Diamond Peak.

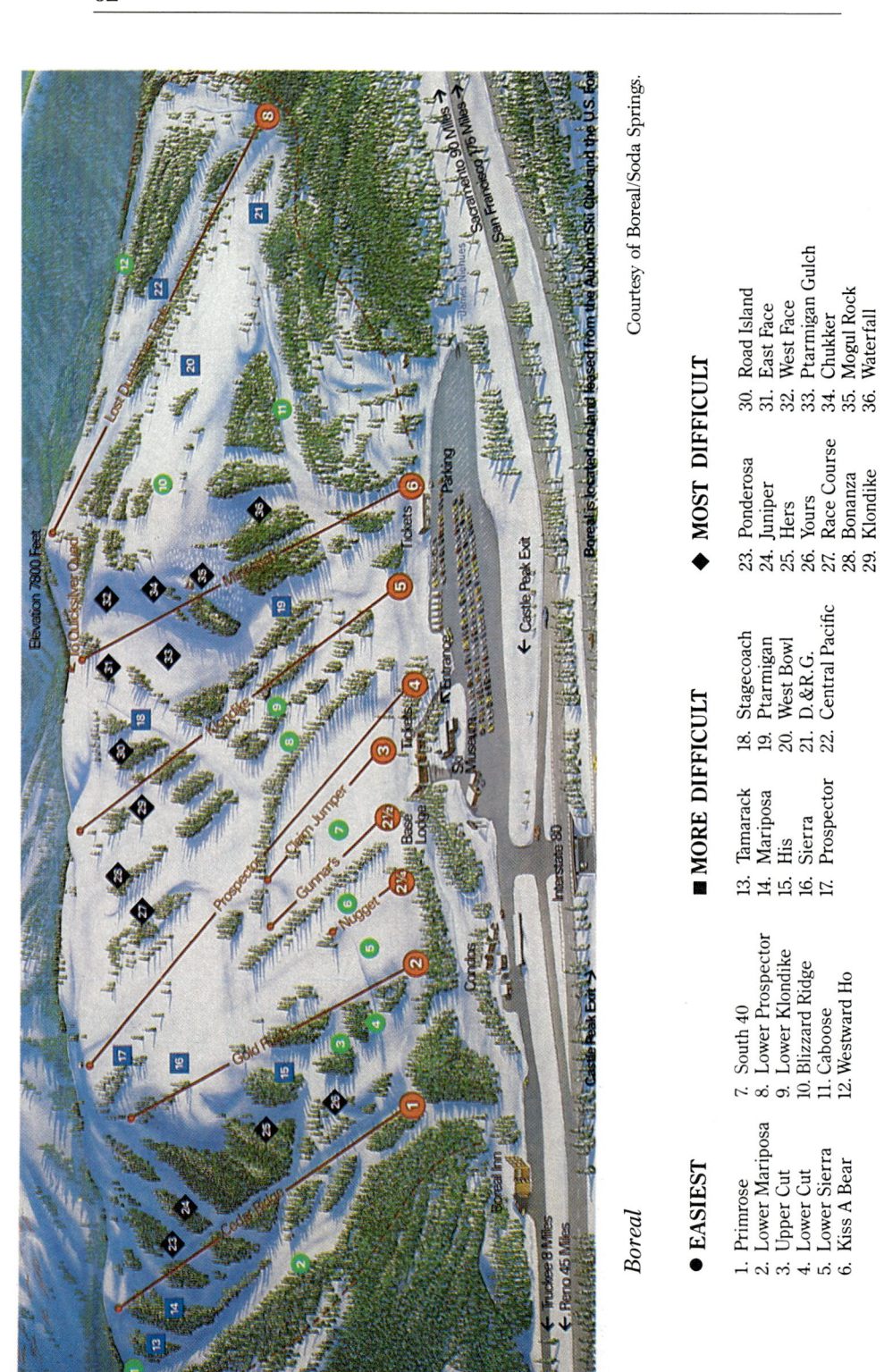

## Boreal

### ● EASIEST

1. Primrose
2. Lower Mariposa
3. Upper Cut
4. Lower Cut
5. Lower Sierra
6. Kiss A Bear
7. South 40
8. Lower Prospector
9. Lower Klondike
10. Blizzard Ridge
11. Caboose
12. Westward Ho

### ■ MORE DIFFICULT

13. Tamarack
14. Mariposa
15. His
16. Sierra
17. Prospector
18. Stagecoach
19. Ptarmigan
20. West Bowl
21. D.&R.G.
22. Central Pacific

### ◆ MOST DIFFICULT

23. Ponderosa
24. Juniper
25. Hers
26. Yours
27. Race Course
28. Bonanza
29. Klondike
30. Road Island
31. East Face
32. West Face
33. Ptarmigan Gulch
34. Chukker
35. Mogul Rock
36. Waterfall

Courtesy of Boreal/Soda Springs.

Courtesy of Tahoe Donner.

*Tahoe Donner*

● Easiest  ■ More Difficult  ◆ Most Difficult (Not Groomed)

*The summit at Kirkwood is only one chair ride away from its base, due to its high base elevation of 7,800 ft.*
Courtesy of Kirkwood.

64

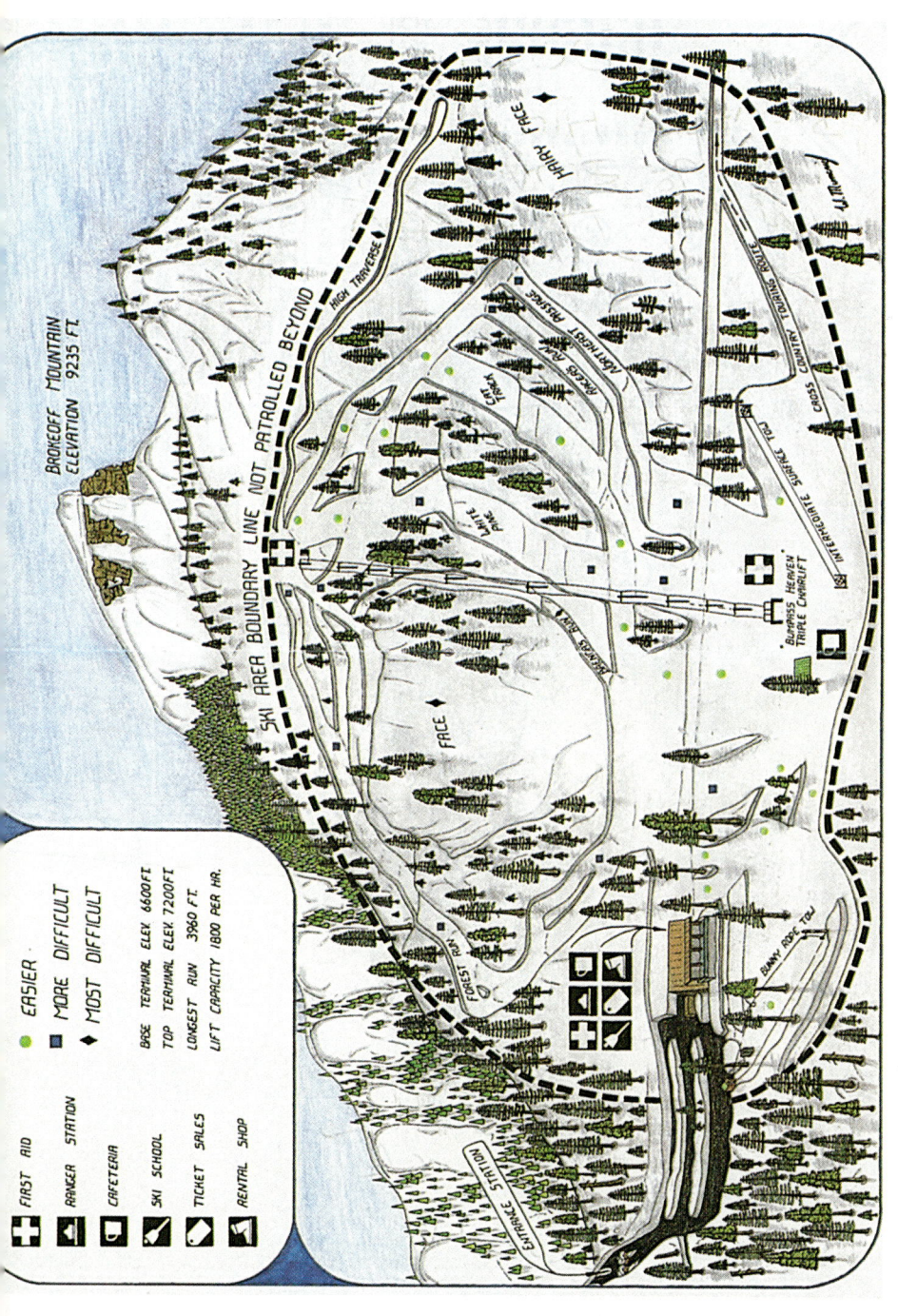

Lassen Park Ski Area

Courtesy of Lassen Park Ski Area.

Courtesy of Mount Rose.

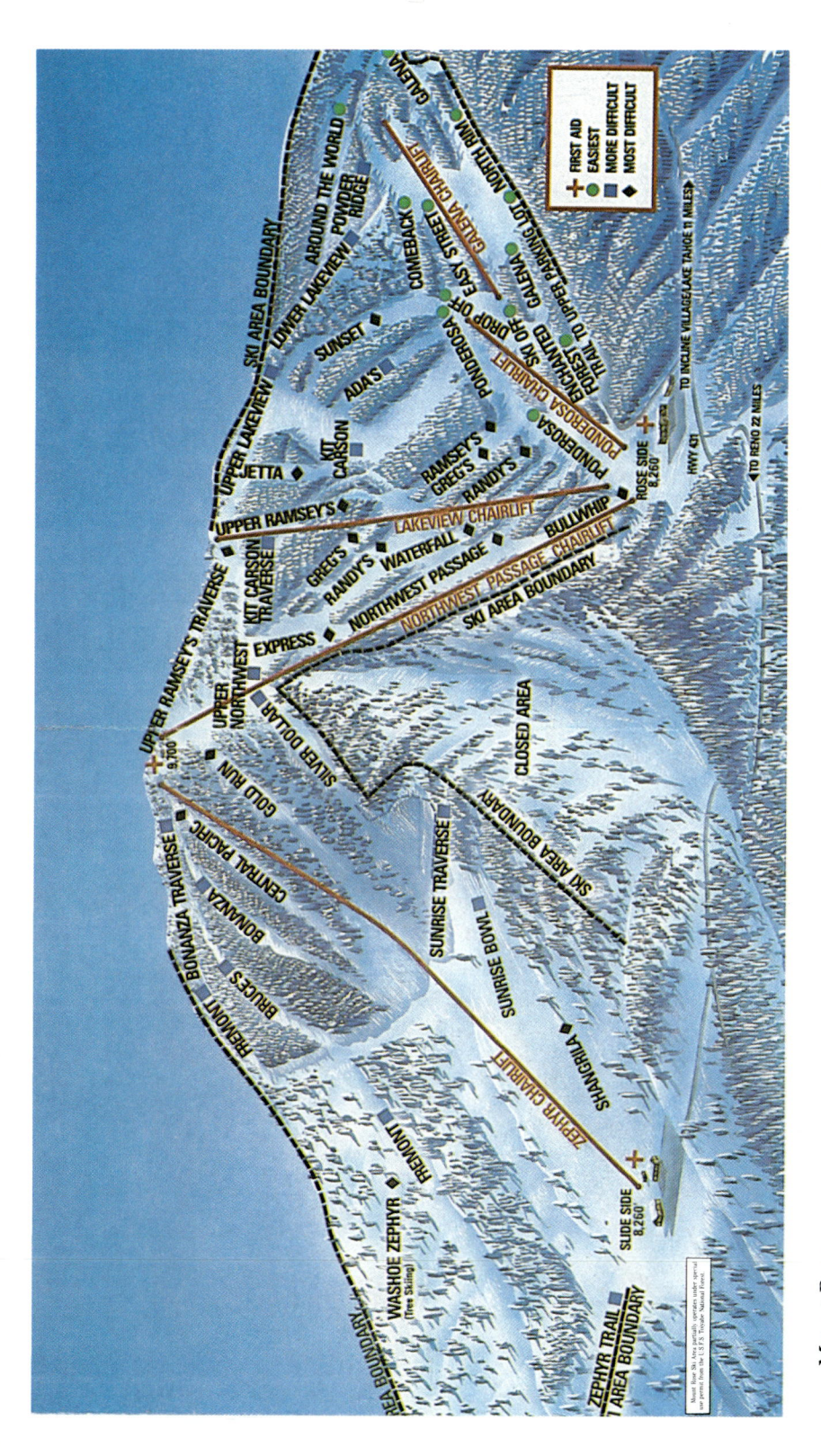

*Mount Rose*

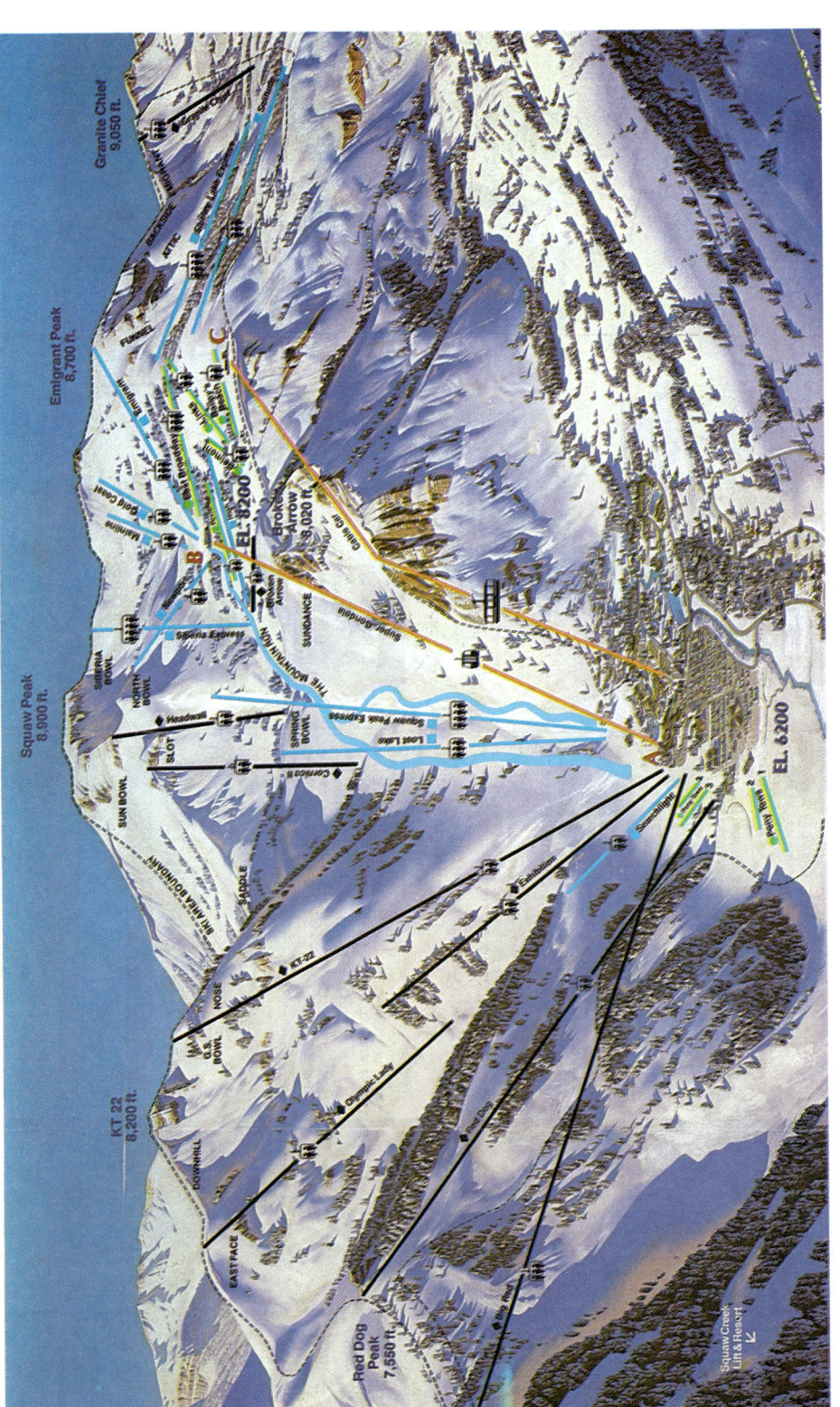

*Squaw Valley*

Courtesy of Squaw Valley USA.

With some of the steepest terrain in the area, Squaw Valley is a great testing ground for advanced ski skills.
Courtesy of Squaw Valley USA.

## Alpine Meadows

### ● EASIER
1. Lower 40
2. Meadow
3. Subway
4. Tiegel

### ■ MORE DIFFICULT
5. Scott Ridge Run
6. Bobby's Run
7. Reily's Run (Sherwood to Lakeview)
8. Return Road (Sherwood to Weasel)
9. Weasel Run
10. Loop Road
11. Yellow Trail
12. Ladies Slalom
13. Red Trail
14. Red-Green Trail
15. Terry's Return
16. Rock Garden
17. Green Trail
18. Blue Trail
19. Alpine Bowl
20. Kangaroo
21. Sherwood Run
22. Standard Run
23. Weasel Chair to Sherwood
24. Lakeview to Weasel
25. Winter Road
26. Weasel to Lakeview
27. Ray's Rut (Lakeview to Sherwood)
28. Leisure Lane (Lakeview to Scott)

### ■ MORE DIFFICULT
29. Mountain View
30. Scott Meadow
31. Scotty's Beam
32. Twilight Zone
33. Shooting Star
34. Outer Limits

### ◆ MOST DIFFICULT
35. Lower 40 Face
36. Gentian Gully
37. Promised Land
38. Chute that Seldom Slides
39. Expert Shortcut
40. Hidden Knolls
41. Lower Saddle
42. Sympathy Face
43. Peril Ridge
44. The Face
45. Waterfall
46. D-8
47. D-7
48. Three Sisters
49. Wolverine Bowl
50. Beaver Bowl
51. Big Bend Bowl
52. SP Bowl
53. Sun Bowls
54. South Face
55. Sherwood Face

### ◆◆ EXPERT ONLY
56. Scott Chute
57. Counterweight Gully
58. Our Father
59. Palisades

*Courtesy of Alpine Meadows.*

*Alpine Meadows' north-facing slopes hold powder late into May, giving new definition to the term "spring skiing."*

Courtesy of Alpine Meadows and Egidio Photography.

*After learning to ski at Alpine Meadows' ski school, kids love to coast down Hot Wheels, a creek-bed gully that feels like a bobsled run.*

Courtesy of Alpine Meadows.

## Trail Marking and Map Legends

- ▌ Ski Lift
- ● Easiest
- ■ More Difficult
- ◆ Most Difficult
- ▬ ▬ Ski Area Boundary (Illegal To Cross)
- ≡ Easiest Way Down
- ⬥ Ski School
- ✦ Ski Rental
- ▌ Ticket Sales
- ⋀ Sport Shop
- ✚ Ski Patrol
- ✱ Walking
- 🅿 Parking
- 🚌 Ski Bus Station
- ✘ Restaurant
- ⛉ Rest Room
- ☎ Phone
- ★ Mt. Top
- ☐ Access Gate

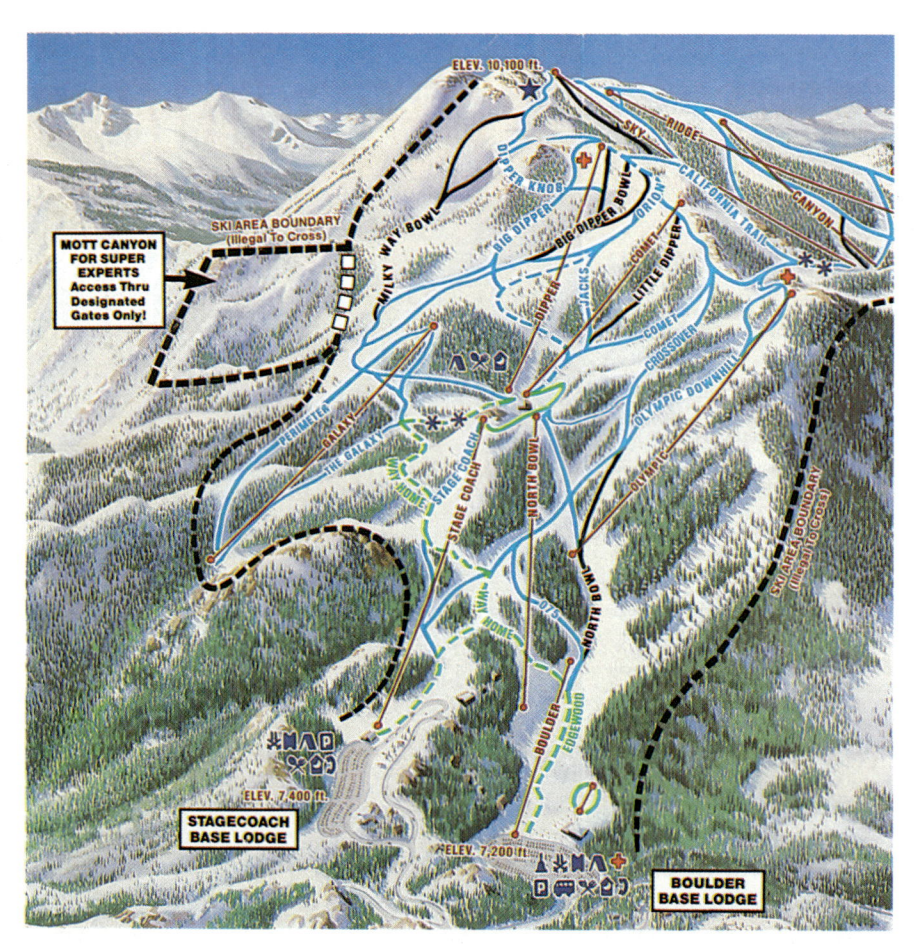

*Heavenly Valley*
*(Heavenly Nevada)*

Courtesy of Heavenly Valley.

*Soaking up sun and enjoying the view are only part of the fun at Heavenly Valley.*  Courtesy of Heavenly Valley.

*Heavenly Valley*
*(Heavenly California)*  Courtesy of Heavenly Valley.

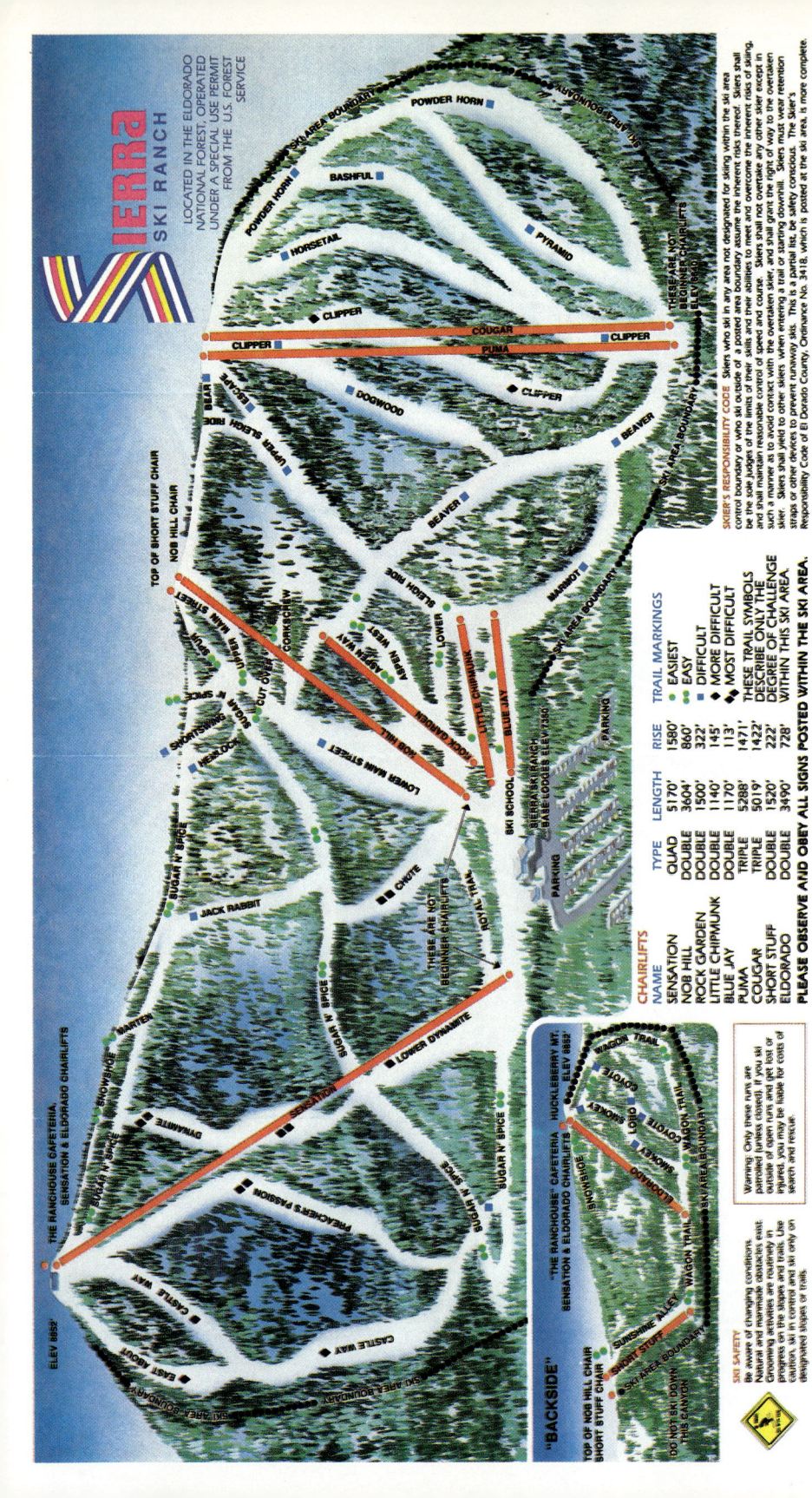

# SIERRA SKI RANCH

LOCATED IN THE ELDORADO NATIONAL FOREST, OPERATED UNDER A SPECIAL USE PERMIT FROM THE U.S. FOREST SERVICE

## CHAIRLIFTS

| NAME | TYPE | LENGTH | RISE |
|---|---|---|---|
| SENSATION | QUAD | 5170' | 1580' |
| NOB HILL | DOUBLE | 3604' | 860' |
| ROCK GARDEN | DOUBLE | 1500' | 322' |
| LITTLE CHIPMUNK | DOUBLE | 1140' | 145' |
| BLUE JAY | DOUBLE | 1170' | 113' |
| PUMA | TRIPLE | 5288' | 1471' |
| COUGAR | TRIPLE | 5019' | 1422' |
| SHORT STUFF | DOUBLE | 1520' | 222' |
| ELDORADO | DOUBLE | 3490' | 728' |

PLEASE OBSERVE AND OBEY ALL SIGNS POSTED WITHIN THIS SKI AREA.

## TRAIL MARKINGS

- ● EASIEST
- ● EASY
- ■ DIFFICULT
- ◆ MORE DIFFICULT
- ◆◆ MOST DIFFICULT

THESE TRAIL SYMBOLS DESCRIBE ONLY THE DEGREE OF CHALLENGE WITHIN THIS SKI AREA.

**SKIER'S RESPONSIBILITY CODE** Skiers who ski outside of a posted area boundary or who ski outside of a posted area boundary assume the inherent risks of skiing, and shall maintain reasonable control of speed and course. Skiers shall not overtake any other skier except in such a manner as to avoid contact with the overtaken skier, and shall grant the right of way to the overtaken skier. Skiers shall yield to other skiers when entering a trail or starting downhill. Skiers must wear retention straps or other devices to prevent runaway skis. This is a partial list, be safety conscious. The Skier's Responsibility Code of El Dorado County, Ordinance No. 3418, which is posted at the ski area, is more complete.

## SKI SAFETY

Be aware of changing conditions. Natural and manmade obstacles exist. Grooming activities are routinely in progress on the slopes and trails. Use caution, ski in control and ski only on designated slopes of trails.

**Warning:** Only these runs are patrolled funless closed. If you ski outside of open runs and get lost of injured, you may be liable for costs of search and rescue.

"BACKSIDE"
TOP OF NOB HILL CHAIR
SHORT STUFF CHAIR
HUCKLEBERRY MT. ELEV 8650'

Courtesy of Sierra Ski Ranch.

*Sierra Ski Ranch*

*Kirkwood*

Courtesy of Kirkwood.

*Homewood*                                                         Courtesy of Homewood.

**MAP LEGEND**

- ● EASIEST (green)
- ■ MORE DIFFICULT (blue square)
- ♦ MOST DIFFICULT (black diamond)
- — CHAIR LIFTS (red line)
- — SURFACE LIFTS (blue line)
- — SLOW SKIING AREA (yellow line)
- ▲ FOOD & BEVERAGE (purple house)
- ✱ MID-STATION/ LOADING ONLY (red star)
- ✚ SKI PATROL (red cross)
- ⌂ SKI SCHOOL MEETING AREA (green house)

*Homewood's tree-lined trails appear to dip right into Lake Tahoe.*
                                             Courtesy of Homewood.

# Part II
## Lake Tahoe Area

# Sugar Bowl

*Sugar Bowl Corporation*
*P.O. Box 5*
*Norden, CA 95724*
*Information: (916) 426-3651*
*Snowphone: (916) 426-3847*

### Driving distances

| | |
|---|---|
| Los Angeles | 476 mi |
| Reno | 44 mi |
| Sacramento | 90 mi |
| San Diego | 595 mi |
| San Francisco | 180 mi |
| San Jose | 207 mi |
| S. Lake Tahoe | 54 mi |
| Tahoe City | 22 mi |
| Truckee | 14 mi |

*For road conditions, call*
*(916) 581-1400, California*
*(702) 793-1313, Nevada.*

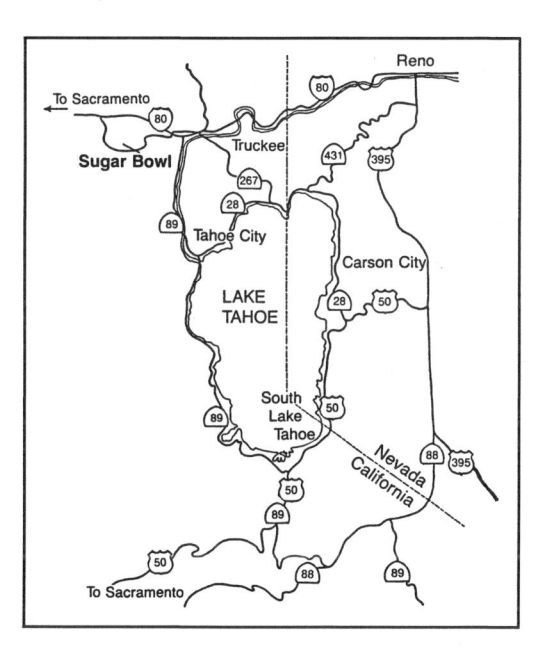

In 1938, the concept for a ski resort was born in the mind of Austrian ski champion Hannes Schroll. His vision took shape with the backing of stockholders that included the likes of Walt Disney, J.D. Zellerbach, chairman of the board of Crown Zellerbach Paper Company, and Jerome Hill, grandson of Great Northern Railroad founder, James Hill.

By 1939, San Franciscans could escape the city on a Southern Pacific transcontinental night train and disembark at Norden Station in Donner Summit the next morning. From there, they were transported by tractors between 25-foot high snow banks into another world, a world where private homes were modeled after Tyrolean chalets and everyone dressed for dinner at the Bavarian-style lodge. The site, chosen for its snow pack, one of the deepest averages recorded in the U.S., was named Sugar Bowl.

Today, Sugar Bowl is less formal, but the romantic notion of a winter escape remains. Although it no longer stops at Norden, the Southern Pacific still chugs

*Built in 1939, the lodge at Sugar Bowl is the oldest in the Lake Tahoe area. (Courtesy of Sugar Bowl Corporation.)*

through the Donner Pass right underneath the "Magic Carpet" gondola that transports skiers from a covered parking lot across the valley to Sugar Bowl. Once there, transport is by foot, ski, or horse-drawn sleigh. Today some still come seeking this temporary isolation from their regular world. But now, more than ever, those who come, come for the "sugar"—the powdery deeps on Mt. Lincoln and Mt. Disney.

## LOCATION

Sugar Bowl is located in Placer County, California, 14 miles west of Truckee. From Reno, 44 miles east, or Sacramento, 90 miles west, Sugar Bowl is reached via the six-lane I-80 to the Nordon/Soda Springs exit. Sugar Bowl's parking lot is less than 3 miles further on Donner Pass Road. (Old SH 40). Donner Pass Road is closed in winter about 2 miles past Sugar Bowl, cutting off access from Donner Lake.

At the parking lot, skiers can purchase a $5 ticket for the gondola or chair lift to Sugar Bowl. The fee is waived for overnight guests, and porters are available to help with luggage.

From Stateline at Crystal Bay in North Lake Tahoe, drive north on SH 267 to Donner Pass Road and I-80. Head west to the Nordon/Soda Springs exit, and then east again on Donner Pass Road, to Sugar Bowl. From Tahoe's West Shore, SH 89 runs north into I-80 at Truckee.

The closest major airport to Sugar Bowl is at Reno, Nevada. Sugar Bowl is also served by the Sacramento airport. Scheduled service to Lake Tahoe Airport in South Lake Tahoe is less frequent and, in heavy weather, flights often land in Reno instead. Four-wheel-drive and cars equipped for skiers are available for rental at all 3 airports.

Amtrak's "California Zephyr" stops in Truckee, as well as in Sacramento and Reno/Sparks. Auto rentals are available in Truckee at the AAA Auto Rental, adjacent to the Amtrak station. Greyhound operates bus service into Truckee and Soda Springs.

## TERRAIN

Sugar Bowl starts where many ski mountains end—at a base elevation of 6,883 ft. With an annual snowfall of 500 in., (the 1982/83 season received a

*With an annual snowfall of 500 in. and a base elevation of 6,883 ft, Sugar Bowl lays claim to the deepest snow pack in the Lake Tahoe area.* (Courtesy of Sugar Bowl Corporation.)

record 896 in.), Sugar Bowl lays claim to the deepest snow pack in the Tahoe area.

Advanced slopes cover 50% of the mountain. There's not much here for beginners. Advanced skiers will find challenging steeps on the right side of Mt. Lincoln, an ungroomed area for experts only. To the left, hair-raising chutes like *Fuller's Folly* appear to plunge straight down the fall line while *Carl's Nose* and *Silver Belt* are mined with moguls. Further below, *Steilhung Gully* and *Hari-Kari Gully* bank through the trees like bobsled runs.

From the top of Mt. Lincoln to the base, intermediate skiers can cruise for 3 miles on *Lakeview*, and on *California Street*, where the pitch is kinder and the trails are wider and well-groomed. Or they can try the open bowls on Mt. Disney. Beginners will feel most comfortable on the *Meadow Runs*, *Sleigh Ride*, or *Harriet's Hollow*.

Even on holidays, lift lines are rarely as long as 10 minutes.

## FACILITIES

In addition to regular lift prices, a midweek ski package Sunday to Friday includes 5 nights accommodations at the base lodge, 5 days of lift passes, daily instruction, videotaping in ski school, night skiing, breakfast and dinner daily, complimentary cordials, and Tyrolean entertainment Thursday nights. Rates start at $510 per person, double occupancy. Children who are beginners should be 6-years-old or older.

## FACILITIES AT A GLANCE

| | |
|---|---|
| *Season:* | Mid-November–Mid-April. |
| *Hours:* | 9 a.m.–4 p.m. daily. |
| *Night Skiing:* | None. |
| *Area:* | 1,000 acres with 47 runs. |
| | Beginner: 20% |
| | Intermediate: 30% |
| | Advanced: 50% |
| *Base Elevation:* | 6,883 ft |
| *Summit Elevation:* | 8,383 ft |
| *Vertical Drop:* | 1,500 ft |
| *Longest Run:* | 3 miles. |
| *Snowmaking:* | None. |

*Snowboarding:* February through closing.
*Lift Capacity:* 7,900 per hr.

*Lifts:* 8 chair lifts (7 doubles, 1 quad) and gondola

| Name | Length | Vertical Rise |
| --- | --- | --- |
| Christmas | 2,000 ft | 498 ft |
| Crow's Nest | 3,170 ft | 902 ft |
| Disney | 3,120 ft | 900 ft |
| Lincoln Access | 2,750 ft | 300 ft |
| Magic Carpet Gondola | NA | NA |
| Meadow | 940 ft | 216 ft |
| Nob Hill | 968 ft | 187 ft |
| Silver Belt | 4,529 ft | 1,307 ft |
| Village Chair | NA | NA |

*Lift Passes:*

| | All Day | Afternoon Only |
| --- | --- | --- |
| | 9 a.m.–4 p.m. | 1 p.m.–4 p.m. |
| Adults | $30 | $20 |
| Children 6–12 | $14 | $11 |
| Children under 6 | FREE | FREE |

*Season Passes:* $575 Adult. $275 Child. $425 midweek only.
*Group Rates:* Available by prior arrangement.

*Food & Drink:* A cafeteria, barbecue deck, restaurant, and cocktail lounge are in the base lodge. Food service and an outdoor barbecue are also located at the Silver Belt Ski Station, at the bottom of the Silver Belt chair.

*Parking & Transportation:* Parking is free at the base parking lot on Old Hwy 40. Covered parking is available at the site for $5 midweek and $10 weekends and holidays. Overnight parking for RVs not permitted. The Donner Summit shuttle operates weekends and holidays and connects Sugar Bowl with Donner Ski Ranch, Soda Springs, and Royal Gorge Cross-Country area.

*Ski Rentals:* The rental shop is located in the main lodge, and open from 8 a.m. to 6 p.m., (916) 426-3683. Includes skis boots and poles.
All day: Adult $16. Child $12. Demos skis and poles: $23.

*Ski School:* (916) 426-3097.
  *Method:* Modified ATM.
  *Ski School Director:* Toni Marth.

*(continued)*

*(continued from previous page)*
*Class Lessons:*   9:45 a.m. and 1:45 p.m.
  $18 (2 hr) adult and child
  $26 (4 hr) adult and child
  $75 five lessons (2 hr)
  $130 ten lessons (2 hr)
  *Beginner Special:*   Includes lesson, rental equipment, and use of beginner lifts. $36 adult. $29 child.
  *Private Lessons:*   $30 an hr. Each additional person $8. $130 all day (4 hr) for 1 to 3 persons. Each additional person $15.
*Races & Clinics:*   Racing clinics Saturdays at 1:45 p.m. with minimum of 3 participants, at class lesson rates. Private clinics by arrangement.
*Day Care:*   None.
*Camper Facilities:*   No overnight RV parking. Camper and tent sites are available 40 miles southeast at Sugar Pine Point State Park, south of Tahoma on SH 89. $10 per night. No hookups. Heated restrooms. Parking.
*Medical:* First aid on mountain. Tahoe Forest Hospital is 14 miles east inTruckee.

The Weekend Special, sold on Saturdays (except those that are also holidays), includes 2 days of lift tickets and 3 half-day lessons. The cost for adults is $72, and for children, $55.

During Interski Week, a special pass permits skiers to ski Boreal, Donner Ski Ranch, and Sugar Bowl for $30. Designed for intermediate and advanced skiers, Boreal is connected with Donner Ski Ranch via the back bowls and an intermediate run. The circle is completed via the shuttle bus that links Donner Ski Ranch, 1 mile east, with Sugar Bowl.

## SPECIAL EVENTS

- *Alpenfest*—March. Employees dress in Tyrolean costumes; music, yodelers and dancing.
- *Silver Belt Ski Race*—March. Masters' division of the USSA.
- *Antique Ski/Longboard Race*—March.
- *Jimmie Heuga Express*—March. Charity skiathon.

# WINTER ACTIVITIES

## Cross-Country

*Royal Gorge Cross-Country Resort* is 2 miles from Sugar Bowl, off Old Hwy 40 at Soda Springs. With 67 trails and 196 miles of track, Royal Gorge is the largest Nordic ski resort in North America. The trails are 39% beginner, 41% intermediate, and 20% advanced. Facilities include snowmaking, double tracks with skating lanes, ski school, rental equipment, ski shop, 2 lodges, 2 cafes, and 7 warming huts.

An all-day pass is $14.50 for adults and $8.50 for children 7 and older. Children under 7 years are free. Half-day passes, twilight passes, and season passes are also available. Adult class lessons are $23, including trail pass. The Pee Wee Snow School, for ages 4 to 9, meets from 10:30 a.m. to 1:30 p.m. $25 includes lesson, rentals, pass, lunch, and supervision.

Royal Gorge participates in the the Ski North Tahoe interchangeable trail pass, along with Diamond Peak Cross-Country, Northstar-at-Tahoe, Tahoe Donner, Spooner Lake, Squaw Valley Nordic, and Tahoe Nordic. Rates are $34 for 4 days, $40 for 5 days, and $45 for 6 days.

Royal Gorge is connected by shuttle buses on weekends and holidays with Sugar Bowl, Soda Springs Ski Area, and Donner Ski Ranch, (916) 426-3871, or 800-634-3086 outside California and Nevada.

*Clair Tappaan Lodge* on Old Hwy 40, 1 mile west of Sugar Bowl, is owned and operated by the Sierra Club, and is open to members and their guests. The lodge maintains a little more than two miles of groomed cross-country trails and offers instruction in both Nordic and telemark techniques, primarily on weekends and holidays. Lessons for adults and children over 8 are $12 for a 1- to 2-hour class, depending on class size.

Skis, boots, and pole rentals are $11 for adults and $7 for children 12 and younger. Rates for "back country" equipment are $14 adults and $12 for children. Use of the trails is free for Sierra Club members. Guests are asked to pay a $4 donation or $2 for children. Bunk-style accommodations and all meals are available at the lodge.

For information on other cross-country trails in the North Lake Tahoe area, see also Tahoe Donner Cross-Country, Squaw Valley, and Northstar-at-Tahoe.

## Snowmobiling

For information on nearby snowmobiling, see Boreal and Tahoe Donner Ski Resort. For snowmobile rentals and guided tours, see Squaw Valley.

### Mountaineering

Montaineering seminars are held nearby at *Alpine Skills International*. See Donner Ski Ranch.

### Sleigh Rides

Horse-drawn sleighs depart from the lodge for 30-minute rides every hour between 4 p.m. and 8 p.m. on weekends and holidays, weather permitting. Midweek rides are by special arrangement. Minimum 10 persons. Advanced reservations required. Adults $6. Children 12 and under $4. Children under 2 are free.

## OTHER ACTIVITIES

**Ballooning:** Mountain High Balloons, Truckee.
**Cinema:** The Martis Valley Theatre, Truckee.
**Fitness:** High Sierra Fitness, adjacent to the Truckee Airport.
**Museums:** Western America Ski Sport Museum—Adjacent to Boreal, 4 miles from Sugar Bowl; Emmigrant Trail Museum, Donner Memorial State Park.
**Sightseeing:** Nevada City and historic Truckee.
**Swimming:** Truckee High School, Truckee.

## SHOPPING

*Klein's Ski Shop*, located at the mountain base, sells ski equipment, apparel, and accessories. Complete cross-country ski equipment and accessories are available at the *Royal Gorge Ski Shop*, 2 miles west. The *High Sierra Ski Shop*, Donner Pass Road, has downhill and cross-country equipment for rent but not for sale, (916) 426-3567. A grocery store and deli are located within a mile of the Sugar Bowl parking lot at Norden House. A general store selling groceries and other items such as car chains is located at the gas station at the Soda Springs/Norden exit off I-80.

## APRÈS-SKI

The *Silver Belt Bar* at the lodge is the place where skiers congregate after a day on the slopes, before or after dinner. An accordion player on weekends adds to the European atmosphere.

The ample bar at the *Donner Summit Lodge* on Old Hwy 40 at I-80 attracts locals and skiers and is open until 2 a.m. There's dancing to a live band every other weekend at the *Serene Lake Lodge*, Baker Ranch Road near Royal Gorge.

## RESTAURANTS

**Engadine Cafe**   $$   *(916) 426-3661*
Rainbow Road in the Rainbow Lodge, about 10 miles west of Sugar Bowl and $1/2$ mile from the Rainbow Road exit off I-80. The Engadine Cafe features Swiss-Italian cuisine in a country-Alpine setting. Selections include pasta, salad, and seafood specials such as Pacific salmon. Open for breakfast, lunch, and dinner. Acoustic guitar entertainment on Friday and Saturday evenings.

**Lodge Dining Room**   $$   *(916) 426-3651*
The lodge dining room at Sugar Bowl is open for dinner daily. Jackets and ties are encouraged but no longer required. Jeans, however, are banned. Continental cuisine is served in a pleasant room with white tablecloths and red accents. For dinner guests not staying on the mountain, there's a valet gondola from the parking area on Donner Pass Road to the Sugar Bowl Lodge until 10 p.m.

**Serene Lake Lodge**   $$   *(916) 426-9001*
Baker Ranch Road, $1^1/2$ miles from Sugar Bowl. Dining selections at the lodge include NY steak, top sirloin, veal piccata, chicken fettucine, and a variety of seafood including swordfish and scallops. Live band for dancing every other weekend. Open daily from 7 a.m. to 10 p.m. for breakfast, lunch, and dinner.

**Hofbrau**   $   *(916) 426-3638*
Donner Pass Road and I-80, in the Donner Summit Lodge. The Hofbrau selections include turkey, roast beef, pastrami, fish, chicken, and homemade pies. Open for breakfast and dinner.

See also restaurant listings in Truckee under Tahoe Donner Ski Resort.

## ACCOMMODATIONS

Housing at the base of Sugar Bowl is limited to 23 rooms at the lodge "Le Grand Hotel" and about 15 individually owned and decorated homes on and around the mountain. The homes range from rustic studio apartments to tastefully decorated 6-bedroom homes with telephones, televisions, or even pianos. A few are ski-in and ski-out locations with the others within walking distance of the lifts. Rates range from moderate to expensive. For reservations, call Sugar Bowl Corporation, (916) 426-3651.

**Donner Summit Lodge**   $$   *(916) 426-3638*
Old Hwy 40 at the Norden/Soda Springs exit from I-80. P.O. Box 115, Soda Springs, CA 95728. Forty moderate but spacious rooms with either king-size or

two double beds, private bathrooms, dressers, small table and chairs, and TV. No phones in rooms. Indoor hot tub and sauna on lower level. Restaurant and bar on premises. Rates are slightly lower midweek (non-holiday).

**Le Grand Hotel   $$**   *(916) 426-3651*
Located in the lodge, Le Grand Hotel consists of 23 basic rooms in the original lodge. Double beds, private bathrooms, balconies, and phones. No TV.

**Rainbow Lodge   $$**   *(916) 426-3871*
Rainbow Road, 1/2 mile off I-80 and 7 miles east of Sugar Bowl, the Rainbow Lodge bed-and-breakfast, decorated with rustic charm, has 20 rooms with shared bathrooms and 10 rooms with private bathrooms. Rooms sleep up to 4. No TV or phones. Restaurant and bar. Meeting rooms available.

**Soda Springs Station   $$**   *(916) 426-9504*
Located on Old Hwy 40, 2 miles west of Sugar Bowl at the turnoff for Royal Gorge cross-country area, these luxury 1-, 2-, and 3-bedroom condominiums, mostly on two levels, are fully equipped with wood-burning stoves, ovens, refrigerators, microwaves, TV, and phones. A sauna and hot tub are located in the building. No maid service during stay.

**Serene Lake Lodge   $**   *(916) 426-9001*
Baker Ranch Road, 1 1/2 miles from Sugar Bowl. Rustic rooms with 1 or 2 queen-size beds and shared baths. No phones or TV in rooms, but guests share a large-screen TV in common lounge area. Two-bedroom cabins with sitting areas and kitchens are also available. Utensils are included, but guests supply own sheets. Daily maid service is provided for lodge rooms but not for cabins. Shuttle bus to Royal Gorge and Sugar Bowl.

For additional nearby accommodations, see also Donner Ski Ranch, Boreal, and Tahoe Donner.

# Donner Ski Ranch

❄

P.O. Box 66
Norden, CA 95724
Information: (916) 426-3635

### Driving distances

| | |
|---|---|
| Los Angeles | 477 mi |
| Reno | 45 mi |
| Sacramento | 91 mi |
| San Diego | 596 mi |
| San Francisco | 181 mi |
| San Jose | 208 mi |
| S. Lake Tahoe | 55 mi |
| Tahoe City | 23 mi |
| Truckee | 15 mi |

*For road conditions, call
(916) 581-1400, California
(702) 793-1313, Nevada*

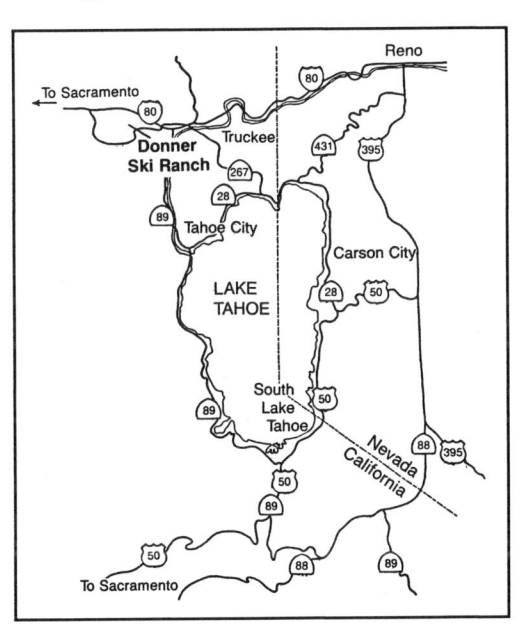

The outstanding feature of Donner Ski Ranch is the efficiency of the mountain's lifts. A quick look at the number of chair lifts—only 4—could easily lead skiers to dismiss the mountain as inconsequential. Each chair, however, has been strategically placed to serve the maximum possible area so that skiers can reach 360° of the mountain. From Chair 1, for example, a skier can reach all 21 runs on the front of the mountain. Two chairs serve the other 21 runs on the back side of the mountain.

While smaller and lower than its next-door neighbor, Sugar Bowl, Donner Ski Ranch still offers a wide range of terrain, from cornices to open bowls. With limits on the number of daily tickets sold, the mountain is rarely crowded, allowing skiers enough space to bask in the casual, unpretentious atmosphere. And for those seeking a ski-week getaway, Donner Ski Ranch offers the convenience of contemporary accommodations right at its base.

## LOCATION

Donner Ski Ranch is on Donner Pass Road (Old Hwy 40), in Placer County, California, 3.5 miles off I-80 at the Norden/Soda Springs exit, 15 miles from Truckee and just 1 mile east of its neighboring ski area, Sugar Bowl. Donner Pass Road is closed in winter on the east side of Donner Ski Ranch, making I-80 the best approach from east or west.

The closest major airport to Donner Ski Ranch is at Reno, Nevada. Donner Ski Ranch is also served by the Sacramento airport. Scheduled service to Lake Tahoe Airport in South Lake Tahoe is less frequent and, in heavy weather, flights often land in Reno instead. Four-wheel-drive and cars equipped for skiers are available for rental at all 3 airports.

Amtrak's "California Zephyr" stops in Truckee, as well as in Sacramento and Reno/Sparks. Auto rentals are available in Truckee at the AAA Auto Rental, adjacent to the Amtrak station. Greyhound operates bus service into Truckee and Soda Springs directly from Sacramento and Reno with connections from a number of other cities.

## TERRAIN

Donner Ski Ranch packs a variety of terrain within its 360 acres, including cornices, mogul fields, bowls, and tree runs. In addition to 3 bottom-to-top lifts, a shorter chair drops novices off midway so they don't have to ride all the way to the top.

Advanced skiers gravitate to *The Palisades*, the cornices to the right of Chair 3, or to *Phil's Run*, the toughest steep on the mountain. The face of Chair 2 is fodder for bump bashers, while those in search of a chute challenge head for *Tower Five*. Powder hounds can still find good powder weeks after a storm in the bowl off Chair 3.

The *half-pipe* is designed for snowboarders and gulley lovers. *Lyla* and *Lyla's Sister*, on the other hand, are casual cruisers for skiers who don't like surprises. The longest run is 1 mile on the South Bowl Trail.

## FACILITIES

Wednesdays are special at Donner Ski Ranch, with all lift tickets going for $12, and group lessons and ski rentals going for $10, for a total savings for adults of $15.

A special program in Norpine instruction (telemark downhill skiing) is offered daily by Mimi and Bela Vadasz of Alpine Skills International.

## FACILITIES AT A GLANCE

| | |
|---|---|
| *Season:* | November 23–April 15. |
| *Hours:* | 8:30 a.m.–4 p.m. daily. |
| *Night Skiing:* | 4 p.m.–10 p.m. Fridays and Saturdays. |
| *Area:* | 360 acres with 40 runs. |
| | Beginner: 25% |
| | Intermediate: 50% |
| | Advanced: 25% |
| *Base Elevation:* | 7,031 ft |
| *Summit Elevation:* | 7,751 ft |
| *Vertical Drop:* | 720 ft |
| *Longest Run:* | 1 mile. |
| *Snowmaking:* | On lower half of front chair lift. |
| *Snowboarding:* | Permitted. |
| *Avg. Annual Snowfall:* | 450 in. |
| *Lift Capacity:* | 5,400 per hr. |

*Lifts:* 4 chair lifts (1 triple, 3 doubles)

| Name | Length | Vertical Rise |
|---|---|---|
| Chair 1 | 2,230 ft | 721 ft |
| Chair 2 | 1,300 ft | 475 ft |
| Chair 3 | 2,410 ft | 525 ft |
| Chair 4 | 1,100 ft | 275 ft |

*Lift Passes:*

| | All Day | Afternoon Only |
|---|---|---|
| | 8:30 a.m.–4 p.m. | 12:30 p.m.–4 p.m. |
| Adults | $18 | $10 |
| weekend/holiday | $22 | $18 |
| Children under 13 | $10 | $10 |
| Seniors 60+ | $10 | $10 |
| Night Skiing, all ages | $5 | |

*Multiday Rates:* None.
*Season Passes:* Adult $330. Child $150.
*Group Rates:* Available for groups of 15+ midweek or 20+ weekend by prior arrangement.

*(continued)*

*(continued from previous page)*

*Food & Drink:*  The cafeteria in the base lodge is open for breakfast and lunch. A sit-down restaurant is open daily for breakfast, and for dinner on weekends and holidays. The bar remains open from 10 a.m. to 9 p.m. midweek, and until midnight on weekends.

*Parking & Transportation:*  Parking is free at the base. Overnight RV parking permitted. No hookups. The Donner Summit Shuttle connects the Donner Ski Ranch with Sugar Bowl, Royal Gorge, and Soda Springs on weekends and holidays.

*Ski Rentals:*  Base lodge shop open 7:30 a.m.–4:30 p.m. daily. Includes skis, boots, and poles.

|  | Adult | Child |
|---|---|---|
| All day: | $14 | $8 |
| Half day: | $ 9 | $6 |
| Demos: | $20 |  |
| Snowboards: | $20 |  |

Cross-country also available.

*Ski School:*  Phone (916) 426-3635.

  *Method:*  ATM.

  *Ski School Director:*  John Hoffman.

  *Class Lessons:*  10:30 a.m. and 1:30 p.m.
    $15 ($1/2$ hr). Ages 11 + .

  *First Timer's Special:*  10:30 a.m. and 1:30 p.m. Includes $1^{1}/_{2}$-hr lesson, use of beginner lift, and equipment rental.
    $30 weekend/holiday. $24 midweek.

  *Kids Klub:*  $35. Ages 5–10. 10:30 a.m. to 12 p.m. and 1 p.m. to 3 p.m. Includes lesson and lift ticket.
    $15 afternoon only, lift ticket not included.
    $175 book of 10 days of lessons, lift ticket not included.
    $300 30 Kids Klub—30-day lift pass.

  *Private Lessons:*  9:15 a.m., 12:15 p.m., 1:30 p.m., and 3 p.m.
    $25 (1 hr). Additional person $10. Limit 3.
    $150 (5 hr). For up to 10 persons. Powder, mogul, and telemark lessons upon request.

  *Snowboard Lessons:*  By appointment. $25 1-hr private, adult or child. $10 each for a second and third person.

*Races & Clinics:*  $150 for 5 hr for up to 8 persons. Reservations required.

  *Jr. Race Team:*  Open to ages 7–17. Contact Ski School.

> *Day Care:* None. A list of baby-sitting services is available from the Truckee Chamber of Commerce, (916) 587-2757 or (800) 548-8388.
>
> *Camper Facilities:* Overnight parking for RVs permitted. No hookups. Camper and tent sites available 35 miles southeast at Sugar Pine Point State Park, south of Tahoma on SH 89. $10 per night. No hookups. Heated restrooms. Parking.
>
> *Medical:* First aid on mountain. Closest hospital is Tahoe Forest Hospital, Truckee, 14 miles east on I-80.

During Interski Weeks in March and April, a special pass permits skiers to ski Donner Ski Ranch, Boreal, and Sugar Bowl for $30. The Interski is designed for intermediate and advanced skiers. Boreal is connected with Donner Ski Ranch via the back bowls and an intermediate run. The circle is completed via the shuttle bus that links Donner Ski Ranch with Sugar Bowl, 1 mile west.

## SPECIAL EVENTS

- *Ski Free Day*—December. Santa Claus hands out 1,500 free lift tickets.
- *USSA/Far West Freestyle, Aerial, Mogul, and Ballet Competition*—January.
- *Anniversary Week*—January. All lift tickets and lessons are $6, and equipment rentals $10, Monday through Friday.
- *Far West Masters' Race*—February.
- *Spring Fling Week*—March. Lift ticket discounts.
- *Family Week*—March. Lift tickets $12, lessons and rentals $10.
- *Snowboard Half-pipe and Giant Slalom Competitions*—Monthly.
- *Donner Summit Interski*—March/April. Intermediate and advanced skiers can ski Donner Ski Ranch, Sugar Bowl, and Boreal in one day on one lift ticket.
- *Golden Egg Hunt*—Easter Sunday. Ski with the Easter Bunny.

## WINTER ACTIVITIES

### Cross-Country

Lessons in Norpine (Nordic downhill skiing), are offered daily for $15 ($1 1/2$ hr). Private 1-hour lessons are $25 for one person, and $10 for each additional person. Nordic rentals available at the base rental shop.

See also Sugar Bowl and Tahoe Donner.

## Snowmobiling

A snowmobile trail is located 5 miles from Donner Ski Ranch at the *Castle Peak* exit off I-80. A Sno-Park permit is required for parking. No equipment rentals on site. See Boreal and Tahoe Donner for additional information.

## Mountaineering

*Alpine Skills International*, located at the Donner Spitz Hutte, less than 1 mile east of Donner Ski Ranch, offers seminars in cross-country, telemark, and extreme skiing techniques. The course covers other skills as well, including descents with ice axe and belay rope, meteorological fundamentals, mountain snow-pack stability evaluation, safe route finding, and evaluation of avalanche-hazard situations. Mini-dorm accommodations and meals are available at the Spitz Hutte. Bunk and Breakfast, $16 per night. Private home, $52, (916) 426-9108.

## Tobogganing, Tubing, and Snow Play

For snow-play information in the North Lake Tahoe area, see Tahoe Donner, Granlibakken, and Squaw Valley.

## Sleigh Rides

Sleigh rides are available 1 mile west at Sugar Bowl. See Sugar Bowl for additional information.

## OTHER ACTIVITIES

**Ballooning:** Mountain High Balloons, Truckee.
**Cinema:** The Martis Valley Theatre, Truckee.
**Fitness:** High Sierra Fitness, Truckee Airport.
**Sightseeing:** Historic towns, Nevada City and Truckee.
**Swimming:** Truckee High School, Truckee.
**Western America SkiSport Museum:** Adjacent to Boreal Lodge.

## SHOPPING

The *Donner Ski Shop*, located in the main lodge, is open from 8 a.m. to 5:30 p.m. and carries ski accessories. A grocery and deli are located less than 1 mile west on Old Hwy 40. *The General Store* at the gas station at the Norden/Soda

Springs I-80 exit carries groceries, tire chains, and sundries. For additional shopping 15 miles east in Truckee, see Tahoe Donner.

## APRÈS-SKI

Skiers socialize in the bar at the base lodge, open until 2 a.m. For après-ski information nearby and in Truckee, see Sugar Bowl and Tahoe Donner.

## RESTAURANTS

**The Old Highway 40 Room   $$**          *(916) 426-3635*
Located in the main lodge at Donner Ski Ranch, the Old Highway 40 Room is open for breakfast and lunch daily, and for dinner on Wednesdays, Fridays, and Saturdays until 9:30 p.m. The menu is limited but offers fish, chicken, veal, and steak entrées.

For additional dining suggestions see Sugar Bowl and Tahoe Donner.

## ACCOMMODATIONS

**The Summit House Hotel   $$**          *(916) 426-3622*
Located at the base of the mountain adjacent to the lodge, the 72-room Summit House offers nicely furnished rooms, studios, suites, and loft suites. All rooms have one queen-size or two extra-long double beds. Studios have queen-size Murphy beds, while suites consist of a hotel room plus a studio, or studio and a loft. Each unit includes a gas fireplace, phone, television, bi-weekly maid service, small refrigerator, and wet bar. Two-night minimum stays apply on weekends and 3-night minimum stays are required on holidays, except Christmas, when a 4-night minimum stay applies.

See additional accommodations under Sugar Bowl, Boreal, and Tahoe Donner.

# Soda Springs

*P.O. Box 39*
*Truckee, CA 95734*
*Information: (916) 426-3666*
*Snowphone: (916) 426-3663*

### Driving distances

| | |
|---|---|
| Los Angeles | 473 mi |
| Reno | 43 mi |
| Sacramento | 87 mi |
| San Diego | 592 mi |
| San Francisco | 177 mi |
| San Jose | 204 mi |
| S. Lake Tahoe | 53 mi |
| Tahoe City | 19 mi |
| Truckee | 13 mi |

*For road conditions, call*
*(916) 581-1400, California*
*(702) 793-1313, Nevada*

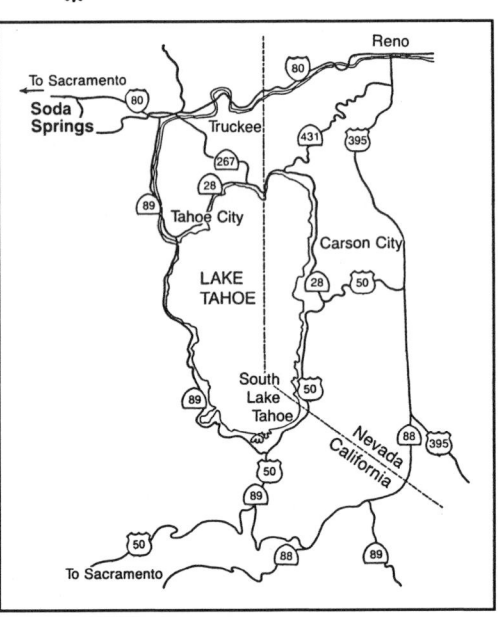

Soda Springs is under the same management as Boreal Ski Area, 3 miles east. But unlike Boreal, which is open night and day, seven days a week, Soda Springs is only open Friday through Monday and holidays. The facility is available for rent the rest of the week.

The mountain attracts skiers who like wide, smooth, well-groomed runs— slope characteristics perfect for learning, improving, and particularly for racing. In addition to special event competitions like the Far West Giant Slalom, local schools, ski clubs, and corporations hold races regularly at Soda Springs.

## LOCATION

Soda Springs is located in Nevada County, California, on Soda Springs Road, south of Old Hwy 40, 1 mile from the Norden/Soda Springs exit from I-80. Just north of the Placer County line, the ski area is adjacent to the Royal Gorge cross-country area, 2 miles west of Sugar Bowl, and 3 miles west of Donner Ski Ranch. The access to Soda Springs via Old Hwy 40 from Donner Lake is cut off in winter with the closure of Old Hwy 40 (Donner Pass Road) between the lake and Donner Ski Ranch.

The closest major airport to Soda Springs is at Reno, Nevada. Soda Springs is also serviced by the Sacramento airport. Scheduled service to Lake Tahoe Airport in South Lake Tahoe is less frequent and, in heavy weather, flights often land in Reno instead. Four-wheel-drive and cars equipped for skiers are available for rental at all 3 airports.

Amtrak's "California Zephyr" stops in Truckee, as well as in Sacramento and Reno/Sparks. Auto rentals are available in Truckee at the AAA Auto Rental, adjacent to the Amtrak station. Greyhound operates bus service into Truckee and Soda Springs.

## TERRAIN

Soda Springs is uniquely set up so that Chair 1 services beginner slopes; Chair 2, intermediate and beginner slopes; and Chair 3, advanced, intermediate, and beginner slopes. Because each chair goes a little higher, beginners don't have to spend time riding a lift to terrain they're not ready to ski. Black diamond runs branch off from the summit to the west and east sides of the face, drawing good skiers away from slower traffic. Intermediate runs head down the fall line in the center of the mountain, while beginner runs are concentrated in front of the base lodge.

## FACILITIES

Soda Springs can be rented for exclusive day use for a party, fundraiser, or employee day on any non-holiday Monday through Thursday during the season and most weekends in April, snow permitting. Cost varies with the number of lifts utilized. Chair 1 is $700; Chair 2, $800; Chair 3, $900. A combination of 1 and 2 is $1,400; 1 and 3 is $1,500; 2 and 3, $1,600; or all three for $2,300 daily.

Families can save $101 on lift tickets, lessons, or equipment rentals at Soda Springs or Boreal when they purchase a book of 20 $10-coupons for $99. Skiers who purchase all-day lift tickets and turn them in by 12:30 p.m. receive a $5 credit or $2 on a child's ticket.

## FACILITIES AT A GLANCE

*Season:* Thanksgiving–Easter.
*Hours:* 9 a.m.–4:30 p.m. Friday through Monday and holidays.
*Night Skiing:* None.
*Area:* 200 acres with 16 runs.
 Beginner: 30%
 Intermediate: 50%
 Advanced: 20%
*Base Elevation:* 6,700 ft
*Summit Elevation:* 7,352 ft
*Vertical drop:* 652 ft
*Longest Run:* 1 mile.
*Snowmaking:* None.
*Snowboarding:* Permitted.
*Avg. Annual Snowfall:* 360 in.
*Lift Capacity:* 4,800 per hr.

*Lifts:* 3 chair lifts (1 double, 2 triples)

| Name | Length | Vertical Rise |
| --- | --- | --- |
| Chair 1 | NA | 300 ft |
| Chair 2 | NA | 400 ft |
| Chair 3 | NA | 650 ft |

*Lift Passes:*

| | All Day | Afternoon Only |
| --- | --- | --- |
| | 9 a.m.–4:30 p.m. | 12:30 p.m.–4:30 p.m. |
| Adults | $20 | $15 |
| Children 5–12 | $11 | $9 |
| Children under 5 | FREE | FREE |
| Seniors 60–69 | $11 | $9 |
| Seniors 70+ | FREE | FREE |

*Military:* 20% off all lift ticket rates.
*Multiday Rates:* None.
*Season Passes:* $200 adults. $110 child. Family rates available.
*Group Rates:* Available by prior arrangement.
*Food & Drink:* A cafeteria with a beer and wine bar is located at the base and is open from 8:30 a.m. to 4:30 p.m.

*Parking & Transportation:* Parking is free at 3 lots, one in front of the base lodge and two across the street. No overnight parking for RVs. Overnight parking without hookups available at Boreal, 5 miles east on I-80.

*Ski Rentals:* Base lodge shop open 8:30 a.m.–4:30 p.m. Includes skis, boots, and poles.
    All day:   Adult $16. Child $11.
    Half day:   Adult $13. Child $10.
    Snowboards:   Adult and child $21.

*Ski School:* Phone (916) 426-3666.
   *Method:* ATM.
   *Ski School Director:* David Barker.
   *Class Lessons:* 10 a.m. and 2:15 p.m.
    $17 (2 hr) Ages 7+.
    $24 (4 hr) Ages 7+.
   *Beginner Special:* Includes use of beginner lift.

|  | Adult | Child |
|---|---|---|
| 2-hr lesson | $25 | $18 |
| with equipment rental | $37 | $28 |
| 4-hr lesson | $32 | $25 |
| with equipment rental | $39 | $32 |

   *Improvement Special:* Includes rentals, lift ticket, and a 2-hr lesson.
    Adult $46. Child $36.
   *Private Lessons:* $35 per hr for 1 or 2 persons. Early bird private, 9 a.m.–10 a.m., $27.
   *Snowboard Lessons:* $27 from 9 a.m.–10 a.m.

*Races & Clinics:*
   *Coin-operated Race Course:* 50¢ per run.
   *Race Lessons:* $35 per hr.

*Day Care:* None.

*Camper Facilities:* Overnight parking for RVs permitted at Boreal, 5 miles east. No hookups. Camper and tent sites available 35 miles southeast at Sugar Pine Point State Park, south of Tahoma on SH 89. $10 per night. No hookups. Heated restrooms. Parking. For information call (916) 525-7982.

*Medical:* First aid at mountain base. Closest hospital is Tahoe Forest Hospital, 13 miles east in Truckee.

*Other:* Locker rental available.

## SPECIAL EVENTS

- *Santa Skis Soda Springs*—December 25.
- *California State Snowboarding Competition*—March.
- *Far West Cup Series*—March. Giant slalom race.
- *Easter Egg Hunt*—Easter.

## WINTER ACTIVITIES

### Cross-Country

Soda Springs is adjacent to the *Royal Gorge* Nordic area, the largest in California. See Sugar Bowl for additional information.

For other activities in the area, see Boreal, Donner Ski Ranch, and Tahoe Donner.

## SHOPPING

A general store is located in the base lodge. For additional shops, see Sugar Bowl, Boreal, and Tahoe Donner.

## APRÈS-SKI, RESTAURANTS, AND ACCOMMODATIONS

*Norden Station Condominiums* are on Donner Pass Road (Old Hwy 40), a couple of blocks from Soda Springs. The *Donner Summit Lodge* is also within a mile. For information on these accommodations as well as après-ski and dining suggestions, see Sugar Bowl, Donner Ski Ranch, Boreal, and Tahoe Donner.

# Boreal

*P.O. Box 39*
*Truckee, CA 95734*
*Information: (916) 426-3666*
*Snowphone: (916) 426-3663*

### Driving distances

| | |
|---|---|
| Los Angeles | 471 mi |
| Reno | 40 mi |
| Sacramento | 90 mi |
| San Diego | 590 mi |
| San Francisco | 175 mi |
| San Jose | 202 mi |
| S. Lake Tahoe | 51 mi |
| Tahoe City | 17 mi |
| Truckee | 10 mi |

*For road conditions, call*
*(916) 581-1400, California*
*(702) 793-1313, Nevada*

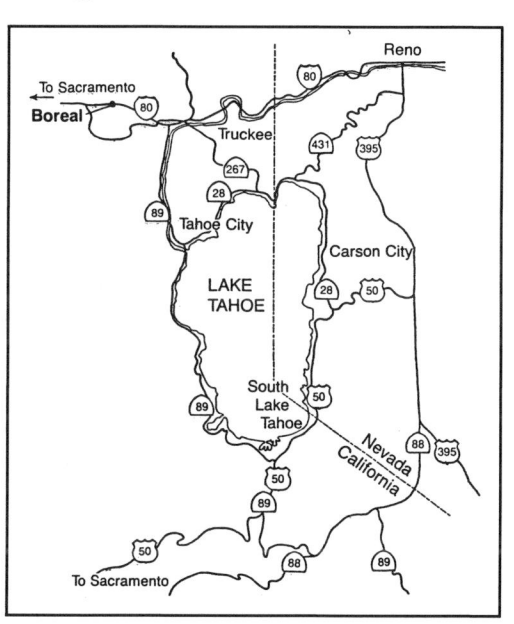

Boreal's major lure is its accessible location in Donner Summit, right at the Castle Peak exit off I-80. There are no precipitous two-lane roads to negotiate in heavy weather. No long hikes, laden with ski equipment, from remote parking areas. And, with quick snow clearance on I-80, road delays are rare. In fact, with snowmaking on 10 runs, and lifts running until 10 p.m., Boreal is like a lighthouse in the snow, beckoning skiers to its slopes almost any time the mood strikes.

Boreal is also the location of the Western America Ski Sport Museum. Admission is free to this unique museum, open Tuesday through Sunday from 11 a.m. to 5 p.m. Exhibits trace the history of skiing in the west from 1849, when the gold rush drew Norwegian immigrants to the Sierras along with their skis, or "snowshoes," as the miners called them.

Today, the modern equipment and facilities at Boreal allow their descendants to fully enjoy the sport of skiing.

## LOCATION

Boreal is located in Placer County off I-80 at the Castle Peak exit, 8 miles west of Truckee, 45 miles west of Reno, and 90 miles east of Sacramento.

From Stateline at Crystal Bay in North Lake Tahoe, drive north on SH 267 to Donner Pass Road and I-80. Head west to the Castle Peak exit. Turn left under I-80 to Boreal on the south side of the Interstate.

From Tahoe's West Shore, SH 89 runs north into I-80 at Truckee.

The closest major airport to Boreal is at Reno, Nevada. Boreal is also serviced by the Sacramento airport. Scheduled service to Lake Tahoe Airport in South Lake Tahoe is less frequent and, in heavy weather, flights often land in Reno instead. Four-wheel-drive and cars equipped for skiers are available for rental at all 3 airports.

Amtrak's "California Zephyr" stops in Truckee, as well as in Sacramento and Reno/Sparks. Auto rentals are available in Truckee at the AAA Auto Rental, adjacent to the Amtrak station. Greyhound operates bus service into Truckee and Norden/Soda Springs, 4 miles west on I-80.

## TERRAIN

Boreal is a softly rounded mountain, devoid of craggy peaks. It plateaus somewhat at the top, allowing skiers to descend from a number of lifts along the crest.

The Mineshaft and Klondike chairs serve most of the black diamond runs on the face, including the steep and bumpy *Waterfall*, *Mogul Run*, and *Chukker*, a short but exciting gulley. Skiers with second thoughts can bail out of this area on *Stagecoach*, the easier way down.

From the summit, skiers can access the advanced and intermediate runs like *Air Shaft* and *Timber Wagon* on the back side of Boreal. These are wide-open bowls at the top that narrow at the bottom. The ride back to the top is via the Quicksilver Quad.

Intermediates will feel at home on boulevards like *Central Pacific* and *Mariposa*, off Chair 8, or on the wide and rolling *Sierra* and *Prospector* runs.

Beginners can cruise from the summit to base on *Westward Ho* or *Primrose*, while the shorter chair lifts will keep them in the lower, gentle meadows. A *half-pipe* for snowboarders is reached via Chair 3.

## FACILITIES

With illumination on 6 runs, Boreal offers the only major night skiing in the Sierras. Three chair lifts run nightly until 10 p.m. and are included in the price of the all-day lift ticket. Lower-priced night-only or afternoon-night combinations are also available.

Families can save $101 on lift tickets, lessons, or equipment rentals at either Boreal or Soda Springs ski area when they purchase a book of twenty $10 coupons for $99.

## FACILITIES AT A GLANCE

| | |
|---|---|
| *Season:* | Late October–End of April. |
| *Hours:* | 9 a.m.–10 p.m. |
| *Night Skiing:* | 6 runs on 75 acres, daily, from late November–April 1. |
| *Area:* | 380 acres with 41 runs. |
| | Beginner: 30% |
| | Intermediate: 55% |
| | Advanced: 15% |
| *Base Elevation:* | 7,200 ft |
| *Summit Elevation:* | 7,800 ft |
| *Vertical Drop:* | 600 ft |
| *Longest Run:* | 1 mile. |
| *Snowmaking:* | 10 runs on 600 acres. |
| *Snowboarding:* | Permitted. |
| *Avg. Annual Snowfall:* | 360 in. |
| *Lift Capacity:* | 14,000 per hr. |
| *Lifts:* | 10 chair lifts (1 quad, 1 triple, 8 doubles) |

| Name | Length | Vertical Rise |
|---|---|---|
| Cedar Ridge | NA | 500 ft |
| Claim Jumper | NA | 250 ft |
| Gold Rush | NA | 500 ft |
| Gunnar's | NA | 200 ft |
| Klondike | NA | 600 ft |
| Lost Dutchman | NA | 600 ft |
| Mineshaft | NA | 600 ft |
| Nugget | NA | 50 ft |
| Prospector | NA | 600 ft |
| Quicksilver Quad | 2,000 ft | 450 ft |

*(continued from previous page)*

| Lift Passes: | All Day | Afternoon Only |
|---|---|---|
| | 9 a.m.–10 p.m. | 1:30 p.m.–10 p.m. |
| Adults | $25 | $18 |
| Children 5–12 | $14 | $12 |
| Children under 5 | FREE | FREE |
| Seniors 60–69 | $14 | $12 |
| Seniors 70+ | FREE | FREE |

*Military:* 20% off all lift rates.

*Multiday Rates:* None.

*Season Passes:* $350 adult. $190 child. Family rates are $350 for the first adult, $280 for the second, and $150 per child.

*Group Rates:* Available by prior arrangement.

*Food & Drink:* The base lodge cafeteria is open from 8 a.m. until 10 p.m. The bar opens at 11 a.m. and closes at 10 p.m.

*Parking & Transportation:* Parking at the base is free, with a short walk to lifts. RVs permitted overnight, no hookups.

*Ski Rentals:* The base lodge rental shop is open from 8:30 a.m.–10 p.m. Includes skis, boots, and poles.
  All day: Adult $16. Child $12.
  Half day: Adult $13. Child $10.
  Snowboards: $21.

*Ski School:* Phone (916) 426-3666.
  *Method:* ATM.
  *Ski School Director:* David Baker.
  *Class Lessons:* 10 a.m. and 2:15 p.m.
    $17 (2 hr) ages 7+.
    $24 (4 hr) ages 7+.
  *Beginner Special:* Includes 2-hr lesson and use of beginner lift.
    $25 (2 hr) adult. $18 child.
    $32 (4 hr) adult. $25 child.
    $37 (2 hr) adult with equipment rentals.
    $28 (2 hr) child with equipment rentals.
  *Improvement Special:* Includes rentals, lift ticket, and a 2-hr lesson.
    $46 adult. $36 child.

*Animal Crackers Ski School:* Ages 4–12.
  Includes lessons, lunch, equipment rental, and lift ticket.
  $32 12:30 p.m.–4:30 p.m.
  $42 8:30 a.m.–4:30 p.m.
*Private Lessons:* $35 per hr.
*Snowboard Lessons:* $35 per hr.

*Races & Clinics:*
  *Race Lessons:* $35 per hr.
  *Sierra Ski Teachers Clinic:* For skiers who wish to become instructors. Covers skiing techniques, methodology, analysis, and class handling. Four weekends, $131, including lift tickets.

*Day Care:* None.

*Camper Facilities:* Overnight parking for RVs permitted. No hookups. Camper and tent sites available 35 miles southeast at Sugar Pine Point State Park, south of Tahoma on SH 89. $10 per night. No hookups. Heated restrooms. Parking. For information call (916) 525-7982.

*Medical:* First aid at the mountain. Closest hospital is Tahoe Forest, 8 miles east in Truckee.

*Other:* Free ski check, game room, service station, ski museum.

During Interski Weeks in March and April, a special pass permits skiers to ski Boreal, Donner Ski Ranch, and Sugar Bowl for $30. The Interski is designed for intermediate and advanced skiers. Boreal is connected with Donner Ski Ranch via an intermediate run in the back bowls. A shuttle bus links Donner Skir Ranch with Sugar Bowl, 1 mile west.

## SPECIAL EVENTS

- *Santa Claus Skis Boreal*—December 24.
- *New Year's Eve Celebration*—December 31. Buffet dinner, music in convention room, torchlight parade, fireworks. Lifts remain open until 1 a.m.
- *California State Snowboarding Competition*—January.
- *Snowboard Slalom and Half-pipe competitions*—January.
- *Sacramento Special Olympics*—February.
- *Ski the Californias Race*—January.
- *Snowfest Winter Carnival*—March.
- *Easter Buffet Brunch*—Easter. Egg hunt, parade.

*Boreal is one of the easiest ski areas to reach, located just off I-80 in Donner Summit.* (Courtesy of Boreal/Soda Springs.)

## WINTER ACTIVITIES

### Cross-Country

The closest cross-country area is on the north side of I-80 at the *Castle Peak* exit. Beginner, intermediate, and advanced areas are ungroomed. A 3-mile trail leads to the Peter Grubb warming hut. Rentals and lessons not available. A Sno-Park permit is required for the limited parking.

*Royal Gorge* Nordic area and the *Clair Tappaan Lodge* cross-country area are about 5 miles from Boreal. For additional information on these Nordic ski areas, see Sugar Bowl and Tahoe Donner.

Additional cross-country trails are located at Northstar-at-Tahoe and Tahoe Donner.

### Snowmobiling

A snowmobiling trail is located across I-80 at the *Castle Peak* exit. A Sno-Park permit is required for parking. Snowmobile rentals and tours are available at

*The Snow Connection* in Truckee, (916) 587-8913. Guided tours with *Eagle Ridge Outfitters*, at Old Hobart Mill, 5 miles north of Truckee on SH 89, range from 2 hours to 2 days, (916) 587-9322.

For additional information on snowmobiling, see Squaw Valley and Diamond Peak.

### Tobogganing, Tubing, and Snow Play

A sledding and snow-play hill is located 5 miles east on Old Hwy 40, just before the Truckee River Bridge. No equipment rentals on site. For information on other snow-play areas in the North Lake Tahoe area, see Granlibakken and Squaw Valley.

### Sleigh Rides

Sleigh rides are available 7 miles from Boreal at the Sugar Bowl ski area on Old Hwy 40, and at Tahoe Donner, 8 miles east.

## OTHER ACTIVITIES

**Cinema:** The Martis Valley Theatre, Truckee.
**Fitness:** High Sierra Fitness, Truckee Airport.
**Sightseeing:** Frontier town of Truckee; Historic gold rush town, Nevada City.
**Swimming:** Truckee High School, Truckee.
**Western America Ski Sport Museum:** Adjacent to Boreal Lodge.

## SHOPPING

*Jo's Ski Shop* at the base lodge sells ski accessories. Groceries can be purchased at the mini mart in the Mobil Station at the east end of the parking lot. Additional shops for sporting goods, gift items, and children's apparel are located 8 miles east in Truckee.

## APRÈS-SKI

The cocktail lounge at Boreal is open until 10 p.m. for night skiers. The closest watering hole for skiers headed west on I-80 is at the *Donner Summit Lodge* at the Norden/Soda Springs exit, open until 2 a.m. A little further west, the *Rainbow Lodge* is a quaint, romantic spot just off I-80, 1/2 mile south on Rainbow Road.

For a livelier atmosphere, skiers can head east on I-80 to Truckee. For additional information on après-ski spots in this historic town, see Tahoe Donner.

## RESTAURANTS

The *Boreal Lodge Cafeteria* is open through the dinner hour for night skiers. For nearby dining information, including in Truckee, see Tahoe Donner and Sugar Bowl.

## ACCOMMODATIONS

**The Boreal Inn**   $$   *(916) 426-3666*
The Boreal Inn is a 36-room lodge within walking distance of the lifts. Moderately-priced rooms with private baths, TV, and phones, each have two queen-size beds. Midweek prices are about $10 less than weekends. Midweek packages from Sunday to Thursday include lift tickets.

For additional lodging information near I-80 and Truckee, see Tahoe Donner and Sugar Bowl ski areas, located a few miles from Boreal.

# Tahoe Donner

P.O. Box 11049
Truckee, CA 95737
Information: (916) 587-9400
Snowphone: (916) 587-9494

### Driving distances

| | |
|---|---|
| Los Angeles | 486 mi |
| Reno | 40 mi |
| Sacramento | 100 mi |
| San Diego | 605 mi |
| San Francisco | 190 mi |
| San Jose | 217 mi |
| S. Lake Tahoe | 49 mi |
| Tahoe City | 19 mi |
| Truckee | 6 mi |

*For road conditions call
(916) 581-1400, California
(702) 793-1313, Nevada*

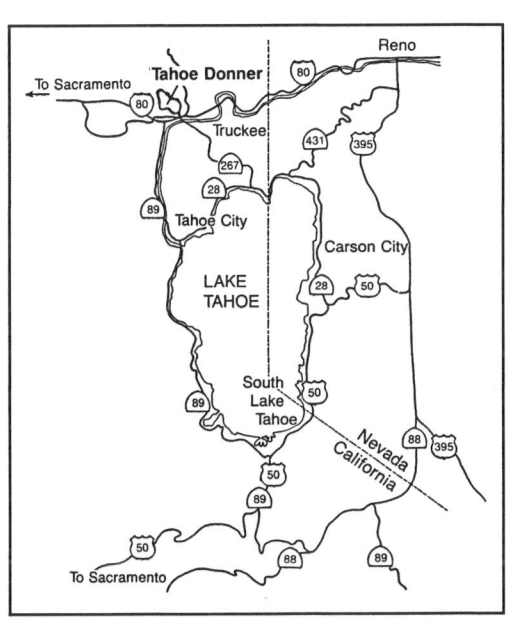

Tahoe Donner is a family resort that goes out of its way to make parents and their children feel comfortable. With condominium lodging within walking distance of the mostly gentle, well-groomed slopes, it's the perfect place to introduce beginners to skiing without worrying about crowded slopes or steep terrain.

Tahoe Donner welcomes small children with its Snowflake Ski School, a play area with figures of Snow White and the Seven Dwarfs, and an immaculate, airy lodge brightened with turquoise and pink pastels.

It's also a place where families can get away together and still be close to other activities, including sleigh rides, snowmobiling, and one of the best cross-country tracks in California. The historic town of Truckee, with its cinema, restaurants, and shops, is only 8 minutes away.

## LOCATION

Tahoe Donner is located in Nevada County, California, on Snowpeak Way, off Northwoods Blvd., 6 miles west of Truckee. From San Francisco and Sacramento, take I-80 to the Donner State Park exit. Turn left over the bridge and I-80, 1/2 mile to Northwoods Blvd. Turn left on Northwoods to Snowpeak Way. From Reno, take I-80 to the SH 89 South exit. Turn right (north) to Donner Pass Road in Truckee and then left 1/2 mile to Northwoods. Turn right on Northwoods, 5 miles to Snowpeak Way.

The closest major airport to Tahoe Donner is at Reno, Nevada. Tahoe Donner is also serviced by the Sacramento airport. Scheduled service to Lake Tahoe Airport in South Lake Tahoe is less frequent and, in heavy weather, flights often land in Reno instead. Four-wheel-drive and cars equipped for skiers are available for rental at all 3 airports.

Amtrak's "California Zephyr" stops in Truckee, as well as in Sacramento and Reno/Sparks. Auto rentals are available in Truckee at the AAA Auto Rental, adjacent to the Amtrak station. Greyhound also operates bus service into Truckee.

## TERRAIN

The runs at Tahoe Donner are wide and almost treeless. With the exception of *Skips Plunge*, the most challenging route down the mountain, runs are groomed and smooth. The absence of mogul runs, chutes, and unpacked powder results in a calm environment for first-timers and novices.

Skiers attempting to acclimate children, siblings, or friends to skiing need not be experts themselves to negotiate the terrain and help others at the same time. Even the longest run on the mountain, *Mile Trail*, is gently sloped so beginners can enjoy the full vertical rise of the mountain.

More confident skiers can move up to the intermediate favorites like *Eagle Rock Bowl* and, ultimately, the *Gulley* and *Skips Plunge*.

## FACILITIES

At Tahoe Donner, midweek lift prices (Monday through Friday) represent a one-third savings over the normal weekend rates. Wednesdays are Women's Ski Days. The cost for a lift ticket, lesson, lunch, video analysis, and après ski session is $35, or $125 for five Wednesdays. Reservations required.

Discounts for students and for the military are sold through the schools and military bases.

## FACILITIES AT A GLANCE

*Season:* Mid-December–Easter.
*Hours:* 9 a.m.–4 p.m. daily.
*Night Skiing:* None.
*Area:* 120 acres with 11 runs.
    Beginner: 50%
    Intermediate: 50%
    Advanced: 0%
*Base Elevation:* 6,750 ft
*Summit Elevation:* 7,350 ft
*Vertical Drop:* 600 ft
*Longest Run:* 1 mile
*Snowmaking:* None.
*Snowboarding:* Permitted.
*Avg. Annual Snowfall:* 300 in.
*Lift Capacity:* 1,500 per hr.

*Lifts:* 3 lifts (2 double-chair lifts and 1 Mighty Mite surface tow)

| Name | Length | Vertical Rise |
| --- | --- | --- |
| Eagle Rock Chair | 3,200 ft | 546 ft |
| Mighty Mite | 100 ft | NA |
| Snowbird Chair | 1,800 ft | 250 ft |

*Lift Passes:*

|  | All Day | Afternoon Only |
| --- | --- | --- |
|  | 9 a.m.–4 p.m. | 1 p.m.–4 p.m. |
| Adults | $12/$18 wkd & hol. | $14/$12 |
| Children 7–12 | $8/$10 | $8 |
| Children under 7* | FREE | FREE |
| Seniors 60–69 | $8/$10 | $8/$10 |
| Seniors 70 + | FREE | FREE |
| Mighty Mite only | $6 | $6 |

*Multiday Rates:* None.
*Season Passes:* Adult $240. Child $120.
  *Ages 6 and under ski free with adult lift pass.

*(continued)*

*(continued from previous page)*

*Group Rates:* Available for groups of 20+ by prior arrangement.

*Food & Drink:* Cafeteria open daily at base lodge with outdoor BBQ on weekends. Bar open until 9 p.m., and sometimes until 10 p.m.

*Parking & Transportation:* Free parking for autos and RVs daytime. No overnight RV parking or hookups.

*Ski Rentals:* Base lodge shop open 8:30 a.m.–4:30 p.m. weekdays, and 8 a.m.–4:30 p.m. weekends and holidays. Includes skis, boots, poles.
    All day: Adult $14. Child $11.
    Half day: Adult $11. Child $9.

*Ski School:* Phone (916) 587-9444.

*Method:* ATM.

*Ski School Director:* Don Frye.

*Class Lessons:* 10:30 a.m. and 2 p.m. daily. $14 ($1^1/_2$ hr) for ages 7 and older.

*Learn-to-Ski Special:* Monday–Friday except holidays. $32 includes class lesson, use of the Mighty Mite, and equipment rentals.

*Snowflake Ski School:* Ages 3–6. Includes lessons and indoor activities, equipment, snack, and lift ticket. $44 all day. Lunch included.
$26 half day. 9 a.m.–12 p.m. or 1–4 p.m.

*Private Lessons:* 9:15 a.m. and 12:30 p.m. daily. $32 per hr. Each additional person $16.

*Handicapped Lessons:* Not available.

*Races & Clinics:* Races, held once a month, are open to novices and intermediate skiers in 12 age groups. Winners receive medals and prizes.

*Day Care:* At the Snowflake Ski School, for ages 3–6. Babysitter referrals are available through the Truckee Chamber of Commerce, (800) 548-8388.

*Camper Facilities:* Overnight RV parking is permitted at the Little Truckee Summit parking lot, 17 miles north of Truckee on SH 89 north and Jackson Meadow Road. No hookups. Camper and tent sites are available 35 miles southeast at Sugar Pine Point State Park, south of Tahoma on SH 89. $10 per night. No hookups. Heated restrooms. Parking. For information call (916) 525-7982.

*Medical:* First aid at the mountain base by ski patrol. Tahoe Forest Hospital is the closest hospital, located 6 miles east in Truckee.

## SPECIAL EVENTS

- *Santa Visits Tahoe Donner*—December 24.
- *Torchlight Parade*—New Year's Eve.
- *Snow Sculpture Contest*—January.
- *President's Torchlight Parade*—February.
- *Fun Medal Race*—alternate Sundays. For novices.
- *Snowfest Fun Day Race*—March. Obstacle races and relays.
- *Spring Carnival*—April. Clowns, games, and races.
- *Easter Bunny Visits*—Easter.

## WINTER ACTIVITIES

### Cross-Country

*Tahoe Donner Cross-Country,* located off Northwoods Blvd. on Alder Creek Road adjacent to the Tahoe Donner downhill area, is open day and night until 9 p.m. Forty miles of track are machine-groomed, with two sets of diagonal tracks and one wide skating track. Thirty-one trails are almost evenly allocated for beginning, intermediate, and advanced skiers.

Instruction includes group and private lessons and the Tiny Tracks Snow School for ages 3–6 and 7–12. Other facilities include a ski shop, rental shop, the Cookhouse, and a cafe open for breakfast and lunch. The Family Room in the day lodge is for relaxing or watching family movies or ski videos. The Old West Kiddie Corral is a ski playground especially designed for kids. A warming hut, located 3 miles into the Euer Valley, offers food and beverage service on weekends.

An all-day pass is $11.50 adult, $9.50 seniors 60+ and teens 13-17, $7.50 children. Half-day (from 1 p.m.), twilight (from 3 p.m.) and night-only (from 5 p.m.) passes are also available, (916) 587-9484.

Tahoe Donner Cross-Country participates in the Ski North Tahoe interchangeable trail pass, along with Diamond Peak Cross-Country, Northstar-at-Tahoe, Royal Gorge, Spooner Lake, Squaw Valley Nordic, and Tahoe Nordic. Rates are $34 for 4 days, $40 for 5 days and $45 for 6 days.

Three miles of beginner and intermediate trails are also located at Donner Memorial State Park, located off I-80 at Donner Pass Road. Parking available. No fees, (916) 587-3841.

For information on other cross-country areas nearby, see also Sugar Bowl, Boreal, Northstar-at-Tahoe, and Squaw Valley.

### Snowmobiling

A snowmobile trail is located 6 miles west of Northwoods Blvd. and Donner Pass Road at the *Castle Peak* exit from I-80. A Sno-Park permit is required for

*Tahoe Donner's many activities for both parents and children make it a great choice for a family ski trip. (Courtesy of Tahoe Donner.)*

parking. At *Little Truckee Summit*, 17 miles north of Truckee at the intersection of SH 89 North and Jackson Meadow Road, marked snowmobile trails follow roads to Webber Lake, Yuba Pass, Bald Ridge Loop, and Treasure Mountain. These 3 routes cover 110 miles and range from beginning to advanced. Parking is available at the Little Truckee Summit parking area. For further information, contact the Truckee Ranger Station, (916) 587-2158.

Snowmobile rentals and tours are available at the *Snow Connection* in Truckee, (916) 587-8913 and at *Tahoe Truckee Sports*, (916) 587-7436. At Old Hobart Mill, 5 miles north of Truckee on SH 89, guided tours with *Eagle Ridge Outfitters* range from 2 hours to 2 days, (916) 587-9322.

For additional information on snowmobiling, see Squaw Valley and Diamond Peak.

## Tobogganing, Tubing, and Snow Play

A hill for sledding and other snow play is located 5 miles north of Tahoe Donner on Old Hwy 40 at *Glenshire*. No equipment rentals on site. Saucers and tubes are rented at *Granlibakken*, 26 miles south. See Squaw Valley and Granlibakken.

## Sleigh Rides

Sleighs drawn by Belgian horses depart from the lodge at the *Tahoe Donner Cross-Country Center*. Thirty-minute rides leave every hour between 4 p.m. and 8 p.m. on weekends and holidays, weather permitting. Midweek rides by special arrangement. Minimum 10 persons. Advanced reservations required, (916) 587-9484.

## OTHER ACTIVITIES

**Ballooning:** Mountain High Balloons, Truckee.
**Cinema:** The Martis Valley Theatre, Truckee.
**Fitness:** High Sierra Fitness, adjacent to the Truckee Airport.
**Swimming:** Truckee High School, Truckee.
**Sightseeing:** Emigrant Trail Museum, Donner Memorial State Park; historic buildings, Truckee.

## SHOPPING

Ski apparel and accessories are available at the *Ski Shop* in the base lodge. A convenience market and deli are located a couple of miles below the ski area on Northwoods Blvd. Less than 10 minutes away in Truckee, an eclectic assortment of stores are clustered on Commercial Row amid restaurants and bars. *Sew-N-Sew-N-Such* has quilts, comforters, dolls, and country furniture. *Ace of Hearts* features antique jewelry and clothing, including vintage wedding dresses. The *Treehouse Children's Clothing and Gifts* carries Wrangler, Oshkosh, and other major clothing brands for infants through teens. Gift items, apparel, and housewares are available at a number of shops, many open 7 days a week.

## APRÈS-SKI

Skiers in search of a lively bar need only head for Commercial Row in Truckee. Spirited spots include *O.B.'s Pub and Restaurant* and the *American*

*Bar*, where the walls are lined with pictures of such notorious figures as John Dillinger and Baby Face Nelson. After dinner on weekends, jazz fans can soak up their favorite sounds at the *Passage Restaurant*, downstairs from the Truckee Hotel. For an evening reminiscent of frontier days, the *Tourist Club*, decked out with stuffed caribou, deer, and antelope, is open until 2 a.m.

## RESTAURANTS

**Left Bank   $$$**                                                    *(916) 587-4694*
On Commercial Row, Truckee. The Left Bank presents continental cuisine in a romantic ambience. Stone walls and dark woods are warmed by fringed lamps, pink tablecloths and burgundy and brass accents. Selections vary from breast of pheasant to seafood entrées, including swordfish in blueberry sauce and tuna grilled with ginger sauce. Open for lunch from 11:30 a.m. to 3:30 p.m., and for dinner 5:30 p.m. to 10:30 p.m., as well as for Sunday brunch. Beer and wine served.

**Josephine's Pasta and Pizza   $$**                                   *(916) 587-9291*
On Commercial Row, Truckee. Josephine's dishes up pizza, fish, pasta, and other Italian specialties in a warm atmosphere of brick, stained glass, and brass lights. Entrées include fettucini carbonara, saltimbocca, and pizzas. Open for dinner daily from 5 p.m. to 9:30 p.m. or 10:30 p.m. weekends. Beer and wine.

**O.B.'s Pub and Restaurant   $$**                                     *(916) 587-4164*
On Commercial Row, Truckee. O.B.'s mix of rustic wood, stained glass, lace curtains, and antiques is as eclectic as its menu. Barbecued ribs, coquilles sardou, chicken teriyaki, seafood, steak, and potato skins. Open for lunch and for dinner from 5:30 p.m. to 10:30 p.m. Breakfast served on weekends. No reservations taken.

**The Passage   $$**                                                   *(916) 587-7619*
Adjoining the Truckee Hotel at Bridge and Commercial Row, the Passage is open for breakfast, lunch, and dinner. The continental and American dining selections include fresh seafood, cornish game hen, pasta de jour, steak, and specials such as catfish and Cajun sausage, or tomato and basil fettucini. A lunch menu offers burgers, sandwiches, and salads.

**China Chef   $**                                                     *(916) 587-1831*
On Commercial Row, Truckee. China Chef serves Cantonese and Szechwan cooking for lunch and dinner from 4:30 p.m. to 10 p.m.

**Copa de Oro   $**                                                    *(916) 587-2161*
1010 Bridge St., Truckee. Mexican cuisine includes burritos, rellenos, and fajitas. Open 4:30 p.m. to 10 p.m. Closed Mondays.

## ACCOMMODATIONS

**Tahoe Donner Condominiums   $$$**   *(916) 587-1236*
Clustered left and right of the base lodge, the Tahoe Donner Condominiums are comfortably decorated 2- or 3-bedroom units with TV, phones, and woodburning stoves. Kitchens are equipped with dishwashers, refrigerators, and coffee makers. Some kitchens have a microwave as well as a conventional oven. Two-night minimum.

**Donner Lake Village   $$**   *(916) 587-6081*
Located on Donner Pass Road (Old Hwy 40), 5 miles west of the Donner Lake exit from I-80. (Old Hwy 40 is closed beyond the west end of the lake in winter.) Modern motel rooms, studios, 1- and 2-bedroom condominium units, some with lake views. Two-bedroom townhouses have 2 bathrooms. All units have TV and phones. Fireside lounge and game room, saunas, gift shop, and conference room on premises.

**Donner Pines East   $$**   *(916) 587-4127*
Donner Pass Road, (Old Hwy 40), Donner Lake, 1 mile off the Donner Lake exit from I-80. Five fully furnished condominiums have living rooms, dining rooms, kitchens, master and guest bedrooms, bathrooms, and half baths. All units have fireplaces, garages, and TV. No phones. Some units have a microwave oven. Lake views.

**Richardson House   $$**   *(916) 587-5388*
10154 High St., Truckee. Sitting on a hill overlooking Truckee, this renovated Victorian has 7 rooms with shared bathrooms. Rates include breakfast and afternoon hors d'oeuvres. Other features include a homey living room with TV, and hot tub.

**Super 8 Motel   $$**   *(916) 587-8888, (800) 843-1991*
11506 Deerfield Dr. on the south side of I-80, just west of the SH 89 exit. The Super 8 Motel has 41 small rooms on 3 floors, with private baths, TV, phones. Sauna and whirlpool on premises. Lobby with fireplace. No elevator.

**Truckee Hotel   $$**   *(916) 587-4444*
At Commercial Row and Bridge Row in downtown Truckee, a 1-minute walk from the Amtrak depot. The Truckee Hotel first opened its doors to guests in 1863 as the Whitney House. Rebuilt after a fire in 1909, the hotel, with its ruby glass lamps, lace curtains, and collection of historic photos, evokes the frontier days of Truckee. Eight of the 29 rooms have private bathrooms with old fashioned tubs. Each room is uniquely decorated. "The Bulette Suite" carries the portrait of Julia Bulette, a famous courtesan of earlier days, and is decorated in Victorian reds with a king-size bed and sofa.

Strains of classical music soothe guests each morning in the breakfast room which doubles in the evening as the television lounge. Owner Rob Sayers has researched much of Truckee's history and regales guests with tales of the areas's past and its more notorious citizens. Continental buffet breakfast included. Two-night minimum stay required during Christmas holidays.

**Alpine Village Motel**   $   *(916) 587-3801, (916) 587-3247.*
I-80 at Donner Pass Road, Truckee. Twenty-six modest units with a variety of king-size, queen-size, and double beds. Private baths, TV, and refrigerators in most rooms. Housekeeping units with kitchens sleep 6 or 7. Senior citizen discounts.

**Gateway Motel**   $   *(916) 587-3183*
On Donner Pass Road, 1 mile west of Truckee, the Gateway Motel has 27 cabins sleeping 2 to 4, available on a first-come basis. No reservations taken. Small, rustic cabins in knotty pine are basic but have private bathrooms with showers. No tubs, TV, or phones. Some kitchens available.

For additional accommodations in the Tahoe Donner area, see also Boreal, Sugar Bowl, and Northstar-at-Tahoe.

# Northstar-at-Tahoe

*P.O. Box 129*
*Truckee, CA 95734*
*Information: (916) 562-1010*
*Lodging: (916) 562-1113;*
*(800) 533-6787*
*Snowphone: (916) 562-1330*

| Driving distances | |
|---|---|
| Fresno | 261 mi |
| Los Angeles | 482 mi |
| Reno | 45 mi |
| Sacramento | 96 mi |
| San Diego | 601 mi |
| San Francisco | 196 mi |
| San Jose | 293 mi |
| S. Lake Tahoe | 38 mi |
| Tahoe City | 8 mi |
| Truckee | 10 mi |

*For road conditions, call*
*(916) 581-1440, California*
*(702) 793-1313, Nevada*

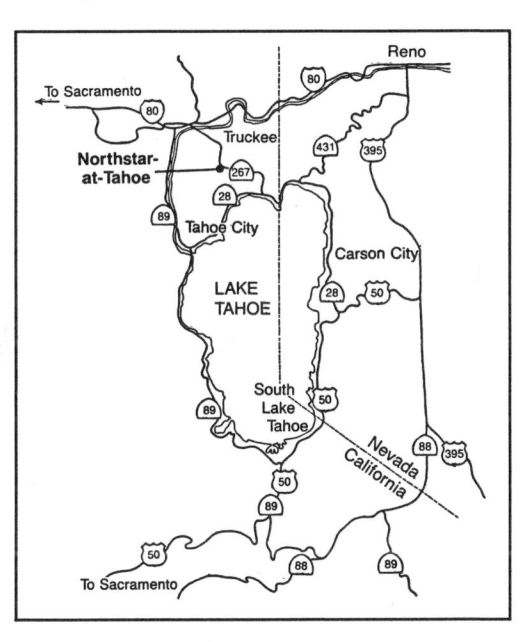

Northstar's distinctive blue-roofed village offers the intimacy and convenience of a self-contained resort within minutes of Tahoe's North Shore gambling action. From the moment skiers park their cars and hop on the complimentary shuttle, there's a sense of a well-run resort with user-friendly facilities. Horse-drawn sleighs and the bustle of skiers in and out of shops, restaurants, and bars add to the winter gaiety.

Skiers can choose from on-site accommodations that range from single rooms to townhouses and spacious homes. Or they can base themselves in the frontier atmosphere of nearby Truckee or the highrise glamour of a North Shore casino hotel.

Wherever they stay, Northstar's well-groomed terrain and beautiful scenery provide both exhilaration and relaxation for the whole family.

## LOCATION

Northstar-at-Tahoe is on SH 267 in Placer County, 6 miles east of Truckee and 6 miles west of North Lake Tahoe. From San Francisco, Sacramento, or Reno, take I-80 to the SH 267 exit. Turn south on SH 267, and go 6 miles to Northstar Dr. and then west 2 miles to the village. From Stateline at South Lake

*Northstar-at-Tahoe's 1,700 acres of skiable terrain, with 50 groomed runs and an abundance of trees, means fun for skiers of all levels.* (Courtesy of Northstar-at-Tahoe.)

Tahoe, drive north on US 50 to SH 28. Go north 32 miles along the east shore to Kings Beach, then 6 miles north on SH 267 to Northstar Dr.

Reno Cannon International Airport is the closest major airport to Northstar-at-Tahoe, which is also served by the Sacramento airport. Scheduled service to Lake Tahoe Airport in South Lake Tahoe is less frequent and, in heavy weather, flights sometimes land in Reno instead. Four-wheel-drive and cars equipped for skiers are available for rental at all 3 airports and at the Truckee-Tahoe airport for private craft on SH 267.

Aerotrans Luxury Vans runs several times daily from the Reno airport to Northstar. The one-way ride is $15 per person with a minimum of 3 people, or a $45 minimum, (702) 786-2376. Sierra Nevada Stage Lines also operates a ski shuttle from the Reno airport to Northstar daily except Saturdays. Adults are $15 and children, 14 and under, are $10, round-trip, (702) 329-1147 or (800) 822-6009.

Cab fare from the Reno airport runs about $55 one way. Limousine service is available from Truckee-Tahoe Limousine and Tours, (916) 587-2160, and from 5 Star Enterprises, Truckee, (916) 587-7651.

Amtrak's "California Zephyr" stops in Truckee, as well as in Sacramento and Reno/Sparks. Autos with chains and racks are available for rent in Truckee at the AAA Auto Rental, adjacent to the Amtrak station. During the busy season, 4-wheel-drive vehicles should be reserved a month or more in advance. Rental car delivery to the train stations in Sacramento and Reno can be arranged through Hertz. Greyhound operates bus service into Truckee and Reno daily.

With 24-hour notice, Northstar provides complimentary shuttle service for lodging guests from the Amtrak or Greyhound depot in Truckee and the Truckee-Tahoe airport, except on Saturdays, Sundays, and holidays, (800) 533-6787. Weather permitting, a free ski shuttle also runs to and from Northstar from South Shore casinos on Tuesdays and Thursdays, except Christmas week. The bus picks up at 7 a.m. and arrives Northstar at 8:30 a.m. The return run to the South Shore departs Northstar at 4:30 p.m., (916) 587-0257.

TART, the Tahoe Area Regional Transit, operates bus service daily around the North and West Shore with stops at Kings Beach, Crystal Bay, Incline, and Truckee, with connections to Reno and South Lake Tahoe, (916) 562-1010.

## TERRAIN

Northstar is shaped like an upside-down pyramid, with most of the runs at the top, narrowing to just 3 runs at the bottom. While this makes for some congestion at the end of the day, the higher altitude for most of the runs ensures better snow conditions than below.

Although Northstar is predominately an intermediate mountain, the back side has 600 acres of advanced terrain and an average slope of 30%. It's the place to be after a storm, when the long, steep, tree-lined trails brim with superlative snow. *Burn Out*, aptly named for its long, moguled runs, tests a skier's endurance. However, the toughest mogul challenge is under the Schaffer Camp Lift on *The Rapids*. On the front side, the Rendezvous Lift drops skiers at the summit of a black-diamond bowl where *The Chute* and adjacent slopes test turning skills on narrow trails.

When it comes to intermediate slopes, a lift ride to the summit provides a glorious cruise down on the 2.9 mile long *West Ridge* and gentle *Village Run*. Lookout Lift serves a mid-mountain area of intermediate fun runs, such as *Hoot Owl* and *The Gully*.

Beginner runs are clustered in front of the mid-mountain lodge by the Chipmunk, Bear Paw, and Bear Cub tows. The longest novice trail is *Village Run*, off the gondola. Beginners heading for *The Gulch* or *Woodcutter* will have to face some intermediate runs as well.

## FACILITIES

Northstar-at-Tahoe limits ticket sales and reservations are recommended, particularly on holidays, when some skiers are turned away. Advance reservations can be made at Northstar for lodging, lift tickets, ski rentals, cross-country ski tickets, rental cars, or ski lessons. Various 2- to 5-night packages combine a choice of accommodations with lift passes and rental equipment. Call (916) 587-0200 or (800) 533-6787 for package rate information.

Frequent skiers can save money on regular lift rates with the use of the Take Ten Card. The rate for 10 days of skiing anytime is $300 adult or $110 child, a savings of $30. For 10 days of midweek skiing, skiers pay $250 and save $80. The card also includes a free run on Northstar's NASTAR race course, free ski corral check, and a 15% savings on the rental of high-performance demo skis.

The Family Membership Club costs $50 and entitles families of 2 or more to discounts on lift tickets, lodging, gasoline, food, and ski lessons. A family of 2 can save up to $11 midweek and $8 weekends. A family of 4 can save up to $21 midweek and $14 weekends.

Northstar participates in the Ski Tahoe North interchangeable lift ticket with Squaw Valley, Alpine Meadows, Diamond Peak, and Mount Rose. The rates are: 3-day $96, 4-day $128, 5-day $160, and 6-day pass $189. The resort also participates in the Ski Tahoe interchangeable lift ticket with Squaw Valley, Alpine Meadows, Heavenly Valley, and Kirkwood. The cost is $160 for 5 days or $192 for 6 days.

# FACILITIES AT A GLANCE

| | |
|---|---|
| *Season:* | Thanksgiving–April 30. |
| *Hours:* | 8:30 a.m.–4 p.m. daily. |
| *Night Skiing:* | None. |
| *Area:* | 1,700 acres with 49 runs. |
| | Beginner: 25% |
| | Intermediate: 50% |
| | Advanced: 25% |
| *Base Elevation:* | 6,400 ft |
| *Summit Elevation:* | 8,600 ft |
| *Vertical Drop:* | 2,200 ft |
| *Longest Run:* | 2.9 miles. |
| *Snowmaking:* | Covers more than 100 acres and 2,200 vertical ft, beginner through advanced terrain. |
| *Snowboarding:* | Permitted Sunday–Friday, non-holidays. |
| *Avg. Annual Snowfall:* | 400 in. |
| *Lift Capacity:* | 17,600 per hr. |
| *Lifts:* | 11 lifts (1 gondola, 2 high-speed detachable quads, 3 triple chairs, 3 double chairs and 2 surface tows) |

| Name | Length | Vertical Rise |
|---|---|---|
| Aspen (high speed) | 5,100 ft | 900 ft |
| Bear Cub (tow) | 750 ft | 120 ft |
| Bear Paw | 790 ft | 120 ft |
| Big Springs Gondola | 4,100 ft | 480 ft |
| Chipmunk (tow) | 280 ft | 28 ft |
| Comstock (high speed) | 5,900 ft | 2,800 ft |
| Echo | 4,890 ft | 710 ft |
| Forest | 5,750 ft | 1,170 ft |
| Lookout | 960 ft | 4,330 ft |
| Rendezvous | 2,900 ft | 650 ft |
| Schaffer Camp | 6,150 ft | 1,860 ft |

*(continued on next page)*

*(continued from previous page)*

| Lift Passes: | All Day | Afternoon Only |
|---|---|---|
| | 9 a.m.–4 p.m. | 1 p.m.–4 p.m. |
| Adults | $33 | $24 |
| Children 5–12* | $14 | $10 |
| Seniors 60–69** | $24 | $24 |
| Seniors 70+ ** | $5 | $5 |
| Gondola Only | $5 | $5 |

*Children under 5 ski free with paying adult.
**Except Saturdays, Sundays, and holidays.

*Multiday Rates:* Saturday start only.

| | Adult | Child |
|---|---|---|
| 2 out of 3 consecutive days | $59 | $26 |
| 3 out of 4 consecutive days | $88 | $35 |
| 4 out of 5 consecutive days | $115 | $44 |
| 5 out of 6 consecutive days | $143 | $55 |
| 6 out of 7 consecutive days | $170 | $66 |

*Season Passes:* Available to Northstar property owners only.

*Group Rates:* Available by prior arrangement for groups of 20 or more.

*Food & Drink:* The Day Lodge Cafeteria is located mid-mountain adjacent to the top of the gondola, along with the Wine and Cheese House and Alpine Bar. In the base village, Schaffer's Mill Restaurant and Lounge offers sit-down service. Specialty foods are available at Pedro's Pizza Parlor, Sam's Deli, and Clara's General Store. The Rendezvous Sports Pub is also in the village.

*Parking & Transportation:* Parking is free in a multitiered lot, with complimentary tram service to the village. Preferred parking in front of the village is $6. No RV overnight parking permitted. Free shuttles operate around the resort and, with advance notice, to Truckee and North Shore hotels and casinos. A shuttle to and from South Shore runs on Tuesdays and Thursdays.

*Ski Rentals:* The village rental shop is open from 8 a.m.–4 p.m. daily. Includes skis, boots, and poles.
   All day: Adult $17. Child $11.
   Half day: Adult $11. Child $7.
   High performance demo skis are available for $28 in the Northsport Ski Shop and the Ski Stalker Northstar rental shop in the Village.

*Snowboards:* $20

*Ski School:* Phone (916) 587-0271.

  *Method:* ATM.

  *Ski School Director:* Mike Iman.

  *Class Lessons:* Morning class at 10 a.m. includes gondola pass for beginners. Lift pass for other levels not included.
  $25 (2$^1$/$_2$ hr) adult.
  $15 child 5–12.
  $40 (4 hr) adult.
  Afternoon class lesson at 2 p.m. includes lift use while in lesson.
  $20 (2 hr) adult. $15 child.

  *Learn-to-Ski Special:* $34, includes 2$^1$/$_2$-hr morning lesson, ski rental equipment, and all-day gondola ticket.

  *3-Day Learn-to-Ski:* Starts Mondays and Wednesdays. Includes 3 half-day (2$^1$/$_2$-hr) class lessons and lift pass.
  $75 first timers. $115 other levels.

  *Starkids:* Ages 5–12. Includes all-day lesson, lift ticket, T-shirt, and lunch.
  $45. With equipment rental, $53.

  *Private Lessons:*  $ 45 one hr. Additional person $20.
  $90 (2 hr). Additional person $40.
  $135 (3 hr). Additional person $60.

*Races & Clinics:* NASTAR races Thursdays, Fridays, and Saturdays from 11 a.m. to 3 p.m. on Drop Off.

  *Recreational Ski Clinic:* $135 includes 3 days of race training sessions and 3 all-day lift passes.

  *Ski Improvement Clinic:* $115. Starts Mondays and Wednesdays. Three days of 2$^1$/$_2$-hr morning lessons and all-day lift passes.

*Day Care:* Minors' Camp Child Care Center. (916) 587-0278. 8 a.m.–4:30 p.m. Ages 2–6. Must be toilet trained. Reservations recommended. Includes art, science, drama, snow play, two snacks, and lunch.
  $30 all day. $20 afternoon only.
  Learn-to-ski options include equipment and 1$^1$/$_2$-hr lesson and lunch.

   Ski Cubs: Ages 3–6. 1$^1$/$_2$-hr lesson $38.
   Super Cubs: Ages 5–6. 2$^1$/$_2$-hr lesson $48.

*(continued on next page)*

*(continued from previous page)*

*Camper Facilities:* Winter camping at Sugar Pine Point State Park, on the West Shore, 26 miles south on SH 89, (916) 525-7982. Sixteen tent/RV sites to 30 ft long. No hookups. $10 per night. Heated restrooms. Parking.

*Medical:* First aid center located at the mountain. The closest hospital is Tahoe Forest, 6 miles north of Northstar in Truckee.

*Other:* Basket and ski check, Clara's Little General Store, Northsport Ski Shop, ski photo shop, gas station, outpost store with VCR and video rentals.

## SPECIAL EVENTS

- *Far West Regional NASTAR Pacesetting Trials*—December.
- *Santa on Skis*—Christmas week. Carolers, races.
- *All American Ski Race*—monthly.
- *Learn to Ski Month*—January.
- *Ski the Californias Races*—February.
- *North Tahoe/Truckee Snowfest Winter Carnival*—March.
- *Volleyball Tourney on the Snow*—March.
- *Far West Ski Association J4 and J5 Ski Race*—March.
- *Easter Bunny on Skis*—Easter. Easter egg hunt, raw egg toss contest.

## WINTER ACTIVITIES

### Cross-Country

*Northstar's Cross Country and Telemark Ski Center* is located mid-mountain, adjacent to the top of the gondola. The 25 miles of machine-groomed trails include a skating lane and double tracks. The trails are primarily beginner and intermediate, with 1 or 2 advanced runs. The longest, Schaffer Camp Trail, is 6 miles long and connects with Schaffer's Camp Lift on the back side of Northstar. A trailhead is also located at the base of the mountain at the cross-country parking lot.

Trail fees are $10 for adults and $5 for children ages 5–12, or $7 and $3 for half-day. Equipment rentals are $12 or $18 for telemark and skating. Demo skis are also available, as well as ski apparel and accessories. Class lessons are $25 adult and $13 child for a 1$^{1}/_{2}$-hr lesson and trail pass, or $29 and $17 with equipment rental. A 3-day Learn-to-Ski program starts Mondays and Wednesdays and includes a daily 1$^{1}$/$_{2}$-hr lesson, rental equipment, and trail fee for $75, adult or child. A 3-day Variety Pack includes track skiing, skating, and telemark lessons. Private lessons are also available. Special classes just for kids are offered weekends. The center is open from 9 a.m. to 4 p.m., (916) 587-0273.

Additional cross-country trails are located at *North Tahoe Regional Park*, on National Ave. and Donner Road, off SH 28, 2 miles south of Kings Beach. The Park has 7 miles of groomed beginner, intermediate, and advanced trails. Trail fees are $4 for adults and children. No rentals or general-public lessons on site. Contact the North Tahoe Public Utilities District, (916) 546-7248.

Northstar participates in the Ski North Lake Tahoe cross-country interchangeable trail pass, good at 7 Nordic ski areas. Rates are 4-days $34, 5-days $40, and 6-days $45. For further information, call (800) 824-6348.

## Snowmobiling

Snowmobile rentals and tours are available 6 miles north at the *Snow Connection* in Truckee, (916) 587-8913, and at *Tahoe Truckee Sports* on SH 267 and Brockway, (916) 587-7436. Guided tours with *Eagle Ridge Outfitters*, on SH 89, 5 miles north of Truckee on SH 89 at Old Hobart Mill, range from

*The open meadows and tree-lined trails at Northstar-at-Tahoe are ideal for a relaxing afternoon or evening sleigh ride after a long day on the slopes.* (Courtesy of Northstar-at-Tahoe.)

2 hours to 2 days, (916) 587-9322. Snowmobiles are also available through *High Sierra Snowmobiling*, SH 267 and SH 28 in Kings Beach. Rates are $25 for ¹/₂ hour and $40 for 1 hour.

For additional information on snowmobiling, see Squaw Valley and Diamond Peak.

## Tobogganing, Tubing, and Snow Play

A snow hill is located in *North Tahoe Regional Park* in Tahoe Vista. Toboggans, saucers, and inner tubes are permitted at no charge. Toboggan rentals are all day, $10; half day, $5, (916) 546-7248.

## Sleigh Rides

A 20-passenger sleigh and a 4-person sleigh pulled by Belgian horses depart daily from the Basque Club Restaurant. The ¹/₂-hr ride around Martis Valley is $8 for adults and $7 for children, (916) 562-0444.

Eight other cross-country ski areas are nearby. For further information on North Tahoe cross-country, snowmobiling, and snow play, see the Squaw Valley, Granlibakken, Tahoe Donner, Boreal, Sugar Bowl, Diamond Peak, and Mount Rose ski areas.

## OTHER ACTIVITIES

**Ballooning:** Mountain High Balloons, Truckee.
**Bowling:** Bowl Incline, Incline Village.
**Cinema:** The Martis Village Cinema, Truckee; Brockway Theater, Kings Beach.
**Fitness:** High Sierra Fitness, Tahoe-Truckee Airport; North Tahoe Beach Center, Kings Beach.
**Gambling and Video Games:** Cal-Neva Lodge, Crystal Bay Club, and Tahoe Biltmore, in Crystal Bay.
**Lake Cruises:** Tahoe Cruises, South Lake Tahoe.

## SHOPPING

Skiers can find equipment and ski apparel at the *Northsport Shop* in the Village or in Kings Beach at *Gunter's Sports Apparel*. Groceries, sundries, souvenirs, beer, and wine are available in the village at *Clara's General Store*. The *Safeway* supermarket is located 6 miles west on SH 28 in Kings Beach. Gift items and cards can be found at *The Heart 'n Home*, 8561 N. Lake Blvd. in Kings Beach, while avid readers will want to check out the 20,000 paperbacks at the *Book Bank*, 5225 N. Lake Blvd. in Carnelian Bay.

For additional information on shopping, see Tahoe Donner and Diamond Peak.

## APRÈS-SKI

Après-ski fun begins on the mountain in the *Alpine Bar*, with live entertainment on weekends. In the village, large-screen TVs and ski videos compete for skiers' attention at the *Rendezvous Sports Pub*. The lounge at the *Schaffer Mill Restaurant* is the place to relax by a romantic fire, and, on weekends, listen to the sounds of guitar music. The bar stays open until 11 p.m., depending on the crowd.

In Carnelian Bay, *Gar Woods* celebrates happy hour with hors d'oeuvres, drink specials, and action videos.

*The Cantina Los Tres Hombres* in Kings Beach on N. Lake Blvd., has live rock music on Fridays from 9:30 p.m. to 1:30 a.m. *Captain Jon's* in Tahoe Vista soothes skiers with live music in the lounge. Eight miles away in Crystal Bay, the *Tahoe Biltmore* has dancing in the Bananas Disco and a large-screen TV for watching sports. The *Crystal Bay Club Casino* offers late-night entertainment and dancing and, along with the *Cal-Neva Lodge*, 24-hour gambling.

## RESTAURANTS

In addition to restaurants in Northstar, a variety of dining options can be found along Tahoe's North Shore, 6 miles south. For dining options in Truckee, 7 miles north, see Tahoe Donner.

**Captain Jon's   $$$**   *(916) 546-4819*
7220 N. Lake Blvd., on the water at Kings Beach, 6 miles south of Northstar. A nautical atmosphere is the setting for lamb, fowl, and seafood, all prepared with a French accent.

**La Cheminee   $$$**   *(916) 546-4322*
8504 N. Lake Blvd., Kings Beach. This small Tahoe restaurant is noted for excellent French cuisine.

**La Playa   $$$**   *(916) 546-5903*
7046 N. Lake Blvd., Tahoe Vista, in the former Kellogg mansion. Fishing nets and marine prints complement the nautical theme at La Playa, whose owner also operates Le Petit Pier. Seafood specialties include mesquite grilled salmon bernaise and scallops sautéed with garlic.

**Le Petit Pier   $$$**   *(916) 546-2508*
7250 N. Lake Blvd., Tahoe Vista, 8 miles from Northstar. Owner Jean Dufau, who hails from the George V in Paris, recreates the ambience of an intimate country inn for his French specialties.

**Basque Club Restaurant**   $$   *(916) 587-0260*
Basque Dr. at Northstar. The Basque Club is a family-style restaurant serving hearty 5-course Basque meals, including steak, paella, lamb, and hare.

**The Bohn House**   $$   *(916) 546-4738*
8160 N. Lake Blvd., Kings Beach. A tradition of continental cooking is carried on with such dishes as roast duck, tournedos of beef, and chicken Kiev. Open from 5:30 p.m.

**Gar Woods Grill & Pier**   $$   *(916) 546-3366*
5000 N. Lake Blvd. in Carnelian Bay. Gar Woods contemporary design pays homage to the wooden boat era. Open for cocktails, dinner, and Sunday brunch, the menu includes steak, veal, chicken, seafood, pasta and "rock cuisine"—a combination of tri-tip, prawns, pork medallions, and vegetables served rare on a hot rock.

**Schaffer's Mill Restaurant**   $$   *(916) 587-0245*
In the Northstar Village. In a tasteful setting, Schaffer's mainly offers American cooking, including steak, chicken, and nightly seafood specials. Open for lunch and dinner.

**Soule Domain**   $$   *(916) 546-7529*
9983 Cove in Crystal Bay, adjacent to the Tahoe Biltmore. A small log cabin with a crackling fire and charming mountain ambience, the Soule Domain serves a memorable repast. The varied menu ranges from New Zealand lamb to fresh vegetables baked en croute, and Norwegian salmon with basil, honey, cilantro, and lemon garlic creme in white wine. Beer and wine list.

**C.B.'s Carnelian Bay**   $   *(916) 546-4738*
5075 N. Lake Blvd. in Carnelian Bay. C.B.'s pizza and deli serves salads, hot dogs, pizza combos, and sandwiches. Open daily 11:30 a.m. to 10 p.m.

**Pedro's Pizza Parlor**   $   *(916) 587-0245*
In the village, Pedro's mixes pizza with Italian pastas and Mexican entrées.

## ACCOMMODATIONS

**Kingswood Village**   $$$   *(916) 546-2501*
SH 167, 4½ miles south of Northstar. All units have full kitchens, fireplaces, and TV. Some units also have phones and spa tubs. Sauna and laundry on premises.

**Tahoe Vista Inn & Marina**   $$$   *(916) 546-4819, (800) 662-3433*
7220 N. Lake Blvd., Tahoe Vista, 8 miles from Northstar. Deluxe 1-, 2-, and 3-bedroom-plus-loft condominiums sleep from 2 to 6. The fully equipped kitchens include microwave and conventional ovens and washer/dryers. Living areas include fireplaces, TV, and views of Lake Tahoe. Complimentary breakfast and valet parking.

**Best Western Truckee Tahoe Inn**   $$   *(916) 587-4525*
*Nationwide, (800) 528-1234*
SH 267, adjacent to the Truckee-Tahoe airport, 1½ miles east of Truckee and 4 miles west of Northstar. The inn's 100 king-size and double queen-size rooms include phones, private bathrooms, TV, and free continental breakfast. Other facilities include an indoor sauna, outdoor spa, and conference rooms. Children under 12 stay free with adult. Complimentary shuttle to Northstar.

**Brockway Springs**   $$   *(916) 546-4201*
101 Chipmunk Ave., Kings Beach. Luxury 1-, 2-, 3-, and 4-bedroom condominiums and townhouses, some with lake views, have fireplaces, TV, phones, and kitchens that include microwave and conventional ovens. Heated pool, saunas, conference room, and laundry on premises. Daily maid service, snow removal, and security gate.

**Cal-Neva Lodge**   $$   *(702) 832-4000*
2 Stateline Dr., Crystal Bay. A first-class, high-rise casino hotel overlooking Lake Tahoe, the Cal-Neva straddles the California-Nevada border. Facilities include a large casino, restaurant, coffee shop, bar, and lounge with dancing. The health club includes a sauna, Jacuzzi, and weight room. An outdoor ice skating rink is planned. Ski packages available. On Northstar shuttle bus route.

**Northstar-at-Tahoe**   $$   *(916) 562-1113, (800) 533-6787*
Northstar-at-Tahoe offers 230 on-site accommodations ranging from hotel-type units to condominiums and homes. A recreation center with an exercise and weight room, serves all lodgers, as do the saunas and outdoor spas. The hotel rooms and suites are located in the village mall with ski-in, ski-out access, TV, phones and daily maid service.

1-, 2-, 3-, and 4-bedroom townhouses are enhanced with high ceilings, fireplaces, and window seats. The spacious units are each furnished with a TV, phone, and washer/dryer unit. Daily maid service. The Ski Trails Condominiums, adjacent to the village mall, offer ski-in, ski-out access.

Homes vary in size and decor. Beaver Pond unit 800, for example, sleeps up to 8 and includes 2 bedrooms and a loft, a rimrock fireplace, 2 sofas, a large kitchen with double oven, and a walk-in closet in the master bedroom.

Available packages include lift tickets, airport transfers, and accommodations. Additional lodging is available along SH 267 and at Lake Tahoe's North Shore. Sierra Vacation Rentals also rents condominiums and homes in the Northstar area, (916) 546-8222 or (800) 521-6656. For accommodations in nearby Truckee, see Tahoe Donner.

**Garni Motor Lodge**   $   *(916) 546-3341*
*(800) 648-2324, (702) 831-4414*
9937 N. Lake Blvd., Crystal Bay, adjacent to North Shore casinos, the Garni has 100 moderate rooms with king-size, queen-size, or twin beds. A 3-bedroom, 2-bath cabin with kitchen and fireplace sleeps up to 8. Rooms have phones, in-room coffee, and TV. Sauna on premises. Located on shuttle bus route.

# Diamond Peak

P.O. Drawer AL
*Top of Ski Way*
*Incline Village, NV 89450*
*Information: (702) 832-1177*
*Snowphone: (702) 832-3211*

### Driving distances

| | |
|---|---|
| Fresno | 287 mi |
| Los Angeles | 508 mi |
| Reno | 35 mi |
| Sacramento | 122 mi |
| San Diego | 627 mi |
| San Francisco | 210 mi |
| San Jose | 239 mi |
| S. Lake Tahoe | 21 mi |
| Tahoe City | 17 mi |
| Truckee | 18 mi |

*For road conditions, call*
*(916) 581-1400, California*
*(702) 793-1313, Nevada*

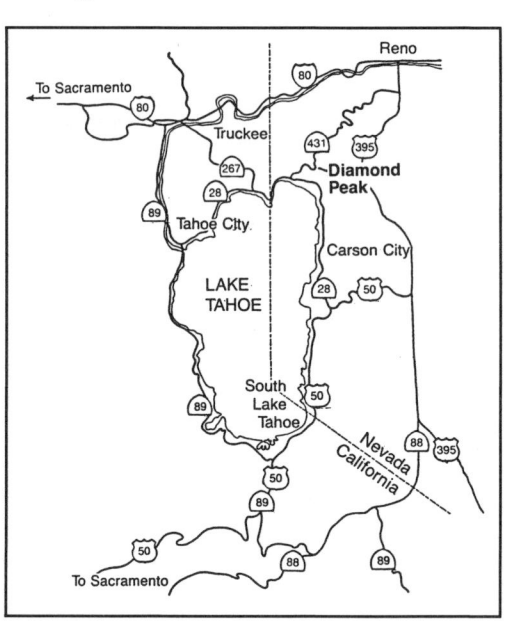

Diamond Peak is a family-oriented ski area that prides itself on convenience and service.

Although the mountain has no on-site lodging, one phone call to Diamond Peak lets skiers reserve their lift passes, round-trip transportation from Reno Cannon International Airport, and accommodations in nearby Incline Village or elsewhere at Lake Tahoe's North Shore.

Diamond Peak also provides special services to acquaint newcomers with the mountain. In addition to regular ski school programs, Diamond Peak conducts guided tours of the terrain. A staff of local seniors, known as Silver Hosts, hands out trail maps and helps with groups.

Diamond Peak is also a convenient ski hub, just 35 miles from the Reno airport, 35 minutes from Tahoe's South Shore and Heavenly Valley, and 25 minutes from Northstar, Squaw Valley, and Alpine Meadows. Located just minutes from Lake Tahoe's North Shore, the mountain also offers sweeping views of Tahoe.

## LOCATION

Diamond Peak is located in Incline Village on the northeast corner of Lake Tahoe in Washoe County, NV. The base is on Sky Way Dr. between SH 28 to the south and SH 431 to the north.

From the Reno airport, take US 395 south 9 miles to SH 431. Head west 25 miles to Country Club Dr. in Incline Village. Turn left on Country Club Dr. and go about 2 miles, then turn right on Sky Way Dr. to the ski area.

From the Lake Tahoe Airport in South Lake Tahoe, turn north on US 50 to Lake Tahoe's South Shore and follow US 50 for 15 miles around the southeast corner of the lake. Turn left or north on SH 28 and continue for about 12 miles to Incline Village. Turn right on Country Club Dr. to Sky Way Dr.

From Sacramento, take I-80 east to the SH 267 exit. Head southeast on SH 267 about 12 miles to SH 28 (N. Lake Tahoe Blvd.) and turn left on Country Club Dr. to Sky Way Dr.

Reno Cannon International Airport is the closest major airport to Diamond Peak. The Sacramento airport is 122 miles west. Scheduled service to Lake Tahoe Airport in South Lake Tahoe is less frequent and, in heavy weather, flights sometimes land in Reno instead. Four-wheel-drive and cars equipped for skiers are available for rental at all 3 airports.

Transfers from the Reno airport to the Hyatt Hotel in Incline Village are available from Tahoe Express 6 to 8 times daily for $14 per person, one way. From Incline, Tahoe Express charges $2 per person to Diamond Peak, with a 2-person minimum. Reservations required, (702) 832-0713. Aerotrans Luxury Vans operates shuttles from the Reno airport to Incline Village and Diamond Peak for $15 per person with a minimum of 3 persons, or for $45, (702) 786-2376.

Cab fare from the Reno airport runs about $45 one way. Limousine service is available from Truckee-Tahoe Limousine and Tours, (916) 587-2160, and from 5 Star Enterprises, Truckee, (916) 587-7651.

Amtrak's "California Zephyr" stops in Truckee, as well as in Sacramento and Reno/Sparks. Autos with chains and racks are available for rent in Truckee at the AAA Auto Rental, adjacent to the Amtrak station. During the busy season, 4-wheel-drive vehicles should be reserved a month or more in advance. Rental car delivery to the train stations in Sacramento and Reno can be arranged through Hertz. Greyhound operates bus service into Reno and Truckee.

Diamond Peak provides complimentary shuttle service to lodges in Incline Village and Tahoe Vista. TART, the Tahoe Area Regional Transit, operates around the lake to Incline Village, (916) 581-6365, CA, and (800) 325-8278, NV.

## TERRAIN

Diamond Peak is really 2 mountains. Runs off the lower peak, topping out at 7,440 ft, are varied but relatively short. The newly developed Diamond Peak is more than 1,000 ft higher and double the vertical of the lower mountain.

For advanced skiers only, *Golden Eagle Bowl* on Diamond Peak's back side is the place to find chutes and challenging pitches, while the heavily-forested front side preserves demanding paths through the trees. Mogul fanciers will find bumps to reckon with on *Thunder* and *Lightning* off *Crystal Ridge*. These runs and others off *Crystal Ridge* feed into *Lodgepole*, which can become congested at the end of the day.

For intermediate skiers, the easiest way off Diamond Peak is a glide on the wide *Great Flume* or a long, scenic cruise on *Crystal Ridge* to *School House*. The trick is to keep an eye on the terrain and not on the spectacular lake views. A wide, unprotected run, *Crystal Ridge* can be windy during a storm. Luckily for skiers, Diamond Peak receives sunshine 80% of the season, but when the wind's blowing, intermediate skiers can head for the Red Fox Lift, where *Delight*, *Bunny*, and *Popular* are all gentle and hospitable.

The beginner runs are limited to *Lodgepole* and *School Yard*. When beginners feel comfortable on these runs, they can try the easier intermediate runs like *Bunny* and *Delight*.

## FACILITIES

Diamond Peak offers several discounts for families. The Campbell's Family Special, for example, includes lift tickets for 2 adults and 1 child (6–12) for $63. Each additional child is $5, holidays excepted. Kids also ski free on a 3-day, 3-night ski package that includes lodging and lift tickets. Rates start at $126 per person.

The Honeymoon Special includes 2 adult lift passes and a designer gourmet picnic basket filled and delivered to the romantic mountain location of the couple's choice, and a color photograph of the couple on the mountain, overlooking Lake Tahoe.

Diamond Peak participates in the Ski Tahoe North interchangeable lift ticket with Squaw Valley, Alpine Meadows, Homewood, Northstar, and Mount Rose. Rates are $96 adult and $36 child for 3 consecutive days; $128 adult, $48 child for 4 consecutive days; $160 adult and $60 child, 5 consecutive days; and $187 adult, $72 child for 6 consecutive days.

## FACILITIES AT A GLANCE

*Season:* Thanksgiving–late April.
*Hours:* 9 a.m.–4 p.m. daily.
*Night Skiing:* None.
*Area:* 1,840 acres with 35 runs.
   Beginner: 18%
   Intermediate: 49%
   Advanced: 33%
*Base Elevation:* 6,700 ft
*Summit Elevation:* 8,540 ft
*Vertical Drop:* 1,860 ft
*Longest Run:* 2.5 miles
*Snowmaking:* Covers 80% of the mountain and 2,000 vertical ft.
*Smowboarding:* Permitted.
*Avg. Annual Snowfall:* 300 in.
*Lift Capacity:* 7,700 per hr.

*Lifts:* 7 chair lifts (6 doubles and 1 quad)

| Name | Length | Vertical Rise |
|---|---|---|
| Coyote | 1,235 ft | 296 ft |
| Diamond Peak | 4,501 ft | 1,478 ft |
| Lakeview | 2,336 ft | 673 ft |
| Lodgepole | 1,576 ft | 226 ft |
| Red Fox | 1,590 ft | 399 ft |
| The Ridge | 1,600 ft | 286 ft |
| School House | 935 ft | 73 ft |

*(continued on next page)*

*(continued from previous page)*

| Lift Passes: | All Day | Afternoon Only |
|---|---|---|
|  | 9 a.m.–4 p.m. | 1 p.m.–4 p.m. |
| Adults | $28 | $19 |
| Children 6–12 | $12 | $10 |
| Children under 6 | FREE | FREE |
| Seniors 60–69 | $12 | $10 |
| Seniors 70 + | FREE | FREE |
| Snowboarder | $18 | $18 |
| Handicapped | $15 | $12 |
| Helper | $15 | $12 |
| Child | $8 | $8 |

*Multiday Rates:* Two consecutive days. Adult $50. Child $20.

*Season Passes:* When purchased prior to November 12: $400 adult, $165 child and senior, $265 student. When purchased November 12 or after: $475 adult, $190 child and senior, $300 student.

*Group Rates:* Available by prior arrangement for 20 or more people.

*Food & Drink:* Base lodge includes cafeteria, deck barbecue, and loft with lounge and bar. Snowflake Lodge at the top of Lakeview Lift contains snack bar, outdoor barbecue, and bar.

*Parking & Transportation:* Parking is free at the base and at an overflow lot at the Incline golf course. No overnight RV parking. Free tram service from the parking lot on busy days. Free shuttles operate daily between Diamond Peak and a number of lodges in Tahoe Vista and Incline Village, and every 1/2 hour from 8:30 a.m. to 1:30 p.m. daily from the Hyatt Hotel.

*Ski Rentals:* The rental and repair shop at the base lodge is open from 8 a.m.–4 p.m. daily. Includes skis, boots, poles.
All day: Adult $14. Child/Senior $10.
Half day: Adult $10. Child/Senior $6.
High performance: $21 all day. $15 half day.

*Ski School:* Phone (702) 832-1130.

*Method:* ATM.

*Ski School Director:* Allen Bitten.

*Class Lessons:* 10:30 a.m. and 12 p.m.
$15 (2 hr). Adult and child.
$24 (4 hr). Adult and child.

*First Tracks:* Powder lesson 8:30 a.m.–10:30 a.m., snow conditions permitting, $20.

*Guided Ski Tours:* 10:30 a.m.–12:30 p.m. and 2 p.m.–4 p.m. $30 all day. $18 half day.

*Learn to Ski Special:* Includes 4-hr lesson, rental equipment, and lift ticket.
$29 adult. $25 child.
$19 adult, half day. $15 child, half day.

*Children's Ski School:* 8:30 a.m.–4 p.m. midweek and 8 a.m.–4 p.m., weekends.

*Child Ski Development Center:* Ages 3–7.
Includes ski instruction, lift ticket, snacks, games.
$35 all day. $25 half day, 3 hrs.
Lunch $5 additional.

*Sierra Scouts:* Ages 7–12. All day 10:30 a.m.–12:30 p.m. and 2 p.m.–4 p.m.
Includes ski instruction, winter safety, and tour of the mountain.
Supervised lunch $5.
$24 all day. $15 half day.

*Private Lessons:* $35, 1 hr. $55, 2 hr.
$175 all day (6 hr). $210 all day 2–5 persons.

*Multi-language Lessons:* Spanish, Japanese, or German on request.

*Races & Clinics:*

*Computerized Race Course:* $1 per run. Seven runs for $5.

*Clinic:* $20 for 2 hr with 5-person minimum.
$10 for 2 hr for groups of 20+.

*Day Care:* Tahoe Tots, 3 miles west in Incline Village accepts children ages 2–12 Monday through Friday from 7:30 a.m. to 6 p.m. $2.50 per hr, lunch included, (702) 831-2486. Rainbow Day Care, 865 Tahoe Blvd., Incline Village, accepts children from 18 months to 5 years from 7:30 a.m. to 6 p.m. on a reservation basis. Diamond Peak guests are $4 per hr and $40 per day on Saturdays and Sundays. Parents provide lunch, (702) 831-8989.

*Camper Facilities:* Winter camping at Sugar Pine Point State Park, on the West Shore, 26 miles south on SH 89, (916) 525-7982. Sixteen tent/RV sites to 30 ft long. No hookups. $10 per night. Heated restrooms. Parking.

*Medical:* First aid center located at the mountain. Helicopter evacuation available. The closest hospital is Lakewood Community Hospital in Incline Village.

*Other:* Ski lockers, sport shop, slot machines in lounge.

## SPECIAL EVENTS

- *Santa on Skis*—Christmas Holidays. Santa Claus, jugglers, string quartets.
- *Far West Ski Association Races*—Weekly.
- *MS Ski Day*—January.
- *Special Olympics*—February.
- *American Cancer Society Ski Day*—February.
- *Snowfest*—March. Children's races, grandparents' races, snowboard competition.
- *Easter Bunny on Skis*—Easter.

## WINTER ACTIVITIES

### Cross-Country

*Diamond Peak Cross-Country* is located 5 miles east of Diamond Peak on Mount Rose Hwy. More than 18 miles of double tracks and skating lanes are groomed for all levels of skiers. A "kinder-track" is a narrower track especially

*The trick at Diamond Peak is for skiers to keep their eyes on the trail, and not on the spectacular lake views.* (Courtesy of Diamond Peak.)

designed for children. Terrain consists of 3 beginner, 3 intermediate, and 2 advanced trails. Four scenic loops offer views of Lake Tahoe.

*Diamond Peak Cross-Country* is open from 9 a.m. to 4 p.m. daily. Trail fees are $9 all day and $5 half day. Seniors age 60–69 and children 6–12 are $6 all day and $4 half day. Seniors 70 and over and children under 6 are free. Lessons are $13 for 1$^{1}/_{2}$ hr. Ski, boot, and pole rentals are $10 for adults and $7 for seniors and children. Half-day rates are available. Package rates for a class lesson, trail pass, and equipment rental are $25 adult and $20 for seniors and children.

Diamond Peak participates in the Ski Tahoe North interchangeable trail pass with Spooner Lake, Northstar, Squaw Valley, Tahoe Donner, Tahoe Nordic, and Royal Gorge cross-country ski areas. Rates are $35 for 4 days, $40 for 5 days, and $45 for 6 days.

Services include food and beverages, accessory shop, and complimentary shuttle service to Incline Village and the Alpine ski area, (702) 832-1177.

## Snowmobiling

*Mountain Lake Adventures, Inc.* conducts guided snowmobile tours from 20 to more than 60 miles. The "Family" adventure lasts 1$^{1}/_{2}$ hr and includes panoramic views of the Sierra Nevada. $65 single, $95 double. The all-day, 6-hr tour takes in the back country, historic Truckee, and Tahoe City, $250 single, $400 double. Sunset and moonlight tours and deep powder tours are also available, (800) 433-5253 or (702) 831-4202.

## Tobogganing, Tubing, and Snow Play

A gentle snow-play hill is located in *Incline Village* adjacent to The Chateau. There is no equipment rental available on site. A steeper hill is located at *Spooner Summit* 9 miles south at the junction of SH 28 and US 50. Sled hills are also located in the meadows and summit at *Mount Rose*, 8 miles east on SH 431.

For additional information on North Lake Tahoe Nordic areas, see Mount Rose, Northstar, Heavenly Valley, Squaw Valley, and Tahoe Donner.

## OTHER ACTIVITIES

**Ballooning:** Aerovision Balloons, Inc., Gardnerville, NV.
**Bowling:** Bowl Incline, Incline Village.
**Cinema:** Incline Cinema, Incline Village.
**Fitness:** Bodytime and Incline Courthouse, Incline Village; North Tahoe Beach Center, Kings Beach.

**Gambling:** Cal-Neva Lodge, Tahoe Biltmore, Crystal Bay.
**Racquetball:** Incline Court House, Incline Village.
**Video Games:** Stateline casinos, Crystal Bay.

## SHOPPING

Skiers can find ski accessories and apparel at the *Ski Shop* at Diamond Peak. Downhill and cross-country equipment and clothes are available in Incline Village at *Rosebud's* in the Country Club Mall, the *Village Ski Loft*, Northwoods and Tahoe Blvd., and the *Outdoorsman* in the Rally Center. The *Potlatch*, 324 Ski Way Dr., takes care of cold feet with all-leather moccasins, and also stocks other Indian art and jewelry.

The *Village Market Pharmacy* at 745 Mays Blvd. in Incline Village, is open 7 days a week. The *Country Club General Store*, across from the Hyatt Hotel in the Country Club Mall, sells a variety of items, from pickles to Pampers.

Women's fashions and shoes are featured at *Jeunesse* in the Incline Center, *Fifth Season Clothing* in the Christmas Tree Village, and *Trish's Ladies Fashions*, 774 Mays. *Kartine's Kasuals*, Country Club Mall, carries men's, women's, and junior sizes, along with gifts and jewelry. *Czyz's*, also in the Incline Center, sells both men's and women's jeans and sweaters. *Interlude International Art & Design Gallery*, is at 930 Tahoe Blvd., Incline Village. Browsers will find antiques and other home furnishings at *Ambience* in the Village Post Office Center, Incline Village, and landscape and western paintings at *Arteliza Galleries*, Tanager Blvd., in Incline Village.

## APRÈS-SKI

At Diamond Peak, skiers gather in the *Loft* bar for après-ski conversation or to try their luck at one of the new poker machines.

As on the South Shore, however, the principal après-ski activity on Tahoe's North Shore is gambling at Stateline casinos and the *Hyatt Hotel*. The casino at the Hyatt is immense and decorated in a fantasy-forest theme with life-size bark trees. The *Savoy Lounge* at the Tahoe Biltmore, Crystal Bay, in addition to gambling features live entertainment on one of the largest stages in the area. A rock-and-roll band livens up the night with dancing nightly except Mondays and Tuesdays. The band at the *Crystal Bay Club*, another Stateline casino, plays top-40 music from 9:30 p.m. to 3 a.m.

At *Testarosa* in Incline Village, skiers dance to the sounds of compact discs late into the night.

## RESTAURANTS

**Hugo's Rotisserie   $$$**   *(702) 831-1111*
In the Hyatt Regency at Lakeshore and Country Club Dr., Incline Village. This newly redecorated eatery features continental entrées including seafood and steak, as well as a salad bar and a dessert bar. Spit-roasted duckling is the specialty of the house.

**Le Bistro   $$$**   *(702) 831-0800*
120 Country Club Dr., #29, Incline Village. Across from the Hyatt Hotel, Le Bistro is a small intimate restaurant with a European atmosphere. The menu offers gourmet selections such as escargots, stuffed braised quail, rack of lamb, cornish game hen, petaluma duck, roast pork loin, steak, and lobster. Open for dinner from 6 p.m. to 10 p.m. Closed Mondays.

**Spatz   $$$**   *(702) 831-8999*
341 Ski Way, Incline Village. Spatz offers fabulous lake views along with its California cuisine. Menu selections include fresh seafood, veal, and chicken. Open from 11:30 a.m. to 2:30 p.m. for lunch, and from 6 p.m. to 8 p.m. (or 9 p.m. weekends) for dinner. Sunday brunch.

**Azzara's   $$**   *(702) 831-0346*
930 Tahoe Blvd., Incline Village. Small, popular restaurant serving tasty Italian and Sicilian dishes, including saltimbocca, lasagna, pizza, chicken, and seafood, in pleasant room enhanced by pastel tiles and hanging plants and flowers. Italian and domestic wines.

**Blue Water Sea Garden   $$**   *(702) 831-2086*
Country Club Mall, Incline Village. Fish tanks set the scene for seafood specialties.

**Bobby's Uptown Cafe   $$**   *(702) 831-0404*
907 Tahoe Blvd., Incline Village. Variety at Bobby's runs from barbecued baby-back ribs to roast turkey dinners.

**Chow Mein Trattoria   $$**   *(702) 831-1111*
In the Hyatt Regency Hotel, Lakeshore at Country Club Dr., Incline Village. The menu at this newly redecorated restaurant is a combination of Italian and Oriental cuisine. Open daily for dinner from 6 p.m. to 10 p.m.

**Ivory's Bar & Grill   $$**   *(702) 831-7373*
Christmas Tree Village, Incline Village. A southwest cantina-style restaurant serving barbecue sandwiches and beef dip, salad, chicken, pork chops, and more. Children's menu.

**La Fondue   $$**   *(702) 831-6104*
Country Club Mall #66, Incline Village, across from the Hyatt. In addition to their famous fondues, La Fondue carries steak, seafood, lamb, and other continental dishes.

**Marie France**  $$ *(702) 832-3007*
907 Tahoe Blvd., Incline Village. Unique entrées include salmon in crust with rhubarb and kiwi, and filet mignon of pork with pears and red wine sauce. Piano music Tuesday through Saturday.

**Schweizer Haus**  $$ *(702) 831-9944*
120 Country Club Dr. in the Country Club Mall, Incline Village, across from the Hyatt Regency Hotel. Swiss cuisine entrées include fondues, Wienerschnitzel, and rahmschnitzel (veal sautéed with mushrooms and cream). Open for lunch and for dinner from 5:30 p.m. to 10 a.m. Closed Tuesdays.

**Sir Charles**  $$ *(702) 832-4000*
In the Cal-Neva Lodge, Crystal Bay. Entrées at Sir Charles vary from the unusual chicken Malibu (breast of chicken sautéed with avocado, swiss cheese, tomato, and madeira wine), to standard steak, pasta, and seafood dishes. Open Thursday through Saturday from 5 p.m. to 10 p.m.

**Stanley's**  $$ *(702) 831-9944*
941 Tahoe Blvd., Incline Village. Steak, seafood stroganoff, and barbecued spareribs are some of the selections served in this old Tahoe house. Open for breakfast and lunch, and for dinner from 5:30 p.m. to 10 p.m. daily.

**China Chef**  $ *(702) 831-0593*
882 Tahoe Blvd., Incline Village. Chinese and Szechuan cuisine is offered in a contemporary setting. Cocktail bar has built-in gaming machines.

**Testarosa**  $ *(702) 831-7373*
881 Tahoe Blvd., Incline Village. Open 24 hours a day, the Testarosa serves pizza, hamburgers, and pasta for lunch and dinner. Dancing nightly.

## ACCOMMODATIONS

Accommodation packages, which include a choice of lodges, condominiums, and private homes on Tahoe's North Shore as well as lift tickets and round-trip transfers from the Reno airport, can be arranged through the Resort at (800) 824-6348 or (800) 468-2463.

Condominiums and homes can also be reserved through the Vacation Station management company, (702) 831-3664 or (800) 841-7443; B.R.A.T. Realty, (702) 831-3318 or (800) 468-2463 ext. 16; and Blue Diamond Realty, (702) 831-7177 or (800) 992-1008.

**Club Tahoe Resort**  $$$ *(702) 831-5750, (800) 527-5154*
SH 28 at Village Blvd., Incline Village, 1 mile from Diamond Peak. Two-bedroom condominiums with lofts all have 2 baths, living rooms with fireplaces, 2 TVs, and 2 phones. Kitchens are fully equipped, including conventional and microwave ovens and washer/dryers. Resort facilities include a sauna, spa and exercise

room, racquetball courts, and game room with billiards. Private deli and cocktail lounge. 2- or 7-night minimums.

**Hyatt Regency Lake Tahoe**    $$$              *(702) 831-1111*
*Nationwide (800) 233-1234*

Country Club Dr. at Lakeshore Dr., Incline Village. A deluxe resort with an 11-story tower and 1- and 2-bedroom lakeside suites with fireplaces and some Jacuzzis. Completely renovated in 1989, rooms now sport a Ralph Lauren lodge look. Rooms all have a phone, TV, and bathroom amenities. Regency Club services are offered on the 10th and 11th floors. The Lakeside Cottages, some with Jacuzzis and wood-burning fireplaces, have been redone in natural wood and river-rock exteriors.

Facilities include a casino with a fantasy-forest theme and life-size bark trees, 3 dining rooms, cocktail lounge, health club, sauna, spa for 24, and heated pool open 24 hours a day. Beauty salon, conference rooms, ballroom. Room service and valet parking. Alpine and Nordic ski rentals. Shuttle bus to ski area and the Reno airport. Ski packages available.

**Coeur du Lac**    $$           *(702) 831-3318, (800) 468-2463*

136 Juanita Dr., Incline Village, 1 mile from ski area. Modern 1-, 2-, 3-, and 4-bedroom condominiums with rustic beamed ceilings, redwood paneled walls, fireplaces, TV, phones, and fully equipped kitchens sleep up to 8. The recreation center has an indoor spa, saunas and showers, heated pool, and lockers. Additional charge for maid service. Free shuttle to Diamond Peak. Ski packages available.

**Haus Bavaria**    $$                     *(702) 831-6122*

593 N. Dyer Circle, Incline Village. This Bavarian-style chalet has 5 rooms with private baths. European breakfast included. No children. Two-night minimum.

**The Inn at Incline**    $$           *(702) 831-1052, (800) 367-7366*

1003 Tahoe Blvd., Incline Village, 2 miles, from the ski area. Spacious rooms and suites with light woods, decorated in beiges and blues, have king-size, queen-size, and twin or double beds, TV, and phones. Refrigerators can be requested. Continental breakfast included on weekends. Indoor pool, spa, sauna, underground parking, and conference room. Ski packages available.

**Lakeshore Condominiums**    $$            *(702) 831-3349*

999 Lakeshore, Incline Village, across from the Hyatt Hotel. Fully furnished 2-, 3-, and 4-bedroom condominiums, all with TV and kitchen, some with phone, washer/dryer, and fireplace. Maid service available at $10 an hr. Two-night minimum. Shuttle bus to Incline stops in front every $1/2$ hour.

**Lakeside Tennis & Ski Resort**    $$     *(702) 831-5258, (800) 222-2612*

977 Tahoe Blvd., Incline Village. Studio, 1-, 2-, and 3-bedroom apartments with fireplaces, kitchens, balconies, queen-size beds, TV, and phones. Extra charge for maid service. Facilities include lounge, hot tub, and conference room. Shuttle bus to Diamond Peak.

**Forest Pines**   $   *(702) 831-1307, (800) 458-2463*
123 Juanita Dr., Incline Village. Fully furnished 1-, 2-, 3-, and 4-bedroom condominiums accommodate up to 8 people. Each unit includes a TV, phone, fireplace, fully-equipped kitchen and a washer/dryer unit. No maid service. Facilities include a recreation room, spa, and sauna.

**Four Seasons**   $   *(702) 831-2311, (800) 322-4331*
807 Alder Ave., Incline Village. Comfortable 1-, 2- and 3-bedroom units with kitchens, sun decks, and fireplaces. No phones or daily maid service. The clubhouse features a heated indoor pool, spa, universal weight center, and meeting rooms. Complimentary shuttle to ski areas.

# Mount Rose

*P.O. Box 2406*
*Reno, NV 89505*
*Information: (702) 849-0704*
*Snowphone: (702) 849-0706*

| Driving distances | |
|---|---|
| Fresno | 298 mi |
| Los Angeles | 519 mi |
| Reno | 22 mi |
| Sacramento | 133 mi |
| San Diego | 638 mi |
| San Francisco | 221 mi |
| San Jose | 250 mi |
| S. Lake Tahoe | 32 mi |
| Tahoe City | 28 mi |
| Truckee | 29 mi |

*For road conditions, call*
*(916) 581-1400, California*
*(702) 793-1313, Nevada*

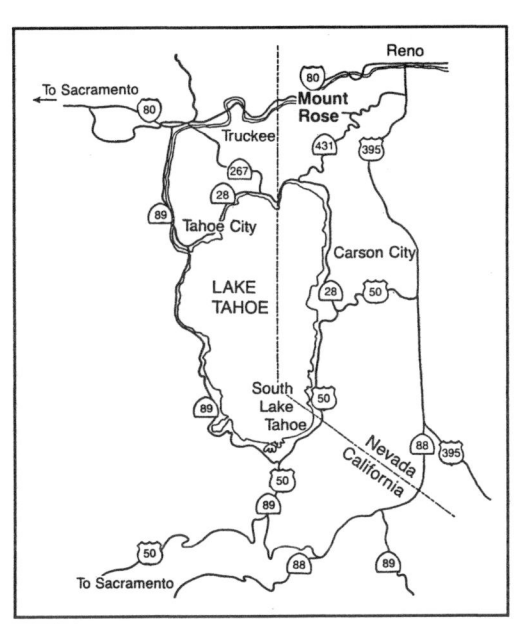

High above the arid Nevada desert, Mount Rose is a haven for the kind of light, dry snow that often eludes its Tahoe neighbors. At 8,250 ft, Mount Rose has the highest base elevation in the Lake Tahoe area and, because of the early snowfall, is traditionally the first to open each year. Due to the high elevation, strong winds sometimes roll in with storms. The trade-off is that when lower slopes in the Lake Tahoe area are melting in the rain or sun, the skiing can be just fine at Mount Rose, even without the aid of snowmaking.

But snow isn't the only trump card that Mount Rose holds. The intermediate and advanced terrain, particularly the steep, smooth runs on the Slide Mountain side, are the kind that advanced skiers like to run again and again: smooth and silky after a good snow, hard and slick in spring, with just enough challenge for a heady thrill.

The best part is that, although only 22 miles from the Reno airport and 11 miles from Tahoe's North Shore, Mount Rose's pleasures are still relatively undiscovered, except by locals. For skiers, that translates to short lift lines, open spaces, and low ticket prices.

## LOCATION

Mount Rose is located off SH 431 in the Toiyabe National Forest in Washoe County, Nevada, 22 miles from Reno Cannon International Airport and 11 miles from Incline Village.

From the Reno airport, take US 395 south 8 miles, then SH 431 west 14 miles to Mount Rose.

From the Lake Tahoe Airport in South Lake Tahoe, turn north on US 50 to Lake Tahoe's South Shore and follow US 50 15 miles around the southeast corner of the lake. Turn left or north on SH 28 and go right 10 miles on SH 431 to the ski area.

From Sacramento, take I-80 east to the SH 267 exit. Head southeast 12 miles to SH 28 (N. Lake Tahoe Blvd.) and then left 5 miles to Incline Village. Turn left at SH 431, 11 miles to the Mount Rose base lodge.

Reno Cannon International Airport is the closest major airport to Mount Rose. Scheduled service to Lake Tahoe Airport, 36 miles southwest, is less frequent and, in heavy weather, flights sometimes land in Reno instead. Four-wheel-drive and cars equipped for skiers are available for rental at both airports and in Incline Village at the Hyatt Regency Hotel, and at Incline Village Compacts, 851 Tanager Road in Incline Village.

See Tahoe Tours operates shuttles from the Reno airport to the Hyatt in Incline Village 6 to 8 times a day. The rate is $15 per person, one way, (702) 832-0713. From Incline Village, Tahoe Express charges $3 per person to Mount Rose with a minimum of 2 people, (702) 832-0713. Aerotrans Luxury Vans also operates between the Reno airport and Incline and Mount Rose for $15 per person and a minimum of 3 persons, or $45, (702) 786-2376.

Cab fare from Incline Village to Mount Rose is about $10 to $15, and $30 from the Reno airport to Diamond Peak. Limousine service is available from Truckee-Tahoe Limousine and Tours, (916) 587-2160, and 5 Star Enterprises, Truckee, (916) 587-7651.

Amtrak's "California Zephyr" stops in Truckee, as well as in Reno/Sparks. Autos with chains and racks are available for rent adjacent to the Amtrak Station in Truckee at the AAA Auto Rental. During the busy season, 4-wheel-drive vehicles should be reserved a month or more in advance. Rental car delivery to the train stations in Reno/Sparks can be arranged through Hertz.

Greyhound also operates bus service into Reno and Truckee.

## TERRAIN

The ski area combines the terrain of 2 mountains: Mount Rose, with terrain for all levels, and Slide Mountain, for intermediate and advanced skiers only. On the Slide side, the most serious pitch is in the center, where *Gold Run*, a demanding bump run, ranks with the steepest slopes in the area. Also on the Slide side, *Washoe Zephyr* offers an abundance of tree-skiing and untracked snow well after a storm. On the Mount Rose side, *Randy's* and *Greg's* are favorite advanced mogul runs.

Intermediate terrain on the Mount Rose side is primarily off the Lakeview Chair where expansive boulevards like *Kit Carson* are perfect for wide, swooping turns. Vistas of Lake Tahoe are best from *Lakeview*, another prime cruiser. On the Slide side, intermediates can head off the lifts to the right and the spacious acres on *Silver Dollar* and *Sunrise Bowl*, or left to timbered runs like *Zephyr Trail*. *Around the World*, a beginner and intermediate run, wraps around the mountain for a long, 2-mile excursion to the bottom.

The beginner runs are strung out on a slant across the bottom of Mount Rose. One of the longest, *Galena*, is wide and open while *Ponderosa*, another longer run, tends to catch faster traffic wooshing off the advanced runs above.

## FACILITIES

Mount Rose has 2 base lodges, the result of once having been 2 separate ski areas. Heading east on SH 431, the Main Lodge and parking area appears first. The second lodge is located 3.5 miles further along the highway at the base of Slide Mountain. The Slide side is for advanced and intermediate skiers only.

Skiers can save midweek when rates are lower. On Tuesdays, except holidays, a free 2-hr class lesson at any level is included with the price of a lift ticket. On Wednesdays, the special includes free rental equipment with the purchase of a lift ticket, holidays excepted.

## FACILITIES AT A GLANCE

| | |
|---|---|
| *Season:* | Mid-November–Mid-April. |
| *Hours:* | 9 a.m.–4 p.m. daily. |
| *Night Skiing:* | None. |
| *Area:* | 900 acres with 55 runs. |
| | Beginner: 30% |
| | Intermediate: 35% |
| | Advanced: 35% |
| *Base Elevation:* | 8,250 ft |
| *Summit Elevation:* | 9,700 ft |
| *Vertical Drop:* | 1,460 ft |
| *Longest Run:* | 2 miles |

*(continued from previous page)*
Snowmaking: None.
Snowboarding: Not permitted.
Avg. Annual Snowfall: 400 in.
Lift Capacity: 8,600 per hr.

Lifts: 6 chair lifts (3 triples and 3 doubles) and 5 surface tows

| Name | Length | Vertical Rise |
| --- | --- | --- |
| Galena | 2,663 ft | 376 ft |
| Lakeview | 3,770 ft | 932 ft |
| Northwest Passage | 4,516 ft | 1,400 ft |
| Overland | 4,950 ft | 1,450 ft |
| Pioneer | 1,450 ft | 1,450 ft |
| Ponderosa | 4,100 ft | 360 ft |

| Lift Passes: | All Day | Afternoon Only |
| --- | --- | --- |
|  | 9 a.m.–4 p.m. | 12:30 p.m.–4 p.m. |
| Adults | $22/$27 wkds/holidays | $16/$21 |
| Children 6–11 | $8/$10 | $10/$7 |
| Children under 5 | FREE | FREE |
| Seniors 62 + | $11/$13.50 | $8/$10.50 |

*Season Passes:* $495 adult. $300 child. $410 student. $250 senior. $900 family of 2. Additional family members $100 each. $295 midweek only.

*Group Rates:* Available by prior arrangement for 20 or more.

*Food & Drink:* A bar and hot-and-cold food service is available in the Main Lodge. A large cafeteria, lounge, and bar are also located in the Slide Mountain Lodge.

*Parking & Transportation:* Parking is free on both sides of the mountain. A free shuttle runs between the 2 base lodges. RV parking is permitted overnight. No hookups.

*Ski Rentals:* The rental and repair shop at the base lodge is open from 8:30 a.m.–4:30 p.m. daily. Includes skis, boots, poles.
  All day: Adult $14. Child $10.
  High performance: $15 all day.
  Children's Rosebud Classes Rentals: $5.

*Ski School:* Phone (702) 849-0704.
  *Method:* ATM.
  *Ski School Director:* Bob Bush.
  *Class Lessons:* 10:30 a.m. and 2 p.m.
    $15 (2 hr). Adult and child.
    $30 (4 hr). Adult and child.
  *Combination:* $42 includes 2-hr lesson, all-day lift ticket, and rental equipment.
  *First Timer:* Includes all-day lesson and rental equipment. Lift ticket not required.
    $33 all day.
    $20 afternoon only.
  *Rosebud's Ski School:* Ages 3-6. 10 a.m.–4:00 p.m. Includes ski instruction and lift ticket. Equipment rental $5 extra. $40 all day. $20 half day.
  *Private Lessons:* $35 1 hr. $65 2 hr. $95 3 hr.
  *Handicapped Lessons:* By arrangement.
  *Powder and Moguls:* Tuesdays.

*Races & Clinics:* For groups only, by arrangement or in private lesson.

*Day Care:* In Incline Village, 11 miles west, at Tahoe Tots, (702) 831-2486, Monday–Friday from 7:30 a.m. to 6 p.m., ages 2–12. $2.50 per hour, lunch included. Rainbow Day Care, 865 Tahoe Blvd., Incline Village, also accepts children from 18 months to 5 years by reservation. 7:30 a.m.–6 p.m. including weekends. $4 per hr. $40 per day, Saturdays and Sundays.

*Camping Facilities:* Winter camping is available at Sugar Pine Point State Park, Tahoma, CA, 26 miles south on SH 89, (916) 525-7982. Sixteen tent/RV sites to 30 ft long. No hookups. $10 per night. Heated restrooms. Parking. Full hookups also available at Virginia City RV Park, 52 miles west, $14. Tent camping is available for $4 per person per night, (702) 847-0999.

*Medical:* First aid center located at the mountain. Helicopter evacuation available. The closest hospital is Lakewood Community Hospital in Incline Village.

*Other:* Ski lockers and sport shop.

## SPECIAL EVENTS

- *Valentine's Day Special*—Valentine's Day. Two-for-the-price-of-one lift tickets.
- *Skiathon*—March.
- *Cup Race*—March.
- *Master's Race*—Late March, early April.

## WINTER ACTIVITIES

### Cross-Country

*Tahoe Meadows* Nordic area is located at the summit of Mount Rose Hwy, 2 miles west of the Alpine area. One 1.8 mile trail is marked for beginners. The second is just over a mile, and primarily intermediate. There are no lessons or equipment rentals on site. No permit is required for parking along the plowed sides of the highway. The trails are generally open from November to May. The area is patrolled by the National Ski Patrol on weekends. For information, contact the Carson Ranger District, (702) 882-2766.

For additional information on Nordic ski areas, see Diamond Peak and Northstar-at-Tahoe.

### Snowmobiling

Snowmobiling is permitted at the summit of Mount Rose Hwy, except in the cross-country area. Contact the Carson Ranger District for information, (702) 882-2766.

Snowmobiles can be rented at the *Reindeer Lodge*, 9000 Mount Rose Hwy, 7 miles east of the Mount Rose Alpine area. Rates for single passengers start at $15 for ½ hour and $25 for 1 hour, on up to $80 for 4 hours. Double passenger rates are $25 for ½ hour, $45 for 1 hour, and $125 for 4 hours, (702) 849-9902.

### Tobogganing, Tubing, and Snow Play

A hill for tobogganing, tubing, and other snow play is located less than a mile northeast of Tahoe Meadows cross-country, near the summit of Mount Rose Hwy. There are no equipment rentals on site. Contact the Carson Ranger District for information, (702) 882-2766.

## Heli-Skiing

*Ruby Mountain* heli-ski tours are conducted daily, from January 15 to April, in the northeast corner of Nevada. Skiers meet in Lamoille, outside of Elko, NV, 350 miles northeast of Mount Rose. The 3-day package consists of guided heli-skiing in the Ruby Mountains, with 10 runs a day, accommodations, breakfast, and lunch. Equipment is available at an extra charge. Cost is $1,300 and participation is limited. Reservations recommended well in advance, (702) 753-6867.

For additional information on Nordic ski areas, snowmobiling, and snow play in the Lake Tahoe Area, see Diamond Peak, Northstar-at-Tahoe, and Heavenly Valley.

## OTHER ACTIVITIES

**Ballooning:** Aerovision Balloons, Gardnerville, NV.
**Gambling:** In Reno and Crystal Bay, Lake Tahoe.
**Sightseeing:** Carson City and Virginia City, NV.

## SHOPPING

The *Mount Rose Ski Shop* at the base lodge sells items such as ski accessories and T-shirts. *Galena Ski Rental*, 16795 SH 341, rents ski equipment.

*Virginia City*, SH 341, 52 miles east, is a source for mining-era antiques, from 19th-century wheelbarrows to miner's hats. Sporting goods, apparel, and gifts are available in Incline Village. See Diamond Peak for more shopping suggestions.

Nearby *Reno* offers a plethora of boutiques and more than 10 shopping malls.

## APRÈS-SKI

Skiers can switch into the après-ski mood at the Mount Rose base lodge. The bar is open until 6 or 6:30 p.m.

Four miles east, it's Christmas all year long at the *Christmas Tree Restaurant and Bar*. Skiers are greeted by a crackling fire and unique libations like "Mrs. Claus' Hot Apple Pie," a mix of apple cider, cinnamon, and tuaca. Potato skins, nachos, and other favorite après-ski hors d'oeuvres can be consumed while listening to live guitar entertainment or a 3-piece Dixie or jazz combo, Wednesdays through Sundays.

Further down the road, 3.5 miles east of Mount Rose, the *Reindeer Lodge* is a funky mountain lodge crowded with moose heads, sofas, and antiques. Offerings include cocktails, beer, and buffalo burgers. On Saturdays, barbecued ribs and chicken are served, followed by entertainment from a live rock-and-roll band.

For glamour and glitz, skiers can head to downtown Reno or Crystal Bay on Tahoe North Shore. Also see Diamond Peak.

## RESTAURANTS

**The Christmas Tree**   $$   *(702) 849-0127*
20007 Mount Rose Hwy (Hwy 431), 4 miles east of the Mount Rose ski area. The Christmas Tree is a rustic steak house that exudes a mountain ambience: a roaring fire in a great stone hearth, Christmas tree boughs hanging from beams, and views of the valley and, occasionally, a deer or grizzly or two. Entrées include lamb chops, steak, and chicken. Vegetarian plate available. Open for dinner from 5 p.m. Wednesday through Sunday.

**Galena Forest Inn**   $$   *(702) 849-2100*
17025 Mount Rose Hwy (SH 431), 15 miles from Mount Rose and 6 miles west of SH 391. Dressier than most mountain-area restaurants, the Galena Forest serves a combination of American and Alpine cuisine in a pretty, open room with views of the forest. In addition to steak, seafood, and a salad bar, menu selections include Weiner schnitzel, rostbraten, escargot, pork piccata, and veal escallop. Closed Mondays and Tuesdays.

## ACCOMMODATIONS

Although there are no accommodations at the ski area, a variety of hotels, condominiums, and lodges are available in nearby *Incline Village* and *Reno*. A number of these properties offer ski packages that include lift tickets at Mount Rose.

Heading east from Mount Rose, the *Reindeer Lodge*, 9000 Mount Rose Hwy, is a bed-and-breakfast inn with 7 basic rooms that sleep from 2 to 7 in double beds or bunks with shared bathrooms. Rates run from $30 to $90. No TV or phones. Limited dining. Lounge with billiards and games. Snowmobile rentals. Entertainment on weekends, (702) 849-9902.

For additional information on accommodations in Incline Village and North Lake Tahoe, see Diamond Peak and Northstar-at-Tahoe.

# Squaw Valley

*Squaw Valley Ski Corp.*
*Squaw Valley USA, CA*
*95730*
*Information: (800) 545-4350,*
*(916) 583-6985*
*Telex: 3718728*
*FAX: (916) 583-5970*
*Snowphone: (916) 583-6955*

### Driving distances

| | |
|---|---|
| Los Angeles | 484 mi |
| Reno | 45 mi |
| Sacramento | 96 mi |
| San Diego | 601 mi |
| San Francisco | 196 mi |
| San Jose | 293 mi |
| S. Lake Tahoe | 40 mi |
| Tahoe City | 8 mi |
| Truckee | 10 mi |

*For road conditions, call*
*(916) 581-1440, California*
*(702) 793-1313, Nevada*

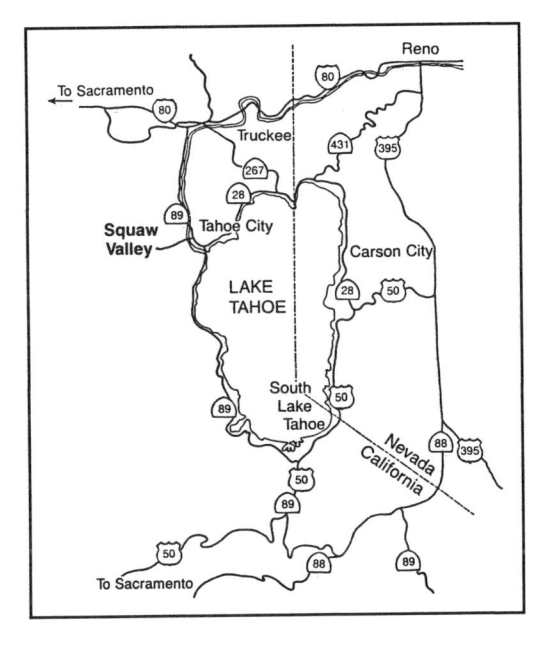

Squaw Valley's "state of the art" facilities, including the largest lift system in the country and slick, modern base lodges, combine with luxury accommodations in the village to make it the most upscale resort in the state.

With new, improved equipment in place, including its 150-passenger cable car, 6-passenger gondola, 3 detachable high-speed express quads, and 27 other lifts, Squaw Valley now boasts one of the largest lift capacities in the industry and reflects the first-class reputation befitting a resort that hosted the 1960 Olympic Winter Games.

As a destination resort with emphasis on top-notch lodging and amenities, Squaw Valley appeals to the more affluent skier, a verity reflected in its upscale prices.

However, Squaw not only draws the skier looking for after-hours comfort, but those in search of a challenge as well. With some of the steepest terrain in the area—KT 22 is the 9th steepest slope in the world—Squaw Valley is one of the best testing grounds for advanced ski skills.

## LOCATION

Squaw Valley is located off SH 89 in Placer County, 8 miles from the west shore of Lake Tahoe, and 10 miles south of Truckee.

From San Francisco, Sacramento, or Reno, take I-80 to the SH 89 exit. Turn south on SH 89 and go 8 miles to Squaw Valley Road, then right 2 miles to the mountain base.

From Stateline at South Lake Tahoe, drive west on US 50 to SH 89. Go north 30 miles along the winding west shore to Tahoe City, then 6 miles west on SH 89 to Squaw Valley Road.

On weekends and during holiday periods, the traffic in and out of Squaw Valley and along SH 89 to Tahoe City tends to be bumper-to-bumper, with the usual 10-minute drive dragging into an hour. Skiers not staying at Squaw can avoid these traffic jams by arriving earlier or later than opening and closing times, or by skiing midweek.

Reno Cannon International Airport is the closest major airport to Squaw Valley, which is also served by the Sacramento airport. Scheduled service to Lake Tahoe Airport, South Shore, is less frequent and, in heavy weather, flights sometimes land in Reno instead. Four-wheel drive and cars equipped for skiers are available for rental at all 3 airports and the Truckee-Tahoe airport on SH 267. Hertz also has a location in the Tram Building in Squaw Valley.

The Squaw Valley Shuttle bus to and from the Reno airport operates by reservation and 24-hr advance notice for $15 one way, (916) 583-5585. Greyline operates service to Squaw Valley from the end of November to the end of March on Mondays, Wednesdays, Fridays, and weekends at 7:30 a.m. and returns at 5:30 or 6 p.m. Adults are $15 round-trip, children under 14, $10 round-trip. Sierra Nevada Stage Lines shuttles adults from Reno to Squaw for $15 and children for $10, (702) 329-1147 or 800-822-6009.

Cab fare from the Reno airport runs about $75 one way. Limousine service is available from Truckee-Tahoe Limousine and Tours, (916) 587-2160, and 5 Star Enterprises, Truckee, (916) 587-7651.

Amtrak's "California Zephyr" stops in Truckee, as well as in Sacramento and Reno/Sparks. Autos with chains and racks are available for rent in Truckee at the AAA Auto Rental, adjacent to the Amtrak station. During the busy season, 4-wheel-drive vehicles should be reserved a month or more in advance. Rental car delivery to the train stations in Sacramento and Reno can be arranged through Hertz. Greyhound operates bus service into Truckee and Reno.

A free shuttle bus stops daily at a number of lodgings along the West Shore and North Shore of Lake Tahoe, including Truckee. The shuttle to the South Shore of Lake Tahoe is $4 round-trip. For reservations, schedules, and bus stops, call Squaw Valley, (916) 583-6985.

Alternatively, skiers staying on the South Shore can take the Tahoe Queen sternwheeler across the lake Tuesdays through Fridays at 8 a.m. and arrive at Tahoe City about 10 a.m. A shuttle bus then deposits skiers at Squaw by 10:30 a.m. The return trip departs Squaw around 4 p.m. and Tahoe City between 4:30 p.m. and 5 p.m. for the South Shore. Cost round-trip is $16.50 adults, $7.50 children, (916) 541-3364.

TART, the Tahoe Area Regional Transit, also operates bus service daily around the North and West Shores.

## TERRAIN

Spread across 6 mountain peaks, 5 of them over 8,000 ft, Squaw Valley's elevation and multiface exposures ensure skiers a long season. With the most challenging terrain concentrated on the left side of the mountain under the KT-22 Peak, experts can ski away from the crowds on favorite advanced slopes like *Olympic Lady*, site of the 1960 Olympic Ladies' Downhill, or the

*Squaw Valley USA, with 8,300 acres of wide-open bowl skiing, offers a peak skiing experience for skiers of all abilities.* (Photo courtesy of Chaco Mohler/Squaw Valley USA.)

formidable KT-22 run, with its electrifying combination of steepness and bumps.

But for some super experts, it's a jump off the cliffs onto the awesome steeps of Squaw Peak *Palisades* that sends the blood racing through the veins. Veteran chute fans can test their nerve on the narrow *Classic Chute* and, when the snow is new, make fresh tracks down the *Funnel*.

Skiers preferring wider spaces will find more comfort in the black diamond *Sunbowl* or intermediate *Siberia Bowl* and *Siberia Lake Express*, site of the Men's Giant Slalom in the 1960 Olympics. The upper portion of *Mountain Run*, the longest run on the mountain, follows the course of the Olympic Men's Downhill from the top of Squaw Peak Tram through Siberia Bowl, all the way down the face. This slope is best enjoyed before traffic starts funneling into it for the run back to base at the end of the day.

The beginner area is unique because of its placement on top of the mountain. At 8,200 ft, beginners are kept out of the way of faster skiers. They can ride the gondola up to the Links and Belmont chairs and go back down them at the end of the day, or take the easiest way down on the 50-ft wide *Home Run*, with its gentle grade of 15%.

Although Squaw Valley's trail map reflects lift names, only a few of the many trail names appear on the map. Planning an exact descent among the numerous possibilities is difficult, especially when friends and family members, who don't all ski at the same speed, are trying to stay together on the slopes. Skiers who are unsure of the mountain can ask for more specific trail information from the hosts and hostesses or at the information booth.

## FACILITIES

Information on Squaw Valley facilities is available at the information booth near the ticket windows. A staff of hosts and hostesses at various locations also offers assistance and conducts mountain tours.

Squaw Valley participates in 2 interchangeable lift tickets: The Ski Tahoe North lift ticket includes Squaw Valley, Alpine Meadows, Northstar-At-Tahoe, Homewood, Diamond Peak, and Mount Rose. The adult and child rates are $96/$36 for 3 days, $128/$48 for 4 days, $160/$60 for 5 days, and $189/$72 for 6 days.

The Ski Lake Tahoe interchangeable lift ticket includes Squaw Valley, Alpine Meadows, Northstar-at- Tahoe, Heavenly Valley, and Kirkwood. The rate is $32 daily for adults or children, and must be purchased for at least 5 days.

Squaw Valley offers a money-back guarantee to skiers if the average wait time in lift lines for their skill category exceeds 10 minutes. To qualify for the refund, skiers must pay $1 to register in the beginner, intermediate, or advanced category. Certain restrictions such as weather conditions and mechanical problems apply.

Squaw also offers a free lift ticket, lesson, and equipment rental to anyone age 13 and over who has never skied before. The "Fun in the Sun" program to encourage new skiers is offered 8 a.m. to 2 p.m. Mondays through Fridays, except holidays. A deposit of $32 is required, but it is refunded when the rental equipment is returned.

Frequent skiers can sign up for Squaw's "Frequent Skier Program" by paying $15 for a special card. Each day that the skier purchases a lift ticket, a circle is added to the card. When 5 Olympic circles are collected, the sixth day of skiing is free.

In addition to the regular beginner specials, Squaw offers an Alpine Package for all ability levels, which includes a 4-hr lesson and equipment rentals. Multiday rates are: adults $84, children $77 for 2 out of 3 days; adults $120, children $108 for 3 out of 5 days; and adults $197, children $177 for 5 out of 7 days.

Squaw Valley ski school is one of the few that teaches freestyle skiing and has a freestyle team.

## FACILITIES AT A GLANCE

| | |
|---|---|
| *Season:* | Mid-November–May. |
| *Hours:* | Weekdays 9 a.m.–4 p.m. |
| | Weekends/Holidays 8 a.m.–4 p.m. |
| *Night Skiing:* | 4 p.m.–9 p.m. Fri and Sat. |
| *Area:* | 8,300 acres with open bowls. |
| | Beginner: 25% |
| | Intermediate: 45% |
| | Advanced: 30% |
| *Base Elevation:* | 6,200 ft |
| *Summit Elevation:* | 9,050 ft |
| *Vertical Drop:* | 2,850 ft |
| *Longest Run:* | 3 miles. |
| *Snowmaking:* | None. |
| *Snowboarding:* | Permitted. |
| *Avg. Annual Snowfall:* | 450 in. |
| *Lift Capacity:* | 47,370 per hr. |

*(continued on next page)*

*(continued from previous page)*

*Lifts:* 32 lifts (150-passenger cable car, 6-passenger gondola, 3 detachable express quads, 16 double chairs, 7 triple chairs, and 4 surface lifts)

| Name | Length | Vertical Rise |
| --- | --- | --- |
| Bailey's Beach | 2,500 ft | 100 ft |
| Belmont | 1,000 ft | 120 ft |
| Big Red | 3,628 ft | 1,300 ft |
| Broken Arrow | 3,000 ft | 1,750 ft |
| Cable Car | 7,500 ft | 2,000 ft |
| Cornice II | 4,500 ft | 1,280 ft |
| East Broadway | 3,200 ft | 301 ft |
| Emigrant | 3,500 ft | 761 ft |
| Exhibition | 3,000 ft | 862 ft |
| Gold Coast | 3,600 ft | 550 ft |
| Gondola | 7,700 ft | 2,000 ft |
| Granite Chief | 4,500 ft | 990 ft |
| Headwall | 4,900 ft | 1,209 ft |
| High Camp | 2,123 ft | 435 ft |
| KT 22 | 4,200 ft | 1,753 ft |
| Links | 3,300 ft | 228 ft |
| Lost Lake Chair | 5,745 ft | 758 ft |
| Mainline | 4,000 ft | 533 ft |
| Newport | 4,200 ft | 467 ft |
| Olympic Lady | 3,800 ft | 1,096 ft |
| Pony Tow I | 150 ft | 150 ft |
| Pony Tow II | 200 ft | 150 ft |
| Pony Tow III | 150 ft | 50 ft |
| Pony Tow IV | 150 ft | 50 ft |
| Red Dog | 4,500 ft | 1,200 ft |
| Riviera | 3,200 ft | 387 ft |
| Searchlight | 900 ft | 240 ft |
| Shirley Lake Express | 3,400 ft | 700 ft |
| Siberia Express | 4,000 ft | 1,000 ft |
| Solitude | 5,000 ft | 660 ft |
| Squaw Creek | 3,800 ft | 1,200 ft |
| Squaw Peak Express | 7,622 ft | 2,000 ft |

| *Lift Passes:* | All Day | Afternoon Only |
|---|---|---|
|  | 9 a.m.–4 p.m. | 1 p.m.–4 p.m. |
| Adults | $35 | $24 |
| night only | $7 | (4 p.m.–9 p.m. Fri/Sat) |
| Children under 13 | $5 | $5 |
| night only | $5 |  |
| Seniors 65+ | $5 | $5 |

*Multiday Rates:*
   $66, 2 out of 3 consecutive days.
   $96, 3 out of 5 consecutive days.
   $150, 5 out of 7 consecutive days.
   $196, 7 out of 9 consecutive days.

*Season Passes:*   $975 adult. $275 child.
   $580 adult midweek only. Discounts for early purchase and for children's passes purchased with an adult pass.

*Group Rates:*   Available by prior arrangement for 20+.

*Scenic Cable Car or Gondola Ride:*   $9 adult. $5 child.

*Food & Drink:*   The Olympic Plaza at the mountain base houses the Olympic Plaza Bar, Hamburger Express, Taco Etc. Etc., Dave's Deli, and Bar 6. Additional restaurants and food concessions are located in the adjacent Olympic Plaza and Valley Mall, including the Sun Deck Cafe, Jimmy's Restaurant (with sit-down service), the Chocolate Mtn. Baking Co., Sierra Scoops Ice Cream, Le Chamois pizza parlor, and the Clocktower Restaurant.

Services at High Camp, located adjacent to the top of the gondola, include the buffet-style Poolside Cafe (named for a planned adjacent outdoor pool and ice rink). An oyster bar and Alexander's Bar and Grill, with sit-down service, are also at High Camp.

Also at the top of the gondola, the 32,000-sq-ft Gold Coast complex has radiant-heated sun decks, the Oasis with the Mermaid Bar, Waterfall Bar, buffet restaurant, and several fast-food concessions, including the Hofbrau and outdoor barbecue.

*Parking & Transportation:*   General parking is free at the base, with a special lane for carpools of 3 or more. Valet parking is $7. Preferred parking, adjacent to the season-passholders' locker room, $150 a year. RV overnight parking not permitted. Free shuttles from North Shore and West Shore hotels, Truckee, and Tahoe City. Round-trip shuttle to South Shore and Heavenly Valley, $4 round-trip.

*(continued on next page)*

*(continued from previous page)*

*Ski Rentals:* The Company Store in the Squaw Valley Mall is open 8:30 a.m.–4 p.m. weekends and holidays and weekdays 8 a.m.–4 p.m. Includes skis, boots, poles.
    All day:    Adult $18.    Child $12.
    Half day:    Adult $13.    Child $8.
    High performance package:    $30.
    Demo skis only:    $22.
    Snowboards:    $28.    High performance: $30.

*Ski School:* Phone (916) 583-0119.

*Method:* ATM.

*Ski School Director:* Leroy Hill.

*Class Lessons:* 11 a.m. and 2 p.m.
    $20 (2 hr) adult and child.
    $30 (4 hr) adult and child.

*Beginner Special:* Free Monday through Friday, except holidays. Includes self-paced lessons, rentals, and beginner lift ticket. $35 deposit against damages.

*Beginner Snowboard Lesson:* Weekends and holidays. $20 includes 2-hr lesson and beginner lift pass.

*Junior Ski School:* Children 6–12. 11 a.m.–4 p.m.
    $41 4-hr lesson, lift ticket, and lunch.
    $20 2-hr lesson and beginner lift ticket.
    $35 4-hr lesson and beginner lift ticket.
    $44 4-hr lesson plus 3-hr pre-ski warm up and tour of the lower mountain.

*Private Lessons:* $42 1 hr. Additional person $15.
    $80 2 hr. Additional person $25.
    $115 3 hr. Additional person $30.
    $225 all day. Additional person $50.

*Powder, Moguls, Freestyle Lessons:* On request.

*Races & Clinics:*

*Coin-operated Race Course:* Located at top of Shirley Express near East Broadway, $1 per run

*Performance Skiing Program:* Available for racers competing in the Masters Division of USSA.

*Women's Way Ski Seminars:* Small, individually-tailored classes taught by women instructors.
$325 3-day midweek program.
$325 3-day weekend seminar.
$525 5-day midweek seminar.

*Racing Clinic:* $425 December to April. Includes season-long coaching and gate training in slalom, giant slalom, and downhill.

*Advanced Clinics:* Intermediate and advanced skiers. Midweek program starts Sundays and focuses on skiing moguls, deep powder, and steep slopes. Includes 5 days of lifts, video feedback, a lunch, and a Thursday night banquet. Offered once a month, December to March, $535.

*Day Care:* Located in the Ten Little Indians School. Reservations required, (916) 583-4743.

*Snow School:* Ages 3–5 (toilet trained). Includes introduction to skiing.

*Diaper Set:* Ages 6 mos–3 yr. 8:30 a.m.–4:30 p.m.
$45 includes lunch, arts & crafts, and snow play.
$35 additional child, same family.
$33 half day, 8:30 a.m.–noon / 1 –4:30 p.m. Includes snack.
$120 three consecutive full days.
$195 book of five all-day coupons.

*Camper Facilities:* Winter camping available 17 miles south at Sugar Pine Point State Park, south of Tahoma on SH 89, (916) 525-7982. Sixteen tent/RV sites to 30 ft long. No hookups. $10 per night. Heated restrooms. Parking.

*Medical:* First aid center located at top of gondola. Medical center in the Portal Building, with doctor on staff. The closest hospital is Tahoe Forest, 8 miles north in Truckee. Medical services are also available in Tahoe City, (916) 583-5320, or through the Physician's Finder Assistance, (916) 587-6011 ext. 485.

*Other:* Complimentary ski checks located at Olympic Plaza, Gold Coast, and High Camp. Article checks at Olympic Plaza, Ticket Portal Building, Cable Car Building, High Camp, and Gold Coast. Exhibit of the VIII Olympic Games 1960 in Cable Car Building.

## SPECIAL EVENTS

- *Corporate Classic Race*—January.
- *Western States Invitational Freestyles and Aerials*—February.

- *Obstacle Race*—February.
- *Far West Freestyle*—February.
- *Jimmy Heuga Express*—March.
- *International Special Olympics Alpine Skiing Competition*—April.
- *Snowfest*—March. Fireworks, laser shows, hot air ballooning, torchlight parade, special races, dress-up-your-dog contest.
- *Skiathon for Multiple Sclerosis*—March.
- *Spring Fling Slalom and Giant Slalom Races*—April.

## WINTER ACTIVITIES

### Cross-Country

*Squaw Valley Nordic Center* is located in the Opera House, the building that houses the General Store and Cinema. The 12 trails on 25 miles of groomed terrain are $1/3$ beginner, $1/3$ intermediate, and $1/3$ advanced. With the base at 6,200 ft and summit at 7,800 ft, the vertical drop is 1,600 ft. Beginner trails have double tracks and 12- to 20-ft-wide skating lanes. Advanced trails are on Juniper Ridge and the trail to Papoose Peak. The trail used by the 1960 Olympic skiers is a wilderness route, which is marked but not groomed. A short Skiathlon course includes downhill slalom, flats, uphill, and jumps. The Skicross course is wide for sprint starts.

Trail fees are $7 adult and $4 for seniors and children. Half-day and group prices are available. Class lessons are $20 for $1^1/2$ hours. Facilities include equipment rental and sales shop and 2 food services, (916) 583-8951.

*Tahoe Nordic* ski area is located 2 miles north of Tahoe City, 10 miles from Squaw Valley via SH 89 and SH 28. Forty-six miles of groomed beginner, intermediate, and advanced trails range from 1.5 miles to 18.7 miles. Trail fees are $9 adult, $4 children. Afternoon and season passes also available. Lessons run $17 for classes and $26 per hr for private. Kiddie Ski School, open weekends and holidays, is $12 for ages 5–10 and $10 for ages 3–5. Equipment rental is $11 all day, with half price for children. Skating and telemark skis, $16. The trailhead lodge has parking, ski school, rentals, restrooms, a retail shop, and a deli with hot and cold snacks and drinks. Two warming huts are located on the course. TART, the public bus, stops hourly within a few blocks.

Also see the cross-country information under Homewood, Sugar Bowl, Tahoe Donner, Northstar, and Heavenly.

### Snowmobiling

Several snowmobile tours are offered in the North Lake Tahoe area. *TC SNO MO'S* offers rides around the Tahoe City Golf Course, (916) 581-3906. *Eagle*

*Ridge Outfitters* at Old Hobart Mill, 5 miles north of Truckee on SH 89, conducts tours lasting from 2 hours to 2 days, (916) 587-9322. *Snowmobiling Unlimited*, in Kings Beach, 10 miles north of Tahoe City and 16 miles from Squaw Valley, offers rides on 2 oval tracks in North Tahoe Regional Park, and conducts guided tours (including moonlight rides) and personalized trips for beginners to advanced, (916) 583-5858. *Mountain Lake Adventures*, Kings Beach, offers trips lasting from 90 minutes to 6 hours. Snowmobile suits, boots, gloves, and helmets are provided, (800) 433-5253. Snowmobile tours are also offered by *The Snow Connection*, 8 miles north in Truckee, (916) 587-8913, and *High Sierra Snowmobiling*, Kings Beach, (916) 546-9909.

### Tobogganing, Tubing, and Snow Play

Sleds and saucers are rented at *Granlibakken* Resort, $8^{1}/_{2}$ miles south of Squaw Valley. Toboggans and tubes are not permitted. See Granlibakken.

Saucers and tubes also rented at *North Tahoe Regional Park* in Tahoe Vista, off SH 28 at the end of National Avenue.

### Ice Skating

Squaw Valley is building an ice skating rink adjacent to a new Olympic-size pool at the High Camp complex midway on the mountain. Accessible by cable car, the 200 ft by 100 ft outdoor skating rink is set for completion for the 1990/91 season.

## OTHER ACTIVITIES

**Ballooning:** Mountain High Balloons, Truckee.
**Cinema:** Opera House Cinema, Squaw Valley; Cobblestone Cinema, Tahoe City.
**Fishing:** Mickey's Big Mack Charters and Kingfish Guide Service, Tahoe City.
**Fitness:** Squaw Valley Lodge, Squaw Valley.
**Racquetball:** Alpine Motor Inn, Alpine Meadows.
**Sea Plane Rides:** Cal-Vada Aircraft, Homewood.
**Sightseeing:** Historic buildings, Truckee.

## SHOPPING

Ski accessories are available mid-mountain at both the Gold Coast and High Camp, and at the base in the Portal Building and Olympic Plaza Gondola Building. *The Squaw Valley Sports Shop*, in the #2 Squaw Valley Mall, carries skis, clothing, and accessories, while the *Company Store* rents and sells standard equipment and demos. The *Mainstreet Boutique,* also in the Mall, features T-shirts, sweaters, and souvenirs. Leathers, furs, and sweaters are the specialty of the *Truckee River Llama Ranch* boutique in the Olympic House.

Sundries are available in the Olympic House and at the *General Store,* located in the Opera House. Open from 8 a.m. to 7 p.m. (8 p.m. weekends), the General Store also carries groceries, including deli meats and cheeses, fresh produce, and liquor. 100 yards away, *Ski Rentals America,* at 1590 Squaw Valley Road, takes advance reservations for equipment rentals, (916) 581-4707 and (800) 828-4484 in CA, and offers free 140-cm ski rentals to children (under 75 lb) accompanied by at least 1 adult renting for 3 or more days. Open from 8 a.m. to 5 p.m. daily. A mini-mart and ski-repair shop are located adjacent to the Red Dog Cafe.

Tahoe City, 6 miles south on SH 89, has the largest number of shops on the West Shore. Skiers who prefer to rent their equipment before they head for the slopes can find downhill and cross-country equipment, snowboards, clothing, and accessories at a number of shops including *Dave's Ski Shop,* 620 N. Lake Blvd., *Alpenglow,* 415 N. Lake Blvd., and *Porter's Outlet Ski and Sport,* 120 N. Lake Blvd., open Friday and Saturday nights until 9 p.m.

Children's apparel at *Ruffels and Ruffnecks,* in the Cobblestone Center, ranges from newborn to size 14. Also in the Cobblestone Center are the *Scandia Down Shop* and *Gundy,* selling fine crystal and ornaments from Scandinavia.

Other specialty shops offering hours of perusing pleasure include the *Alpine Archives* in the Lighthouse Mall, which harbors 6,000 volumes, including used and rare books, and *Geared for Games* located in the Boatworks Mall, which stocks games for all ages, including puzzles, chess sets, and snow toys, and is open from 10 a.m. to 10 p.m.

Southwest art is featured at the *Sierra Galleries* and *Keeley's Tahoe Rug Co.,* upper level in the Boatworks Mall.

## APRÈS-SKI

Skiers in search of an après-ski ambience don't have to go far. *Bar I* in the Olympic House bustles with energy fortified by music (live or deejay), and convivial conversation. The *Olympic Plaza Bar* in the Gondola Building is spacious and less frenzied, a place to relax and watch ski videos on big-screen TV, recap the day's exciting moments with friends, or simply gaze out the 2-story windows at the mountain view.

Downstairs in the Olympic House, *The Beer Garden,* with pool table and peanut-littered floor, is a popular casual spot. Anyone over 20 is banned from the *Let's Dance* disco and video game room, so teens can have it all to themselves.

*Squaw Valley USA boasts one of the largest lift capacities in the industry, with 32 lifts, including a 150-passenger cable car.* (Courtesy of Squaw Valley USA.)

The busy bar at the *Squaw Valley Inn*, across from the Cable Car Building, draws a chic, young crowd to tables set around a central fireplace. The bar, with occasional live music, stays open until 10 p.m. weeknights and 1 a.m. on Fridays and Saturdays.

The *Last Run* in the Grand Lodge at the Olympic Valley Inn serves potato-skin appetizers and the like before dinner. The adjacent lounge is an inviting spot, with cushy furniture near a large stone fireplace and tall windows facing the snow scene outside. Later in the evening, the lounge is enlivened with a band or a comedian. Although not billed as a singles mixer, Local's Night at the Olympic Valley Inn attracts a crowd in their twenties and thirties who line up to join the action and dance to hot rock. There is a cover charge.

Skiers who define après-ski as margaritas and quesadillas will savor the happy-hour menu served between 4 and 5 p.m., at the *Clocktower Cafe* in the #1 Squaw Valley Mall.

A number of restaurants in Tahoe City have live entertainment. Tuesday nights, it's live music and dancing at *Rosie's*, beginning at 9:30 p.m. The *Pierce Street Annex*, behind Safeway, has dancing nightly from 9:30 p.m. to 1:30 a.m. with top-40 and rock-and-roll sounds.

The smell of beer permeates the bar at *Emma Murphy's*, but the crowd that gathers to dance Thursdays through Sundays doesn't seem to notice. The *Hacienda de la Sierra*, near the Boatworks Mall, is another hot spot, while *Pete and Peters* down the street is quieter, a place for locals to hang out and play pool.

Live music is featured at the *Sunnyside Restaurant and Lodge*, lakeside, 2 miles south of Tahoe City, Wednesday through Saturday.

Skiers headed to the South Shore relax aboard the *Tahoe Queen*. A bus transfers skiers from Squaw Valley around 4 p.m. for the 2-hour cruise back to South Shore. Live music, dancing, appetizers, and a full-service bar await them on board. Reservations required, (916) 541-3364. In California, (800) 238-2463.

Casino gaming and entertainment is 18 miles away in Crystal Bay on the North Shore, where the *Cal-Neva, Tahoe Biltmore* and the *Crystal Bay Club* come together. See Northstar and Incline.

For après-ski suggestions in Truckee, see Tahoe Donner.

## RESTAURANTS

In addition to restaurants in Squaw Valley, restaurant choices in Tahoe City, just 8 miles south of Squaw, range from casual dinners to elegant gourmet feasts.

**Benton's**   $$$   *(916) 583-1576*
Located in the Squaw Valley Inn, Squaw Valley. Named for Garth Benton, the artist who painted the Fox & Hounds mural that dominates the dining room, Benton's offers a variety of fare, from blue-cheese filet and pasta Alfredo with

duck, to grilled swordfish and roasted Cornish game hen. Open for breakfast, lunch, and dinner.

**Wolfdales   $$$**                                                  *(916) 525-7833*
Located adjacent to the Boatworks Mall at 640 N. Lake Blvd., Tahoe City. Wolfdales is open for dinner only. The limited but unique gourmet menu includes some Japanese specialties, as well as lobster and duck.

**Chart House   $$**                                                 *(916) 583-0233*
700 N. Lake Blvd., Tahoe City, in the Roundhouse Mall overlooking the lake. Steaks, seafood, prime rib, salad bar, and famous mud-pie dessert are served in a pleasant room decorated with light woods and glass.

**Chez Fritch   $$**                                                 *(916) 581-2215*
This small restaurant, located in the Opera House adjacent to the Squaw Nordic Center, Squaw Valley, is a pleasant spot. Diners can look at the mountain as they dine on French-influenced dishes, including chicken, beef, and fish.

**Christy Hill   $$**                                                *(916) 583-8551*
Located on the lake at 115 Grove St. in the Lakehouse Mall, Tahoe City. Standard menu options are presented with a California flair. Fresh Hawaiian ahi is broiled with orange, jalapeño, and cilantro butter. Domestic lamb loin is featured with an apricot-ginger chutney, and fresh king salmon is baked with fresh basil pesto.

**Creekside   $$**                                                   *(916) 583-2614*
At the Olympic Valley Inn, Squaw Valley. The Creekside provides fine dining in a soft, candlelit setting overlooking the swimming pool and waterfall. Seafood, fowl, and beef dishes include variations such as veal medallions sautéed with ginger and champagne, topped with pecans and hearts of palm. Vegetarian plate also available.

**Jake's on the Lake   $$**                                          *(916) 583-0188*
Adjacent to the Boatworks Mall at 780 N. Lake Tahoe, Tahoe City. Jake's on the Lake serves steak and seafood in a wood, brass, and glass nautical atmosphere. Children's menu available.

**Jimmy's   $$**                                                     *(916) 583-2614*
Located on the upper level of the Olympic House, Squaw Valley, Jimmy's has a modern, upscale feeling, with comfortable seating and a large fireplace. Entrées include tournedos, broiled swordfish, calamari, steak, lamb, chicken, and pasta. Open for dinner from 4 p.m. to 10 p.m.

**Pfeifer House   $$**                                               *(916) 583-1377*
Located at 760 River Road, 1/4 mile north of Tahoe City, the Pfeifer House was first established in 1939 and is one of Lake Tahoe's old favorites. German cuisine, served in a charming Alpine setting, includes smoked pork tenderloin, Vienna schnitzel, steak tartar, escargot bourguignon, and sauerbraten, as well as fowl and seafood.

**River Ranch   $$**   *(916) 583-4264*
SH 89 at Alpine Meadows Road, 1 mile south of Squaw Valley Road. Scottish plaid fabrics, warm woods, and views of the Truckee River create a picturesque ambience at this popular restaurant. Specialties include wild game, steak, veal, and fresh fish, such as ono, flown in daily.

**Rosie's Cafe   $$**   *(916) 583-8504*
At 571 N. Lake Blvd., adjacent to the Big Trees Mall, Tahoe City. Rosie's is open for breakfast, lunch, or dinner. An assortment of old skis, sleds, bicycles, Indian rugs, a moosehead hung above the bar, and grey-and-white checkered tables add to the informal atmosphere. A large fireplace dominates the usually busy room. Dinner selections include steak, fresh fish, vegetarian stir-fry, and chicken.

**Sunnyside Restaurant & Lodge   $$**   *(916) 583-7200*
Located at 1850 West Lake Blvd., 2 miles south of Tahoe City, the multilevel Chris Craft dining room at Sunnyside Restaurant and Lodge is beautifully situated, with lake views from almost every table. Outfitted with rich mahogany and brass, the attractive room overlooks the marina and snow-capped peaks across the lake. Known for its seafood and steaks, entrées include roast prime rib, fettucini pescatore, and lobster. Open for breakfast, lunch, and dinner daily. Sunday brunch.

**Clocktower Cafe   $**   *(916) 583-1458*
Located in #1 Olympic Mall, Squaw Valley, the Clocktower is open for lunch and après-ski cocktails and appetizers until 5 p.m. A limited dinner menu includes Mexican specialties such as fajitas, burritos, tacos, and taco salads.

**Last Run Cafe   $**   *(916) 583-1501*
Adjacent to the bar in the Olympic Valley Inn, Squaw Valley. The Last Run is open for breakfast, lunch, and dinner from 5:30 to 9:30 p.m. Limited menu includes hot and cold sandwiches, along with a few daily specials.

**Le Chamois   $**   *(916) 583-4505*
Located in the #2 Squaw Valley Mall, Squaw Valley. In spite of the French name, the mainstay of this bright cafe is pizza on the spot or to go, and oven-baked sandwiches.

**Red Dog Cafe   $**   *(916) 581-4306*
This small, casual diner located at 1602 C Squaw Valley Road, across from the Squaw Valley parking lot, mainly has counter-top seating, with a few tables and overhead TV. Open for breakfast, lunch, and dinner. Dinner menu offers steak, cajun prime rib, chicken chardonnay, and lasagna.

**Za's   $**   *(916) 583-1812*
At 395 N. Lake Blvd., Tahoe City, in the rear of Pete & Peters pub, Za's is a small trattoria offering usual and unusual pizza, pasta, salad and calzone. Selections include spaghetti putanesca, a spicy mix of marinara, olives, capers, anchovies and red pepper flakes; homemade Italian sausage, with mushrooms, onions, and tomatoes served with corkscrew pasta; and gorgonzola pizza. Bar adjacent.

## ACCOMMODATIONS

Squaw Valley Reservations, (916) 583-6985 or (800) 545-4350, can reserve space at the main properties in Squaw Valley and nearby.

"The Great Escape" is an all-inclusive midweek package that starts on Sundays and includes round-trip transfers from Reno Cannon International Airport, 5-nights' lodging, breakfast daily at choice of 5 restaurants, dinner 3 nights at Squaw Valley restaurants, a welcome reception, mountain orientation, ski hot-wax, 5-days' lift tickets, 12 hours of lessons, and a farewell party with awards and videos. Prices range from $525 to $713 per person, double occupancy.

The "Mountain Experience" Package, from $330 to $455, includes airport transfers, 5 nights' lodging, 5 days' lift passes, and 3 days of ski lessons. Packages are not available during the Christmas holidays.

Accommodations and packages are also available through North Lake Tahoe Reservations, (800) 824-6348, and the airlines serving Reno. Some condominiums are available through a variety of realty offices, including Squaw Valley Realty, (916) 583-3451. In some cases, one or more realty offices represent different owners in the same complex.

Additional accommodations listed below are located farther south along SH 89 and in Tahoe City, 6 miles south at the junction with SH 28 (N. Lake Blvd.). For accommodations in Truckee, 8 miles north on SH 89, see Tahoe Donner ski area.

**Blue House Inn**   $$$    *(916) 582-8415, (800) 548-6526*
7660 SH 89, 5 miles from Squaw Valley. The 5 rooms at this bed-and-breakfast exude individual charm. The Bordeaux Room includes a canopied country-French queen-size bed, wood stove, and private bath. Two other rooms downstairs share a bath and dressing area. Upstairs, the Charleston Room and the Sleigh Room share a bath and a sitting area, and together can be reserved separately or as a suite. A living and dining area and spa are also at guests' disposal.

**Christy Hill Condominiums**   $$$    *(916) 583-3451*
Located on Squaw Valley Road, diagonally across from the Squaw Valley parking lot, these well-appointed 2-bedroom, 2-bath condominiums are individually decorated. All have TV, phone, and fireplaces. Kitchens have full ovens, refrigerators, and washer-dryers. No maid service.

**Olympic Village Inn**   $$$    *(916) 583-1501, (800) 845-5243*
1900 Squaw Valley Road, Olympic Village, Squaw Valley. Ninety 2-room suites in a 3-story complex each have a bedroom, bath with shower, tub and amenities. In each suite, a small parlor is furnished with a sofabed, dining table, fireplace, TV, stereo, phone and mini-kitchen, featuring range-top stoves, small refrigerators and dishwashers. The Swiss-provincial motif is carried out with hand-painted

floral tiles and sinks, European armoires in bleached pine, and wallpaper with old-world stenciling.

A few larger, corner suites are available through Squaw Valley Realty. Services include daily light housekeeping, babysitting by arrangement, 5 outdoor spas, large swimming pool (open from 10 a.m. to 10 p.m.), 2 restaurants, bar and piano lounge, sundry shop, alcove library, and ski service center. Free shuttle to the lifts operates from 8 a.m. to 5 p.m. and to Alpine Meadows once a day.

**Resort at Squaw Creek    $$$**                    *(916) 583-6300, (800) 327-3353*
1000 Squaw Creek Road, Squaw Valley, at the base of the mountain with ski-in, ski-out access. The 405-room, 9-story resort is a $100-million deluxe property scheduled to open mid-December 1990. All rooms include work/study areas, TV, and 2 telephones. Suites and penthouse suites have small kitchens. The resort features 33,000-sq-ft of conference space, a pool with a water slide, an ice skating rink, and a promenade with 7 retail shops. Restaurant facilities include *Glissandi* for fine dining, *Cascades*, with a deluxe buffet, and the *Hardscramble Creek Bar and Grill*, which converts to a disco at night. Two lounges provide live entertainment. Other amenities include valet parking, daily maid service, and concierge.

**Rocky Ridge    $$$**                                            *(916) 583-3723*
1877 N. Lake Tahoe, SH 28, $1/2$ mile north of Tahoe City. Set on a hill overlooking the lake, Rocky Ridge townhouses range from 2 to 4 bedrooms plus family room, each with 2 to 3 bathrooms. Individually decorated units feature open-beam ceilings, stone fireplaces, and wet bars. Kitchens have refrigerators, self-cleaning ovens, dishwashers, and washers/dryers. Sauna and hot tub on premises. Two night minimum. Maid service available at extra charge.

**Squaw Tahoe Resort    $$$**                    *(916) 583-7226, (800) 874-1030*
Located at the base of the mountain near the Red Dog and Pony lifts, the Squaw Tahoe Resort has well-furnished studios, and 1- and 2-bedroom condominium units with refrigerators, ovens, microwaves, coffee makers, dishwashers, washer/dryers, fireplaces, dining tables, balconies, TV, and phones. Decorated in blues and grays, studio units each have a sofa bed and a Murphy bed to accommodate 4.

On-site facilities include saunas on every floor, two spas, fitness room with Nautilus equipment, recreation room with TV, and covered parking. On-site manager and maid service. Snow conditions sometimes permit ski-in convenience. Three-night minimum during high season and holidays.

**Squaw Valley Inn    $$$**                        *(916) 583-1576, (800) 323-7666*
Located across from the Gondola Building in Squaw Valley, the Inn has 60 spacious rooms decorated in soft pinks and blues, each with 2 double beds, TV, phone, and bathroom with tub/shower combination. A few rooms have kitchenettes. A lounge area is warmly decorated with light woods and forest greens. Facilities include a bar, restaurant, whirlpools, swimming pool, conference facilities, and ski rental and accessories shop.

**Squaw Valley Lodge   $$$**  *(916) 583-5500, (800) 922-9970 CA*
*(800) 992-9920 Nationwide*
Located at the base of the mountain, with ski-in, ski-out convenience, these luxury units sleep from 4 to 6 in studio, studio plus loft, and 1-bedroom condominiums. All units are designer decorated in a contemporary motif. Studios (some with loft) and 1-bedroom units all have TV, phones, microwaves, range top stoves, refrigerators, goose-down comforters, and ample drawer and closet space. One-bedroom corner suites are larger. Continental breakfast served in lobby. Other amenities include fitness center with aerobics, Nautilus equipment, bicycles, steam room, men's and women's locker and shower room, 3 indoor whirlpools, and 1 outdoor. Maid service, bellman and concierge, and complimentary ski check. Covered parking.

**Tavern Inn Condominiums   $$$**   *(916) 583-1504*
203 Squaw Valley Road, Olympic Valley. Twenty-nine Tudor style 1-, 2-, and 3-bedroom luxury townhouses, some with dens, offer all the appointments of a modern home including private patio or balcony, laundry room, stone fireplace, wet bar, ceramic tile baths, walk-in closets, TV, phones, and garage. Kitchens are fully equipped with dishwashers, refrigerators, microwave ovens, and cooktop ranges. Units are spacious—2-bedroom units with den have 2,000 sq ft and sleep from 4 to 10. Spa and sauna on premises. Bi-weekly maid and linen service.

**Chinquapin   $$**   *(916) 583-6991*
3600 N. Lake Blvd., 3 miles east of Tahoe City, Chinquapin's cedar and redwood townhouses consist of a variety of 1- to 4-bedroom condominiums on 95 acres, with 1 mile of beachfront. Nicely decorated units are fully furnished with washers, dryers, TV, and woodburning fireplaces. Lake views. Saunas. Additional charge for maid service during stay.

**Cottage Inn   $$**   *(916) 581-4073*
1690 N. Lake Blvd., 2 miles south of Tahoe City. This bed-and-breakfast, originally built in 1935, has 7 studios and 8 one-bedroom suites in separate cottages, with pine furniture. All have private baths and some have fireplaces. Homey touches include breakfast in bed, hot cider by the fire, and a full cookie jar in the kitchen. Sauna on premises. Shuttle to Squaw Valley and Alpine Meadows. Discount lift tickets.

**Mayfield House   $$**   *(916) 583-1001*
236 Grove St., Tahoe City. This pleasant bed-and-breakfast has 6 rooms that share 2 bathrooms. Each is individually stocked with goose-down pillows and comforters, velour robes, fresh flowers, and a supply of paperback books. Breakfast is served downstairs or in the room. After skiing, guests enjoy conversation and games around the fireplace.

**Pepper Tree Inn   $$**   *(916) 583-3711, (800) 824-5342 CA*
*(800) 624-8590 Nationwide*
645 N. Lake Blvd., Tahoe City. The Pepper Tree has 51 comfortable rooms, some with lake views. Room features include king-size beds, hair dryers and other amenities in the bathrooms, showers (but no tub), in-room coffee makers, TV,

phones, alarm clocks and parking. Heated pool, indoor spa, coin-operated laundry, and 2,000-sq-ft conference room on premises. Package rates with lift tickets are available. Shuttle bus to Squaw Valley stops twice a day.

**River Ranch** $$ *(916) 583-4264, (800) 535-9900*
SH 89 at Alpine Meadows Road, 3 miles from Squaw Valley. This 2-story bed-and-breakfast has 22 small but charming rooms with antiques and country-style wallpaper, with coordinated bedspreads and drapes. Rooms have 1 or 2 double beds, private bathrooms, balconies, TV, and phones. Continental breakfast is included in the rate. Other facilities include a spacious restaurant and bar overlooking the Truckee River. Ski packages available. Shuttle bus stop for Squaw Valley and Alpine Meadows.

**Sunnyside Resort Lodge** $$ *(916) 583-7200, (800) 822-2754*
At 1850 West Lake Blvd., Sunnyside Resort Lodge is 2 miles south of Tahoe City. This lakefront lodge has 23 rooms and designer-decorated suites with country motifs, high ceilings, and light woods. All rooms have TV, phones, and private baths. Some rooms have a rock fireplace. Restaurant with seafood bar and lounge on premises.

**Tahoe Marina Lodge** $$ *(916) 583-2365*
At 270 N. Lake Blvd., Tahoe City. The Tahoe Marina is within walking distance of restaurants, the movie theater, and shops. Spacious, well-appointed 1- and 2-bedroom condominiums are decorated in bright colors. Bedrooms, with queen-size or twin beds, have large closets. Living areas have TV, fireplaces, clock radios, and full kitchens with refrigerators, dishwashers, ovens, washers/dryers, and phones.

**Travelodge** $$ *(916) 583-3766, (800) 255-3050*
Located at 455 N. Lake Blvd., in Tahoe City between Emma Murphy's restaurant and the Cobblestone Mall. Forty-seven pleasant rooms have queen- or king-size beds, TV, phones, coffee in room. Hot tub on premises. Conference room for 12 to 15.

# Alpine Meadows

*Box 5279
Tahoe City, CA 95730
Information: (916) 583-4232,
(800) 824-6348
Snowphone: (916) 583-6914*

| Driving distances | |
|---|---|
| Los Angeles | 497 mi |
| Reno | 46 mi |
| Sacramento | 111 mi |
| San Diego | 616 mi |
| San Francisco | 198 mi |
| San Jose | 228 mi |
| S. Lake Tahoe | 39 mi |
| Tahoe City | 9 mi |
| Truckee | 11 mi |

*For road conditions, call
(916) 581-1400, California
(702) 793-1313, Nevada*

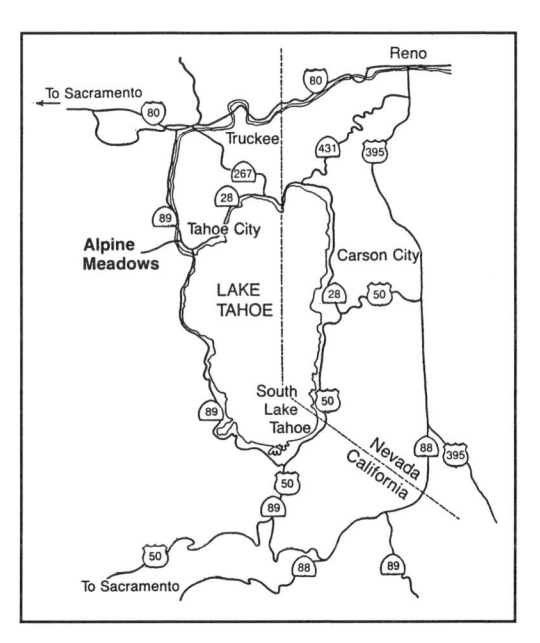

Long runs through open bowls, wide meadows, and forested paths add up to a recreational skier's heaven at Alpine Meadows. This ski area may not be the highest, steepest, or biggest, but it comes close in all categories, making it one of the prime all-around mountains in the state. Intermediate and advanced-intermediate skiers, in particular, have a wide range of choices, from classic cruising slopes to exciting open snowfields.

Less than a mile from Squaw Valley (6 miles by car), Alpine Meadows is not content to live in the shadow of its Olympic neighbor, but, instead, lays claim to the most reliable snow in north Lake Tahoe. Sitting on the Sierra Ridge, new snow on the south and west slopes is softened by the sun in winter. When snow is meager elsewhere, Alpine's north-facing slopes hold powder late into May, giving new definition to the term "spring skiing."

Lacking a village of its own, Alpine operates shuttle buses to and from Squaw Valley and nearby Tahoe City and Tahoe's West Shore.

*Children and parents alike enjoy* Yellow Trail *and the other 58 runs at Alpine Meadows.* (Courtesy of Alpine Meadows.)

## LOCATION

Alpine Meadows is located off SH 89 in Placer County, 6 miles from the west shore of Lake Tahoe and 12 miles south of Truckee.

From San Francisco, Sacramento, or Reno, take I-80 to the SH 89 exit. Turn south on SH 89, and go 12 miles to Alpine Meadow Road, then right 3 miles to the mountain base.

From Stateline at South Lake Tahoe, drive west on US 50 and turn north on SH 89. Follow SH 89 along the winding west shore 32 miles to Tahoe City, where SH 89 turns northwest, and continue 6 miles to Alpine Meadows Road.

Reno Cannon International Airport is the closest major airport to Alpine Meadows, which is also served by the Sacramento airport. Scheduled service to Lake Tahoe Airport in South Lake Tahoe is less frequent and, in heavy weather, flights often land in Reno instead. Four-wheel-drive and cars equipped for skiers are available for rental at all 3 airports.

Daily shuttles with Sierra Nevada Stage Lines depart the Reno airport at 7:10 a.m. and return at 4:30 p.m. Rates are $15 round-trip for adults and $10 for children age 14 and under, (702) 329-2877.

Cab fare from the Reno airport runs about $70 one way. Limousine service is available from Truckee-Tahoe Limousine and Tours, (916) 587-2160, and 5 Star Enterprises, Truckee, (916) 587-7651.

Amtrak's "California Zephyr" stops in Truckee, as well as in Sacramento and Reno/Sparks. Auto rentals are available in Truckee at the AAA Auto Rental, adjacent to the Amtrak station. Although there are no car rental agencies at the Sacramento and Reno train stations, rental car delivery to the station can be prearranged with some auto agencies. Greyhound also operates bus service into Truckee and Reno.

Alpine's free shuttle bus picks up and delivers to more than 30 stops along the West and North Shores of Lake Tahoe. A free shuttle also operates to the South Shore Monday through Friday, with pickup at 13 stops along the South Shore at 7:45 a.m. and returns at 4:30 p.m. Call Alpine Meadows, (916) 583-4232.

TART, Lake Tahoe's public bus system, also operates bus service daily around the North and West Shores.

Alternatively, skiers staying on the South Shore can take the Tahoe Queen sternwheeler across the lake Tuesday through Friday at 8 a.m., and arrive at Tahoe City about 10:30 a.m. A bus then takes skiers to Alpine Meadows. The return trip departs the ski area about 4 p.m.

## TERRAIN

Alpine Meadows extends beneath 2 adjacent mountain peaks, with 3 distinctive ski areas. *Sherwood Bowl*, on the back side of Sherwood Peak, is an advanced area, while the back side of Scott Peak is all intermediate. Terrain for all levels extends down the front side, with most of the black-diamond descents at the higher elevations and the beginner slopes at the bottom.

*Our Father*, a hair-raising chute for experts only, is steep, narrow, and bumpy but generally holds good snow. Competing with it for "toughest" ranking is *Keyhole*, a convex run that starts steep and gets steeper. *Scott's Chute*, a demanding bump run, faces west where the snow can be hard or soft and full of surprises.

Powder hounds longing to make fresh tracks in virgin snow can access the *Sun Bowl* by a high traverse. The tree-runs off *Scott's Peak* are generally good powder paths.

Alpine's abundant blue slopes include favorites like *Sherwood Run* and *Lakeview*, both wide-open runs with room for everyone. Skiers waltz easily through turns on *Dance Floor's* smooth contours, while *Outer Limits* is slicker and faster, for those who like to fly.

Kids love *Hot Wheels*, a creek-bed gully that feels like a bobsled run. Beginners already comfortable on the 4 novice runs can step up to an easier blue run like *Kangaroo*. The longest trail down starts at the top of Alpine Bowl and winds 2½ miles down the middle of the mountain.

## FACILITIES

Alpine Meadows participates in 2 interchangeable lift tickets: The Ski Tahoe North lift ticket includes Alpine Meadows, Squaw Valley, Homewood, Northstar-at-Tahoe, Diamond Peak, and Mount Rose. The adult and child rates are $96/$36 for 3 days, $128/$48 for 4 days, $160/$60 for 5 days, and $189/$72 for 6 days.

The Ski Lake Tahoe interchangeable lift ticket includes Squaw Valley, Northstar-at-Tahoe, Heavenly Valley, and Kirkwood. The rate is $32 daily for adults or children and must be purchased for at least 5 days.

## FACILITIES AT A GLANCE

| | |
|---|---|
| *Season:* | Mid-November–End of May/June. |
| *Hours:* | 9 a.m.–4 p.m. |
| | Spring 8:30 a.m.–4 p.m. |
| *Night Skiing:* | None. |
| *Area:* | 2,000 acres with 59 runs. |
| | Beginner: 25% |
| | Intermediate: 40% |
| | Advanced: 35% |
| *Base Elevation:* | 6,835 ft |
| *Summit Elevation:* | 8,637 ft |
| *Vertical Drop:* | 1,802 ft |
| *Longest Run:* | 2.5 miles. |
| *Snowmaking:* | 1,000 vertical ft on 125 acres with 7 lifts. |
| *Snowboarding:* | Not permitted. |
| *Avg Annual Snowfall:* | 340 in. |
| *Lift Capacity:* | 16,000 per hr. |

*Lifts:* 13 lifts (1 quad, 2 triples, 8 doubles, 2 surface lifts)

| Name | Length | Vertical Rise |
|---|---|---|
| Alpine Bowl | 2,810 ft | 960 ft |
| Kangaroo | 1,780 ft | 470 ft |
| Lakeview | 2,550 ft | 840 ft |
| Meadow | 1,200 ft | 175 ft |
| Roundhouse | 3,850 ft | 980 ft |
| Scott | 2,630 ft | 1,060 ft |
| Sherwood | 3,810 ft | 955 ft |
| Subway | 1,130 ft | 120 ft |
| Summit (express) | 5,500 ft | 1,555 ft |
| Tiegel (poma) | 1,000 ft | 125 ft |
| Weasel | 6,080 ft | 610 ft |
| Yellow | 2,060 ft | 585 ft |

| *Lift Passes:* | All Day | Afternoon Only |
|---|---|---|
|  | 9 a.m.–4 p.m. | 1 p.m.–4 p.m. |
| Adults | $34 | $24 |
| Children 6–12 | $12 | $8 |
| Children under 6 | $5 | $5 |
| Seniors 65–69 | $24 | $24 |
| Seniors 70 + | FREE | FREE |

*Multiday Rates:*
  Adult $96, 3 out of 4 consecutive days.
  Child $33, 3 out of 4 consecutive days.
  Adult $150, 5 out of 6 consecutive days.
  Child $50, 5 out of 6 consecutive days.

*Season Passes:* For midweek, non-holidays, and daily after April 1. $330 if purchased by July 31, $425 if purchased by September 30, and $480 if purchased after September 30. Family rates available.

*Group Rates:* Available by prior arrangement.

*Food & Drink:* The Base Lodge cafeteria serves Italian, Mexican, and deli selections, as well as burgers. Kealy's Pub, adjacent to the Compactor Bar, offers sit-down luncheon service, appetizers, and cocktails. A mid-mountain chalet has soups and deli foods, while the Boulangerie at the base offers cookies, croissants, and espresso.

*(continued on next page)*

*(continued from previous page)*

*Parking & Transportation:* Parking is free at the base. Weekends and holidays, free shuttles operate from the Bridge lot, on SH 89 in Tahoe City across from the Bridgetendor, and from the lot across from Sunnyside Lodge on SH 28. Free shuttles pick up daily from various West and North Shore hotels. For schedules, call (916) 581-8341. A shuttle also meets TART, Tahoe Area Regional Transit, (916) 581-6365, from CA, (800) 325-8278. For groups, unscheduled stops, or service to Truckee, phone at least 1 day ahead. Complimentary South Shore shuttle Monday through Friday.

*Ski Rentals:* The rental shop is open 8:30 a.m.–5 p.m. weekdays, and 8 a.m.–5 p.m. weekends and holidays. Includes skis, boots, poles.
  All day: Adult $18. Child $13 (6–12).*
  Half day: Adult $15. Child $11.*
  High performance package: $29/$25 half day.
    No limit to number of demo skis tested in a day.
  *Children under 6, $8 all day and $7 half day.*

*Ski School:* Phone (916) 581-8221.
  *Method:* ATM.
  *Ski School Director:* Greg Felsch.
  *Class Lessons:* 10 a.m. and 2 p.m.
    $19 (2 hr) adult and child (ages 6–12).
    $32 (4 hr) adult and child.
    $130 5 (4 hr) lessons.
    $150 10 (2 hr) lessons.
  *Beginner Special:* Includes 4-hr lesson and use of beginner's lift and equipment rentals.
    $48 adult. $35 child.
    $38 adult. $25 child, without equipment rental.
    $30 adult. $20 child, afternoon only, without equipment rental.
  *Family Pack:* Includes lift ticket for adults and 2-hr class lesson for children ages 6–12.
    $49 1 adult and 1 child.
    $80 2 adults and 1 child.
    $98 2 adults and 2 children.

*Children's Snow School:* (916) 581-8240.
 Ages 3–6 yrs. Must be toilet trained.
 8:30 a.m.–4:30 p.m.
 $48 includes lessons, boots and skis, lift privileges, lunch, snacks, and snow play.
 $40 additional child in family.
 $36 half-day session.

*Private Lessons:* Every hour on the hour.
 $42 per hr, 3 or more persons $15 each.
 $40 per hr for 2 or more hrs.
 $34 Early Bird Special, 9–10 a.m.

*Powder and Mogul Lessons:* On request.

*Handicapped:* Offered daily for the physically and mentally challenged, (916) 581-4161.

*Races & Clinics:* *Coin-operated Race Course:* At top of Kangaroo Lift.

 *Thursday Series:* Single pole, giant slalom races every Thursday. Open to all skiers, including lower intermediates. Prizes. Entry fee $7.

 *Monday Motorvation:* For serious competitors. Slalom, giant slalom, and Super G. Team and individual races for prizes at award parties. Entry fee $8.

 *Junior Development Program:* Ages 5–12. Weekends, December 10th to April 8th. $50 includes 4-hr coaching Sat. and Sun. $65 with lunch included.

 *Lake Tahoe Ski Team:* Weekends, Thanksgiving to April. Includes a season pass. $720 ages 6–12. $790 ages 13–18. Includes 5-hr training Sat./Sun. and holidays, season pass, and locker space. Full session includes 3 extra midweek sessions, $1,260 all ages.

 *Adult Masters Program:* Daily 10 a.m.–1 p.m. Skiers participate in as many or few days as desired. $450 full time; $400 midweek or weekends/holidays only. $130 for book of 5 lessons. Includes free skiing and gate training.

*Day Care:* None. See Snow School for ages 3–6. Day care for 6 months to 3 yrs located 6 miles away at Squaw Valley.

*Camper Facilities:* Winter camping available 17 miles south at Sugar Pine Point State Park, just south of Tahoma on SH 89, (916) 525-7982. Tent and RV sites to 30 ft long. No hookups. $10 per night. Heated restrooms. Parking.

*(continued on next page)*

> *(continued from previous page)*
> *Medical:* First aid center on mountain staffed by registered nurses. Doctors available by beeper or through the Physician's Finder Assistance, (916) 587-6011 ext. 485. Closest hospital is Tahoe Forest, 12 miles north in Truckee.
> *Other:* Lockers 50¢ a day. $1.25 overnight.

## SPECIAL EVENTS

- *Thursday Race Series*—Thursdays. For lower-intermediate ability and above.
- *Men's and Women's Pro-tour Slalom and Giant Slalom*—December.
- *USRSA*—January. GS open to the public.
- *Monday Motorvation*—Mondays. Team racing with prizes.
- *National Brotherhood of Skiers Western Region Winter Carnival*—Martin Luther King's birthday weekend.
- *Molson Fun Race*—Obstacle course open to public.
- *National Handicapped Sports "Learn-to-ski" Clinics*—February.
- *North Tahoe Snowfest*—March. Winter carnival.
- *USSA Telemark Series*—March.
- *Corporate Ski Challenge*—March.
- *Family Ski Challenge*—March.
- *USSA Masters Finale/Preb Motley Memorial*—April.

## WINTER ACTIVITIES

### Cross-Country

The closest cross country ski areas are *Squaw Valley Nordic Center*, 6 miles from Alpine, and *Tahoe Nordic*, 2 miles north of Tahoe City. For further information, see Squaw Valley.

### Snowmobiling

Several snowmobile tours and rentals are offered in the North Lake Tahoe Area. See Squaw Valley.

## Tobogganing, Tubing, and Snow Play

The closest snow-play areas are located at *Granlibakken* and *North Tahoe Regional Park*. See Squaw Valley and Granlibakken.

## Ice Skating

An outdoor ice skating rink is located 6 miles north at *Squaw Valley*. Situated on the mountain, the rink is accessible via aerial tram. For additional information, see Squaw Valley.

## Sleigh Rides

Sleigh rides are offered near Truckee at *Tahoe Donner* and *Northstar-at-Tahoe*.

## OTHER ACTIVITIES

**Cinema:** Opera House Cinema, Squaw Valley; Cobblestone Cinema, Tahoe City.
**Seaplane Rides:** Cal-Vada Aircraft, Homewood.
**Fishing:** Mickey's Guide Service and Kingfish Guide Service, Homewood; Mac-A-Tac, Tahoe City.
**Racquetball:** Alpine Racquet Club, Alpine Meadows.

## SHOPPING

*Breeze Ski Rentals*, with locations at the mountain and at SH 89 and Alpine Meadows Road, sells ski equipment and apparel. See Squaw Valley for shopping information in Tahoe City, 9 miles south.

## APRÈS-SKI

On weekends, the *Compactor Bar* is a raucous place, with live rock music and skiers packed beer mug to beer mug. The adjacent *Kealy's Pub* is quieter and classier. Both bars are open until 6 or 6:30 p.m.

Nearby, the *River Ranch* is a favorite spot. No live music, but good views and overhead TV. See Squaw Valley for additional après-ski suggestions.

## RESTAURANTS

**The Twain Station**   $$   *(916) 583-6896*
One of the closest restaurants to Alpine Meadows, the Twain Station is located at the corner of Alpine Meadows Road and SH 89. Open for breakfast and dinner, it serves pasta dishes and deli. Espresso bar.

Numerous restaurants in close proximity to Alpine Meadows include the *River Ranch* and restaurants in *Squaw Valley*. See Squaw Valley for a variety of dining options 9 miles south in Tahoe City.

## ACCOMMODATIONS

Although Alpine has no lodging right at its base, numerous accommodations are just minutes away. Ski-week packages offered by Alpine include 5 nights at Granlibakken Ski and Racquet Resort, the Cal-Neva Lodge in Crystal Bay, or lodges in Tahoe City. The packages also include a 5-day lift pass, 20 hours of instruction, shuttle transportation from lodging to the ski area, and continental breakfast.

Early season warm-up packages are available prior to the Christmas holidays. For reservations, call (916) 583-4232 or (800) 543-3221 in California. Additional packages are available through the Tahoe North Visitors and Convention Bureau, (916) 583-3494 or (800) 824-6348.

**Alpine Meadow Condominiums**   $$$   *(916) 583-8213*
Located within walking distance of the Alpine Meadow lifts. 2-, 3-, and 4-bedroom units with fully equipped kitchens, as well as fireplaces, TV, and garages. Some units have phones. Two-night minimum.

**Alpine Motor Inn**   $$   *(916) 583-4266*
On Alpine Meadow Road at the junction with SH 28, 3 miles from Alpine Meadows. The Alpine Motor Inn is the closest motel to the ski area. All rooms have private baths, TV, queen-size or 2 double beds, and sleep 2 to 4. Units with kitchens are not equipped with dishes, pans, or flatware. Continental breakfast included. Spa, steam room, and racquetball court in adjacent building. No phones.

**River Run Condominiums**   $$   *(916) 583-0137*
Alpine Meadows Road at SH 89. River Run is 3 miles from Alpine Meadows ski area and Squaw Valley. Condominiums with 1-, 2-, and 3-bedrooms are trimmed with natural woods and have wood-burning fireplaces, TV, and phones. Washer/dryers in most units. Additional charge for maid service. Weekly rates available.

# Granlibakken

*Granlibakken Resort*
*P.O. Box 6329*
*Tahoe City, CA 95730*
*Information: (916) 583-4242,*
*(800) 543-3221, CA*

### Driving distances

| | |
|---|---|
| Los Angeles | 504 mi |
| Reno | 48 mi |
| Sacramento | 117 mi |
| San Diego | 623 mi |
| San Francisco | 205 mi |
| San Jose | 235 mi |
| S. Lake Tahoe | 33 mi |
| Tahoe City | $1/2$ mi |
| Truckee | 15 mi |

*For road conditions, call*
*(916) 581-1400, California*
*(702) 793-1313, Nevada*

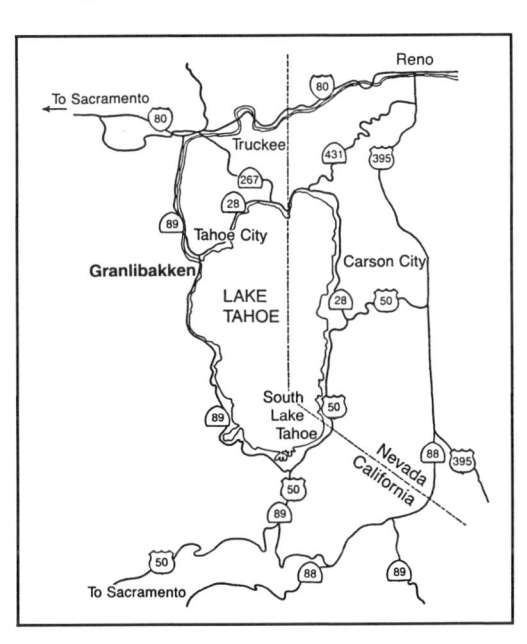

Granlibakken, which translated from Norwegian means "a hill sheltered by fir trees," is a condominium complex and resort. Among its amenities are a small ski slope with an adjacent snow-play hill and cross-country trails. The site was chosen for development by Kjell Rustad, a retired sea captain and renowned Norwegian ski jumper who came to the west shore of Lake Tahoe when it provided one of the few ski jumps around. The ski jump, which was the site of the 1932 Olympic tryouts, is no more, but Rustad's legacy lives on.

Today (for a small price) Granlibakken offers beginners a convenient place to learn to ski without waiting in line, getting lost, or maneuvering through traffic on the slope. And that spells "fun" in any language.

## LOCATION

Granlibakken is located in Placer County, on Granlibakken Road, off SH 89, $1/2$ mile south of Tahoe City, 9 miles south of Squaw Valley and Alpine Meadows, and $6^1/2$ miles north of Homewood.

From I-80, turn south at Truckee onto SH 89 and go 15 miles, then turn right on Granlibakken Road and continue on to the resort. From S. Lake Tahoe, head west on US 50 and north on SH 89 along the winding west shore of Lake Tahoe, past Homewood to Granlibakken Road.

For additional information on air, bus, and train transportation, see Squaw Valley.

## TERRAIN

Although the slope at Granlibakken is short, with a vertical drop of only 280 ft, the pitch on the top half of the hill is more intermediate than novice. Beginners, however, can drop off the poma or rope tow half way up to practice their turns. The ride down may be short, but there's no lift line at the bottom.

An adjacent hill on the left side is fenced off for snow play and saucer rides. Three miles of groomed Nordic trails lie on the opposite side of the hill.

## SPECIAL EVENTS

- *Torchlight Parade and Santa Claus*—Christmas Eve.

## FACILITIES AT A GLANCE

| | |
|---|---|
| *Season:* | Mid-December–March. |
| *Hours:* | 9 a.m.–4 p.m. |
| *Night Skiing:* | None. |
| *Area:* | 10 acres, 1 run |
| | Beginner: 50% |
| | Intermediate: 50% |
| *Base Elevation:* | 6,330 ft |
| *Summit Elevation:* | 6,610 ft |
| *Vertical Drop:* | 280 ft |
| *Longest Run:* | 300 ft |
| *Snowmaking:* | None. |
| *Snowboarding:* | Not permitted. |
| *Avg. Annual Snowfall:* | 96 in. |

| *Lift Capacity:* | 500 per hr. | |
| --- | --- | --- |
| *Lifts:* | 2 surface lifts (1 poma & 1 T-Bar) | |
| Name | Length | Vertical Rise |
| Poma Lift | 300 ft | 280 ft |
| T-Bar | 300 ft | 280 ft |

| *Lift Passes:* | All Day | Afternoon Only |
| --- | --- | --- |
| | 9 a.m.– 4 p.m. | 1 p.m.– 4 p.m. |
| Adults | $10 | $6 |
| Children under 12 | $6 | $4 |

Registered hotel guests receive 50% discount on lift tickets.

*Food & Drink:* Ski hut at base has snacks, hot and cold drinks, beer, and wine.

*Parking & Transportation:* Parking lot for hotel guests is at the lodge above the slope. General parking limited to curbside along access road to Granlibakken. No overnight RV parking. A shuttle to Squaw Valley and Alpine Meadows runs twice in the morning with returns in the afternoon.

*Ski Rentals:* Located at ski hut at base of slope. Includes skis, boots, and poles.
   All day: Adult $14. Child $12.
   20% discount for 5 days when specified on first day of rental.

*Ski School:* Weekends and holidays.
   *Class Lessons:* 10 a.m., 11:15 a.m., and 1:30 p.m.
      $15 (1 hr) adult and child.
   *Private Lessons:* $25 per hr.
   *Semi-private Lessons:* (2 persons) $40 per hr.

*Races & Clinics:* None.

*Day Care:* Day care available at Squaw Valley, 9 miles north.

*Camper Facilities:* Overnight camping available 8 miles south at Sugar Pine Point Park, on SH 89, (916) 525-7982. Tent and RV sites to 30 ft long. No hookups. $10 per night. Heated restrooms. Parking.

*Medical:* Medical clinic $1/2$ mile north in Tahoe City. Doctors available through the Physicians' Finder Assistance, (916) 587-6011 ext. 485. Tahoe Forest hospital is 23 miles north in Truckee.

## WINTER ACTIVITIES

### Cross-Country

The *Granlibakken* Nordic course has 3 miles of flat beginner terrain, and intermediate terrain that includes a hill for telemark turns. The resort also offers tours of the adjacent, ungroomed *Paige Meadows*. Prices for equipment rentals are $10 adults and $8 for children. Lessons are the same as Alpine skiing. Guided back-country and moonlight tours are also available.

Two Nordic trails are located at *Sugar Pine Point State Park*, 8.5 miles south and at Squaw Valley, 10 miles north. See Homewood and Squaw Valley.

### Snowmobiling

Snowmobile trails are located 5.5 miles south on SH 89 at *Blackwood Canyon Sno-Park*. Parking with Sno-Park permit. See Homewood.

For additional listings, also see Squaw Valley.

### Tobogganing, Tubing, and Snow Play

Granlibakken's snow-play hill is adjacent to the Alpine slope. Fee for all day is $3. Plastic saucers and sleds are available for rent for $2. Fifty percent discount for hotel guests. No inner tubes or toboggans permitted.

### Ice Skating

An outdoor ice skating rink is located north of the resort at *Squaw Valley*. Situated on the mountain, the rink is accessible via aerial tram. For additional information, see Squaw Valley.

### Sleigh Rides

Sleigh rides are offered near Truckee at *Tahoe Donner* and *Northstar-at-Tahoe*.

## OTHER ACTIVITIES

For additional activities in the Granlibakken area, see Squaw Valley, Homewood, Tahoe Donner, and Northstar-at-Tahoe.

## SHOPPING

Granlibakken is less than 1 mile south of Tahoe City. For shopping information, see Squaw Valley.

## APRÈS-SKI

There's no bar at Granlibakken, but the *Tahoe House*, at the corner of Granlibakken Road and SH 89, is only a couple of minutes away. The comfortable lounge has a fireplace and is open until 10 p.m. The *Sunnyside Resort* at 1850 W. Lake Blvd. is also nearby. For additional après-ski suggestions, including in Tahoe City, see Squaw Valley.

## RESTAURANTS

Granlibakken provides breakfast only for guests, and catering for groups. The closest restaurant is *The Tahoe House*, at the junction of SH 89 and Granlibakken Road. For additional dining highlights, see Squaw Valley, Alpine Meadows, Homewoood, and Tahoe Donner.

**The Tahoe House   $$**   *(916) 583-1377*
625 W. Lake Blvd., Tahoe City. This restaurant features Swiss cuisine prepared with German, French, and Italian accents, including Swiss bratwurst, rahmschnitzel, and tournedos Helder. Pleasant ambience.

## ACCOMMODATIONS

**Granlibakken   $$**   *(916) 583-4242, (800) 543-3221 CA*
Granlibakken has a variety of first-class accommodations including rooms, studios, and 1-, 2-, 3-, and 4-bedroom condominium units. Studio units are large rooms with twin beds, each with a sitting area with fireplace and dining table. Kitchens have stove-top ranges and ovens, dishwashers, and refrigerators. Balconies, phones, and TV. One-bedroom units have king-size beds and 1 bathroom each.

Larger condo units are townhouses and sleep up to 8. Spa on premises and men's and women's saunas on each floor. Conference rooms and a ballroom theater accommodate up to 540.

The resort offers 3-, 5-, and 7-night packages that include lodging, full breakfast, and a Ski Tahoe North interchangeable lift ticket. Midweek and weekend packages with lift tickets for Alpine Meadows are also available. Free shuttle to Squaw Valley and Alpine Meadows. Two-night minimums apply mid-December to Christmas and all weekends. Five-night minimums Christmas and New Year's weeks.

For additional accommodations in the area, see Squaw Valley, Alpine Meadows, and Homewood.

# Homewood

P.O. Box 165
Homewood, CA 95718
Information: (916) 525-7256
Snowphone: (916) 525-7256

### Driving distances

| Los Angeles | 508 mi |
| Reno | 54 mi |
| Sacramento | 122 mi |
| San Diego | 628 mi |
| San Francisco | 209 mi |
| San Jose | 239 mi |
| S. Lake Tahoe | 19 mi |
| Tahoe City | 6 mi |
| Truckee | 22 mi |

*For road conditions, call (916) 581-1400, California (702) 793-1313, Nevada*

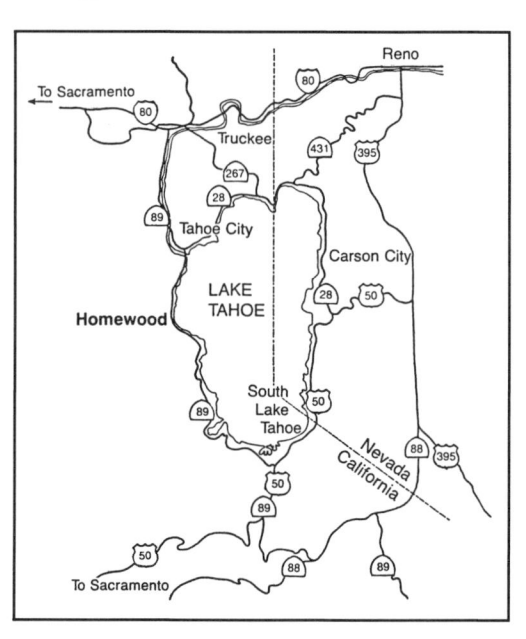

Rising from Lake Tahoe's West Shore, south of Squaw Valley and Alpine Meadows, Homewood is a quiet, forested mountain with breathtaking views of the lake. In an area where spectacular scenery is not uncommon—Squaw Valley, Alpine Meadows, Heavenly, and Diamond Peak all offer wonderful vistas—Homewood tops them all with almost 180° views from 90% of its slopes. Some trails appear to dip right into the water, an illusion that recurs each time the skier reaches another crest. Occasionally, when it's snowing on the summit and raining at the shore, the sun splashes a wide rainbow of blue and purple, yellow and red across the lake, distracting skiers with nature's artwork.

In warmer weather, some skiers bypass Homewood because the bottom slopes look bare. Skiers in the know, however, enjoy plenty of the "white stuff" on the uncrowded and tranquil slopes off the upper lifts.

During the press of holiday traffic and congestion elsewhere on the lake, Homewood's lift lines are rarely longer than 8 minutes, and midweek there's a sense of having the mountain to yourself, the perfect setting for a romantic rendezvous on the slopes.

## LOCATION

Homewood sits on SH 89 on the West Shore of Lake Tahoe, approximately halfway between the North and South Shores. Located in Placer County, Homewood is about 15 miles south of Squaw Valley and Alpine Meadows, 22 miles south of Truckee, and 19 miles north of South Lake Tahoe.

From San Francisco, Sacramento, or Reno, take I-80 to the SH 89 exit. Turn south on SH 89, and go 14 miles to the junction with SH 28. Stay on SH 89 by turning right, or south, and continue 6 miles to Homewood.

From Stateline and Heavenly Valley at South Lake Tahoe, drive west on US 50, then 17 miles north along the winding west shore of SH 89 to Homewood.

Reno Cannon International Airport is the closest major airport to Homewood, which is also served by the Sacramento airport. Scheduled service to Lake Tahoe Airport in South Lake Tahoe is less frequent and, in heavy weather, these flights sometimes land in Reno. Four-wheel-drive and cars equipped for skiers are available for rental at all 3 airports. Limousine service is available from Truckee-Tahoe Limousine and Tours, (916) 587-2160, and 5 Star Enterprises, Truckee, (916) 587-7651.

Amtrak's "California Zephyr" stops in Truckee, as well as in Sacramento and Reno/Sparks. Auto rentals are available in Truckee at the AAA Auto Rental, adjacent to the Amtrak station. Rental car delivery to the train stations in Sacramento and Reno can be arranged through Hertz. Greyhound also operates bus service into Truckee.

*Spectacular views of Lake Tahoe are visible from 90% of Homewood's slopes. (Courtesy of Homewood.)*

TART, the Tahoe Area Regional Transit bus, picks up along Lake Tahoe's North and West shores and stops at Homewood. The $1 bus fare can be deducted from the price of a lift ticket at Homewood.

Alternatively, the Tahoe Queen cruises from the South Shore to the West Shore Tuesdays through Saturdays beginning in January. A glass-bottom paddlewheeler departs from Ski Run Marina on Ski Run Blvd. and arrives in Tahoe City about 10 to 10:30 a.m. Round-trip rates are $16.50 adults and $8 for children under 12. Breakfast, dinner, and cocktails available, (916) 541-3364. In California, 800-238-2463. From Tahoe City, skiers can take the TART bus to Homewood.

## TERRAIN

Most of Homewood's runs are tree-lined trails that roll off Upper Rainbow Ridge. The powder lasts the longest between the trees on black-diamond runs like *White Lightning* and *Ivory Face*, but the most challenging slopes are the double diamonds on *Quail Face*. Although short, the *Nose*, under the Madden Ridge Chair, is almost as steep as KT-22 at Squaw. Chock-full of moguls, it's as lumpy as rocky-mountain candy. The adjacent *Face* is another steep mogul slope.

Skiers who like a bit of bounce but less pitch can take the shorter *Glory Hole*, or can avoid the rougher stuff altogether by cutting left sooner onto *Last Resort*.

The long, 2-mile run starts at the top of the quad chair along *Lake Louise* to *Pot of Gold* and *Ore Car*. *Minors*, *Bonanza*, and *High Grade* are favorite intermediate cruisers, but the most scenic panorama is from *Upper Rainbow Ridge* to midmountain.

Although snowboarders are welcome anywhere on the mountain, the half-pipe on *White Lightning*, is designated just for them.

Because of its position, lower altitude, and lack of snowmaking equipment, Homewood's season is shorter than either Squaw Valley or Alpine Meadows. However, Homewood often remains open when these areas close due to heavy storms or high winds.

## FACILITIES

Homewood has 2 base lodges and parking zones, the result of having once been 2 separate ski areas, Homewood and Tahoe Ski Bowl. A shuttle van runs continually along SH 89 between the 2 parking areas. Due to limited parking at the base, lift lines are generally non-existent.

Homewood participates in the Ski Tahoe North interchangeable lift ticket that includes Homewood, Squaw Valley, Alpine Meadows, Northstar-at-Tahoe,

Diamond Peak, and Mount Rose. Rates are $96 for 3 days, $128 for 4 days, $160 for 5 days and $189 for 6 days.

## FACILITIES AT A GLANCE

*Season:* Thanksgiving–Easter.
*Hours:* 9 a.m.–4 p.m.
*Night Skiing:* None.
*Area:* 1,260 acres with 55 runs.
   Beginner: 15%
   Intermediate: 50%
   Advanced: 35%
*Base Elevation:* 6,230 ft
*Summit Elevation:* 7,880 ft
*Vertical Drop:* 1,650 ft
*Longest Run:* 2 miles.
*Snowmaking:* On lower slope.
*Snowboarding:* Permitted.
*Avg. Annual Snowfall:* 96 in.
*Lift Capacity:* 8,500 per hr.
*Lifts:* 5 chair lifts (1 quad, 2 triples, 2 doubles) and 6 surface lifts (2 T-bars, 3 poma lifts, and a Mighty Mite)

| Name | Length | Vertical Rise |
| --- | --- | --- |
| Alpine Poma | 100 ft | 560 ft |
| Ellis Canyon | 1,087 ft | 4,513 ft |
| Madden Canyon | 960 ft | 4,020 ft |
| Madden Ridge | 1,040 ft | 3,804 ft |
| Mighty Mite | 25 ft | 200 ft |
| North Poma | 100 ft | 600 ft |
| Quail Lake | 762 ft | 2,450 ft |
| Ski Bowl T-Bar | 250 ft | 900 ft |
| South Poma | 100 ft | 600 ft |
| Spring Chair | 250 ft | 1,000 ft |
| Tailings T-Bar | 450 ft | 2,000 ft |

*(continued on next page)*

*(continued from previous page)*

| Lift Passes: | All Day | Afternoon Only |
|---|---|---|
|  | 9 a.m.–4 p.m. | 1 p.m.–4 p.m. |
| Adults | $27 | $20 |
| Children under 12 | $9 | $6 |
| Seniors 60+ | $9 | $9 |
| Handicapped | $3 |  |

| Multiday Rates: | Adult | Child |
|---|---|---|
| 3 out of 4 consecutive days | $74 | $24 |
| 4 out of 5 consecutive days | $92 | $28 |
| 5 out of 6 consecutive days | $105 | $32.50 |
| 6 out of 7 consecutive days | $123 | $36 |

*Season Passes:* $295 midweek. $500 full week.
$250 full week ages 12–16.
$170 full week, seniors and children under 12 yrs.
$235 transferable corporate pass, and $170 for second member.

*Group Rates:* Available by prior arrangement for 25 or more.

*Food & Drink:* A cafeteria is located at each base lodge, at the north and south parking lots. Light dinners and wine are offered weekends and holidays. The warming hut on the mountain at Lower Rainbow Ridge has hot and cold foods, beverages, and a sun deck.

*Parking & Transportation:* A free shuttle runs continually between the parking areas at the north and south parking lots on SH 89. No overnight RV parking. TART, the Tahoe area bus, stops at Homewood and is equipped with ski racks, (916) 581-6365.

*Ski Rentals:* Rental shops at both base lodges are open from 8 a.m.–5 p.m. Includes skis, boots, and poles.
  All day: Adult $18. Child $11.
  Half day: Adult $14. Child $10.
  Snowboards: $16.

*Ski School:* Phone (916) 525-7256.
  *Method:* ATM.
  *Ski School Director:* Brad Leary.
  *Class Lessons:* 10:30 a.m. and 2 p.m.
    $19 (2 hr) adult and child (ages 6–12).
    $28 (4 hr) adult and child.
    $80 5 days, 2-hr lessons.
    $125 5 days, 4-hr lessons.

*Beginner Special:* Includes use of beginner's lift and equipment rentals.
   $29 2 hr, adult. $25 child.
   $35 4 hr, adult $29 child.
*Pre-school:* Ages 4–6, 10:30 a.m., 11:30 a.m., and 2 p.m. daily.
   $12 per hr.
*Private Lessons:* Every hour on the hour.
   $30 1 hr. Additional person $10 per hr.
   $50 2 hr.
   $75 3 hr.
   $150 6 hr.
*Snowboard Lessons:* 10:30 a.m. $19, 2 hr. $28, 4 hr.
*Beginner Snowboard Lesson:* Purchase by 10:00 a.m.
   $35 includes 4-hr lesson, lift ticket, and equipment.
   $29 includes 2-hr lesson, lift ticket, and equipment.
*Powder and Mogul Lessons:* Upon request, conditions permitting.
*Races & Clinics:*
*Race Clinics:* Available for groups of 20+.
*Individual Coaching:* Same rate as private lesson.
*Super Sliders:* Ages 5–14. Seven Sundays with 7 4-hr race lessons, $85.
*Snowboard Series:* Every other Sunday beginning in January. Registration includes lift ticket and shirt, $16.
*Day Care:* Ages 2–10. 8 a.m.–5 p.m. South-side base lodge. Includes supervised snow play. Lunch not included.
   $25 all day. $20 half day.
*Camper Facilities:* Overnight camping 3 miles south at Sugar Pine Point State Park on SH 89, (916) 525-7982. Tent and RV sites to 30 ft long. No hookups. $10 per night. Heated restrooms and parking.
*Medical:* First aid on mountain by pro patrol. Clinic 6 miles north in Tahoe City. Doctors available through the Physicians' Finder Assistance, (916) 587-6011 ext. 485. Closest hospital is Tahoe Forest, 22 miles north in Truckee.

## SPECIAL EVENTS

- *Homewood Snowboard Series*—January, February, March, and April.
- *Far West Super G Race*—February.

- *Far West Freestyle Mogul Competition*—February.
- *USSA Masters Race*—February.
- *USSA Far West Rondele Super G*—February.
- *Snowfest Tahoe*—March. Localman Winter Triathalon: install auto chains, split wood, and shovel snow.
- *Snowfest Bob Everson Junior Memorial Race*—March.

## WINTER ACTIVITIES

### Cross-Country

Cross-country trails through open meadows can be found at *Blackwood Canyon Sno Park* 1/2 mile north of Homewood. Parking by Sno-Park permit.

Two miles south at *Sugar Pine Point State Park*, 11 miles of beginner and intermediate trails are located on both sides of SH 89. Parking $3. Heated restrooms. No lessons or rentals on site.

Other cross-country areas nearby include *Squaw Valley Nordic*, *Granlibakken*, *Tahoe Nordic*, and *North Tahoe Regional Park*. See Squaw Valley, Northstar-at Tahoe, Sugar Bowl, and Heavenly Valley.

### Snowmobiling

Snowmobile trails are located 1/2 mile north of Homewood on SH 89 at *Blackwood Canyon Sno-Park*. Parking with Sno-Park permit.

For guided snowmobile tours, see Squaw Valley.

### Tobogganing, Tubing, and Snow Play

Sleds and saucers are rented at *Granlibakken Resort*, Granlibakken Road off SH 89, 5.5 miles north of Homewood. See Granlibakken.

### Ice Skating

An outdoor ice skating rink is located north of Homewood at *Squaw Valley*. Situated on the mountain, the rink is accessible via aerial tram. For additional information, see Squaw Valley.

### Sleigh Rides

See Tahoe Donner and Northstar.

## OTHER ACTIVITIES

**Cinema:** The Cobblestone Cinema, Tahoe City.
**Gambling:** Cal-Neva Lodge, High Sierra, Tahoe Biltmore, and Crystal Bay Club, Stateline.
**Seaplane Rides:** Cal-Vada Aircraft, Homewood.
**Sightseeing:** Truckee.

For listings on fishing, fitness and racquetball, and other activities, see Squaw Valley and Alpine Meadows.

## SHOPPING

At Homewood, ski shops are located at both base lodges. Groceries, liquor, and deli meats can be purchased at the *Tahoma Market*, 2 miles south on SH 89. Additional shopping can be found in Tahoe City and Truckee. See Squaw Valley and Tahoe Donner.

## APRÈS-SKI

Après-ski time is a warm, comfortable experience at *Sunnyside*, SH 89, 4 miles north of Homewood. Elegantly nautical in theme, the spacious lounge features an oyster bar, large stone fireplace, and tall windows overlooking the lake. Ski videos run on overhead TVs but are not obtrusive. Drinks are 1/2-price at happy hour, 3:30 to 5 p.m., Monday through Friday. Live music is offered Wednesdays, Thursdays, and Fridays.

For additional après-ski suggestions in nearby Tahoe City, see Squaw Valley.

## RESTAURANTS

**The Captain's Alpenhaus**   $$   *(916) 525-5000*
Located in Tahoma at 6941 W. Lake Blvd. (SH 89), the Alpenhaus is open for breakfast, lunch, and dinner. Wednesday night is Basque night, with family-style dining, accordion music, and sing-a-longs. The Bavarian-style menu includes beef fondue bourguignonne, swiss fondue, sauerbraten, beef stroganoff, Vienna schnitzel, and fresh fish. Full bar.

**Swiss Lakewood Restaurant   $$**   *(916) 525-5211*
5055 W. Lake Blvd. (SH 89) Homewood. The Swiss Lakewood Restaurant dates back to 1918 and is the oldest restaurant in Tahoe in continual use. The award-winning owner/chef presents excellent continental cuisine in an attractive dining room that features a cozy fireside lounge. Continental entrées include beefsteak tartar, chateaubriand, pheasant, duck, lobster, osso buco, pasta primavera, escargots bourguignonne, steak, and seafood. The extensive wine cellar houses up to 1,000 bottles.

The *Sunnyside Resort and Restaurant* and the *Tahoe House* restaurant are about 5 miles north of Homewood on SH 89. See Granlibakken and Squaw Valley for additional information on these and other restaurants in the Tahoe City area.

## ACCOMMODATIONS

Although Homewood has no lodging of its own, the nearby motels and cabins along SH 89 (W. Lake Blvd.) between Tahoma and Tahoe City, are mainly of the rustic variety and too numerous to mention. For listings in the Homewood Area, contact the Westshore Association at (916) 583-2371. Three, five, and seven-night packages are available through the Tahoe North Visitors and Convention Bureau, (916) 583-3494, (800) 824-6348. A few highlights are listed here.

**Chambers Landing   $$$**   *(916) 525-5227*
6400 W. Lake Blvd., Homewood. On a sandy beach, 1 mile south of the Homewood ski area, a handful of these individually-owned, luxury townhouses are available for rent directly from their owners. Each home ranges from 2,262 to 2,875 sq ft and has 3-4 bedrooms, 2-3 baths, oakwood floors, brass fixtures, river-rock fireplace, skylights in arched cedar ceilings, "cook's" kitchen, sun deck, indoor spa tub, custom tiles, covered carport, and 24-hr security. Chambers Landing housekeeping at renter's expense. TART bus stop.

**The Captain's Alpenhaus   $$**   *(916) 525-5000*
6941 W. Lake Blvd., Tahoma. Named for its owner, Captain Joel Butler, who spent 25 years in the navy, the Alpenhaus bed-and-breakfast was built in the 1930s. Its country-style rooms and cottages all have private baths. Two family suites each have 2 bedrooms, a kitchen, and a small living area and sleep from 4 to 6. Both suites can be rented as a 4-bedroom unit. Restaurant and bar downstairs. Spa on premises.

**Sugar Pine Lakeside   $$**   *(916) 525-7042*
7021 W. Lake Blvd, 2 miles south of Homewood. 3-bedroom, 2-bath condominiums with lake views, TV, fireplaces, phones, and kitchens with conventional ovens. Units sleep 6 to 8. Covered parking provided. Guests supply own linens and towels.

**Tavern Shores**  $$ *(916) 583-3704*
300 W. Lake Blvd., 1/8 mile south of Tahoe City. 2–4 bedroom condominiums with kitchens, including washers/dryers, stone fireplaces, TV, and phones. Extra charge for linens and maid service. A 2-night minimum applies in winter, with 7-night minimum at Christmas and New Year's.

**Sugar Pine Park**  $ *(916) 525-7042*
7110 W. Lake Blvd., adjacent to Sugar Pine Point State Park. Moderate 3-bedroom, 2½-bath condominium units with fully equipped kitchens, TV, phones, washer/dryer units, and balconies. Guests supply own linens and towels. Additional charge for maid service.

For additional listings nearby, see Granlibakken and Squaw Valley.

# Heavenly Valley

❄

P.O. Box 2180
Stateline, NV 89449
Information: (916) 541-1330
Snowphone: (916) 541-7544

### Driving distances

| | |
|---|---|
| Las Vegas | 463 mi |
| Los Angeles | 465 mi |
| Reno | 55 mi |
| Sacramento | 112 mi |
| San Diego | 586 mi |
| San Francisco | 202 mi |
| San Jose | 229 mi |
| Tahoe City | 35 mi |
| Truckee | 43 mi |

*For road conditions, call
(916) 577-3550, California
(702) 793-1313, Nevada*

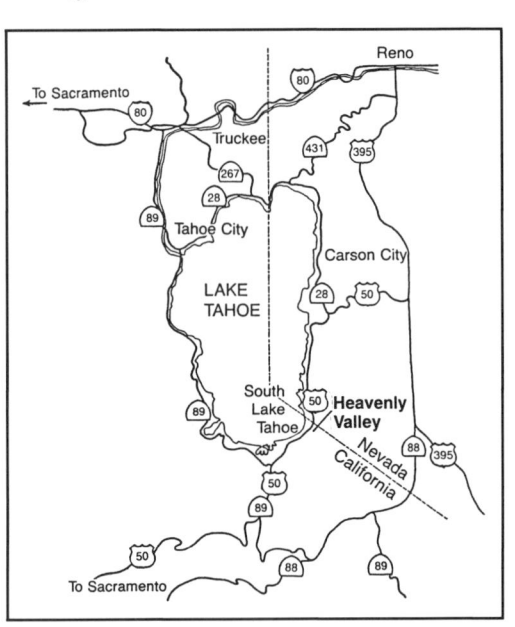

With 12,800 acres spanning across two states—California and Nevada—Heavenly Valley is the nation's largest ski resort with the world's largest snowmaking system. Not only is it vast, it's high, 10,100-ft high, the highest ski resort in the Tahoe area, with the longest run (5 1/2 miles) in the state. It's sunny 84% of the season. And it's glitzy, with nonstop casino action and entertainment just minutes from the slopes.

Heavenly is a contradiction to the usual images of remote serenity and village-like homeyness conjured up by most Alpine ski areas. On top, it's quiet with scenic vistas of Lake Tahoe encircled by white-tipped evergreens to the north, and the rich earthtones of the Nevada desert to the east. But lower down, Heavenly is loud and brassy, presenting a unique dichotomy that enhances the enjoyment, especially for those who have the energy to ski all day and play all night.

Variety, the spice in Heavenly's recipe for fun, is everywhere: In the terrain, from bunny slopes to experts-only; in the lodging, from luxury resorts and condos to rustic cabins and cozy bed-and-breakfasts; in dining options, from Cajun to sushi; and in activity choices, from cross-country to blackjack.

With so much to offer, and relatively easy access from Reno's Cannon International Airport, it's no surprise that Heavenly draws crowds from as far away as Japan.

## LOCATION

Heavenly Valley is located in South Lake Tahoe on the border of California and Nevada, 55 miles south of Reno and 112 miles east of Sacramento. The California base is located in El Dorado County, at the end of Ski Run Blvd., $1/2$ mile south of US 50. The 2 Nevada-side bases lie in Douglas County, east of Stateline and 3 miles south of US 50.

From Sacramento, US 50 is a 4-lane road to Riverton, where it narrows to 2 lanes and becomes winding and somewhat precipitous around Echo Summit, west of the town of Meyers. US 50 turns right at the junction with SH 89. Three miles beyond, Ski Run Blvd. is a right turn $1/2$ mile to Heavenly's California side. To reach the Nevada side, stay on US 50 past Stateline to Kingsbury Grade (SH 207) just past the Stateline casinos. Turn right and go 3 miles to Tramway Drive and continue to the end of the road, where it branches right to the Boulder Base Lodge or left to the Stagecoach Base Lodge.

From Reno, take US 395 south 29 miles to US 50. Turn southwest on US 50, and proceed 22 miles to Kingsbury Grade (SH 207). Turn left on Kingsbury Grade and go 3 miles to Tramway Drive. From North Lake Tahoe, SH 28 south on the east shore is generally shorter than SH 89 on the west side of the lake.

The Lake Tahoe Airport is 6 miles from Heavenly Valley, with scheduled service direct from San Francisco and San Jose and connections from other California cities. Depending on weather conditions, these flights sometimes bypass the airport and land in Reno. Shuttle transportation is available from Lake Tahoe Airport to the South Shore and Heavenly with Dial-A-Ride, (916) 577-7000. Reo's Wonder Mile charges $5 for the transfer service, (916) 544-3333. Showboat Lines transfers American Airlines passengers to the casino hotels at Stateline for $3.50 one way, (702) 588-5300. Tahoe Limousine, (916) 544-2200 or (800) 334-1826, and Alpine Limousine and Tours, (916) 577-2727, provide private transfers by reservation. Taxi fare is about $10.50.

Cannon International Airport in Reno is the closest major airport to Heavenly Valley, which is also serviced by the Sacramento airport. Four-wheel-drive and cars equipped for skiers are available for rental at all 3 airports.

Scheduled airport shuttle service is available 8 times a day from Reno via LTR Stage Lines to South Lake Tahoe. The $1^{1}/_{2}$-hr drive is $11.75 one way, (916) 541-1330 ext. 5103 or (702) 323-3088.

Cab fare from the Reno airport runs about $75 one way. Limousine service is available from Tahoe Limousine, (916) 544-2200 or (800) 334-1826, Bell Limo, (702) 786-3700 or 800-235-5466, and Dial-A-Ride, (916) 577-7000.

Amtrak's "California Zephyr" stops in Truckee, as well as in Sacramento and Reno/Sparks. Train service from Los Angeles to Reno is also daily. Autos with chains and racks are available for rent in Truckee at the AAA Auto Rental, adjacent to the Amtrak station. During the busy season, 4-wheel-drive vehicles should be reserved a month or more in advance.

Greyhound operates bus service into South Lake Tahoe 6 to 8 times daily.

Skiers staying on the North Shore can take the Tahoe Queen sternwheeler from Tahoe City across the lake Tuesday through Friday in the late afternoon, stay overnight, and return the next day. The round-trip cost is $16.50 adults and $7.50 children, (916) 541-3364.

Free shuttle bus service also operates all along the South Shore to the California Base Lodge every 1/2 hour.

## TERRAIN

The first glimpse of Heavenly from the California side can send shivers through the average skier. Squaring off on the face, the notorious *Gunbarrel* is rough, tough, and steep. And, like an outlaw who knows no mercy, Gunbarrel's big, bad bumps start at midmountain and go on and on. Along with other advanced runs on the lower mountain, *Gunbarrel* demands respect when the snow is forgiving, and gets meaner when the powder waxes hard and slick.

The recreational skier need not worry, however. Heavenly Valley is primarily an intermediate ski area, and there are plenty of friendly slopes on the upper mountain and Nevada side, including *Ridge Run*, with its eagle's-nest views of Tahoe. In fact, the main beginner runs like *Maggies* and *Mombo* sit right above the black-diamond trails. At the end of the day, intermediate skiers can bypass the advanced slopes on the bottom via *Roundabout*, a long trail that criss-crosses the mountain and affords a beautiful angle on the lake. Beginners can download on the Gunbarrel or West Bowl chairs, or take the aerial tram for a scenic ride to the base.

Favorite cruising runs like *Olympic Downhill* and *Comet* roll down from the top on the Nevada side where the terrain is predominantly intermediate. Exceptions are the advanced *Milky Way Bowl*, aptly named for its usually bountiful fresh powder and *Mots Canyon*. Entrance to *Mots Canyon*, an ungroomed and sometimes unstable area, is through special gates for experts only. Once headed down, there's no bail-out until bottom. The canyon has 2,000 vertical ft of steep bowls, canyons, and chutes. Although a lift is planned for the Canyon in the near future, at present, skiers are hauled by snow-cat shuttle to the perimeter road. As conditions vary, Mots Canyon may be open or closed. The shuttle only operates when the gates are open at the top.

Heavenly Valley's 20 sq miles of terrain straddle 2 states and 9 mountain peaks. To ski from Nevada to California, take the Olympic or Comet Chair to *Von Schmidt Trail* or the Dipper Chair to the *California Trail*. To ski from California to Nevada, take the Sky Chair to the top and *Skyline Trail* to *Nevada's Dipper Knob Trail*. The longest glide down is 5$^1$/$_2$ miles from the top of the Sky Chair to the Nevada base.

## FACILITIES

Heavenly Valley participates in the Ski Tahoe interchangeable lift ticket with Kirkwood, Northstar, Squaw Valley, and Alpine Meadows. Rates for 5 nights' accommodations and a 5-day lift pass start at $245 per person, double occupancy.

Complete ski packages that include accommodations as well as lift tickets are available through Heavenly's central reservations, (800) 243-2836.

## FACILITIES AT A GLANCE

| | |
|---|---|
| *Season:* | Mid-November–May. |
| *Hours:* | Weekdays 9 a.m.–4 p.m. |
| | Weekends/holidays 8:30 a.m.–4 p.m. |
| *Night Skiing:* | None. |
| *Area:* | 12,800 acres with 60+ runs. |
| | Beginner: 25% |
| | Intermediate: 50% |
| | Advanced: 25% |
| *Base Elevation:* | 6,550 ft, CA; 7,200 ft, NV |
| *Summit Elevation:* | 10,100 ft |
| *Vertical Drop:* | 3,600 ft |
| *Longest Run:* | 5.5 miles. |
| *Snowmaking:* | One of largest systems in the world, 62% of runs covered, including all runs on the California side and 100 acres on Nevada side. |
| *Snowboarding:* | Nevada side only. |
| *Avg. Annual Snowfall:* | 375 in. |
| *Lift Capacity:* | 31,000 per hr. |

*(continued on next page)*

*(continued from previous page)*

*Lifts:* 24 lifts (50-passenger aerial tram, 1 high-speed quad, 7 triple chairs, 9 double chairs, and 6 surface lifts)

| Name | Length | Vertical Rise |
|---|---|---|
| Aerial Tramway | 2,000 ft | 1,700 ft |
| Boulder | 2,980 ft | 400 ft |
| Boulder Mighty Mite | 448 ft | 79 ft |
| Canyon | 3,925 ft | 1,100 ft |
| Comet (high speed) | 3,586 ft | 1,000 ft |
| Dipper | 5,127 ft | 1,300 ft |
| Galaxy | 5,890 ft | 1,100 ft |
| Groove | 1,138 ft | 350 ft |
| Gunbarrel | 3,720 ft | 1,700 ft |
| North Bowl | 5,286 ft | 1,400 ft |
| Olympic | 3,552 ft | 1,000 ft |
| Patsy's | 1,220 ft | 300 ft |
| Pioneer Poma | 709 ft | 132 ft |
| Powder Bowl | 1,138 ft | 1,100 ft |
| Ridge | 4,865 ft | 1,000 ft |
| Sky | 4,663 ft | 1,500 ft |
| Stagecoach | 5,815 ft | 1,500 ft |
| Waterfall | 3,548 ft | 1,200 ft |
| West Bowl | 4,082 ft | 1,800 ft |
| West Bowl Poma | 1,090 ft | 200 ft |
| World Cup | 1,167 ft | 350 ft |
| Other Pomas | NA | 250 ft |

*Lift Tickets:*

| | All Day | Half Day |
|---|---|---|
| | 9 a.m.–4 p.m. | 1 p.m.–4 p.m. |
| Adults | $35 | $23 |
| Children under 12 | $14 | $14 |
| Seniors 65+ | $14 | $14 |
| Weekend Sat/Sun | $58 | |
| Scenic Tram only | $ 9/5 adult/child. | |

*Multiday Rates:* $81, 3-day pass.*
$108, 4-day pass.*
$145, 5-day pass.*

*Consecutive days*

*Season Passes:*  When purchased by September 15—$650 any day, $375 midweek, $375 student (ages 13–18), $175 child and senior age 65+. When purchased by October 15—$750 unlimited, $450 midweek, $425 student, $200 child and senior. When purchased after October 15—$850 any day, $575 midweek, $475 student, $225 child and senior.

*Group Rates:*  Available for 25+ by prior arrangement.

*Food & Drink:*  A cafeteria, bar, and sun deck are located at each of the 3 base lodges. Food services are also located on the mountain at the bottom of the Comet chairs. The Governor's Room Restaurant under the top of the tram has seated service, a cocktail lounge, and sun deck. Sky Meadows at the base of Sky Chair offers sandwiches, drinks, wine, beer, and an outdoor barbecue.

*Parking & Transportation:*  General parking is free at the California base and at both lots on the Nevada side at Boulder Base and Stagecoach Base. No RV overnight parking permitted.

*Ski Rentals:*  Heavenly Sports rental shops, located at all 3 base lodges, are open from 8:30 a.m. to 5 p.m. midweek and 7:30 a.m. to 5 p.m. on weekends and holidays. Includes skis, boots, and poles.

All day:  Adult $15. Child $9.

High performance skis:  $16.

Demo skis also available.

Multiday rates available.

*Ski School:*  Phone (916) 544-1330.

*Method:*  ATM.

*Ski School Director:*  Stu Campbell.

*Class Lessons:*  10 a.m. and 1:30 p.m.

$20 ($2^{1}/_{2}$ hr) adult and child.

*Beginner Special:*  10 a.m. and 11 a.m. Includes lessons and lifts during lessons.

$25 (4 hr) adult or child.

$17 (2 hr) adult or child.

*Little Angels:*  Ages 4–12. 9 a.m.–3:45 p.m. Includes lessons, lunch, and children's lift ticket.

$48 all day.

$27 half day (12:30 p.m.–3:45 p.m.).

*Private Lessons:*  $40 1 hr. Additional person $18.

$200 5 hr. Additional person $50.

*Powder, Moguls, Freestyle Lessons:*  On request.

*(continued on next page)*

*(continued from previous page)*

*Races & Clinics:*
  *Coin-operated Race Course:* Located on Jack's. $1.00 per run.
  *NASTAR Races:* $25. Groups only.
  *Clinics:* $17, 2 hr, 10 a.m. and 1:30 p.m. Groups by arrangement.

*Day Care:* Located at California Base Lodge. Ages 2–4. Must be toilet trained. Includes lunch, arts and crafts, and snow play.
  $35. All day 9 a.m.–3:45 p.m.
  $20. Half day 1 p.m.–3:45 p.m.

*Camper Facilities:* Lakeside RV Park at 3987 Cedar Ave., Stateline, has full hookups, showers, and laundry and is 50 yards from the free casino and ski bus stop. Sites are up to 55 ft long and $22 per night, (916) 544-4704. Chris Haven RV and Mobile Home Park, US 50 & E St., has hookups, showers, and laundry. Rate is $17, (916) 541-1895. Zephyr Cove, 6 miles northeast of Heavenly, has full hookups for self-contained vehicles. Campers are $12, tents $8, (702) 588-6644. Tent and RV sites for self-contained RVs are available at the KOA Kampground, US 50 in Tahoe Paradise, 6 miles from Heavenly. $20 per night with hookups or $15 per night without. Restroom, laundry, and showers are closed in winter, (916) 577-3693.

*Medical:* A first aid center is staffed by ski patrol and nurses. Helicopter evacuation available. Closest Hospital is Barton Memorial in South Lake Tahoe.

*Other:* Locker rental available at all 3 base locations.

## SPECIAL EVENTS

- *US Men's Pro Tour*—January.
- *Top Gun Mogul, Freestyle, and Aerial Exhibition*—February or March.
- *Celebrity Ski Class*—February.

## WINTER ACTIVITIES

### Cross-Country

*Spooner Lake* Nordic ski area is 13 miles north of Stateline on the Nevada side of Lake Tahoe on SH 28, about halfway between Tahoe's North and South

Shores. The 15 miles of groomed beginner, intermediate, and advanced trails include a side track for skating. The main lodge houses food services, a rental shop, and ski school. A warming hut is located between the Moonlight Loop Trail and the Spooner Meadow Trail. Parking is free at the base.

Trail fees are $7 adults, $4 for children, and $3.50 for seniors 60 and over. Children under 6 and seniors over 70 are free. Discounts apply for students and military with 2-for-1 specials on Tuesdays and Wednesdays. An adult trail pass and rental package is $17.50. Morning, afternoon, and twilight passes are also available.

On weekends and holidays, Spooner Lake also offers $1^1/_2$-hr lessons for $15. An inclusive rate of $23 includes a lesson, trail pass, and equipment rentals. A children's ski school includes a lesson, trail pass, and equipment for $14 for ages 4 and 5, or $16 for ages 6–10. Skating lessons and private lessons are also available. Free moonlight tours are conducted on various evenings during the season from 6:30 p.m. to 10 p.m. Equipment rentals are $5 for the evening, (702) 749-5349.

Spooner Lake participates in the Ski Tahoe North Interchangeable trail pass with Royal Gorge, Northstar, Squaw Valley, Tahoe Nordic, Tahoe Donner, and Diamond Peak cross-country. Rates are $34 for 4 days, $40 for 5 days, and $45 for 6 days.

When snow conditions permit, *Lake Tahoe Winter Sports Center*, 3071 US 50, offers about 9 miles of cross-country track and lessons at the Lake Tahoe Country Club. Usage fee $5, equipment rentals $13. A lesson, equipment rentals, and usage fee package is $20, (916) 577-2940.

More than 3 miles of groomed trails are located on the golf course at the *Bijou Cross-Country Center*, US 50 at Johnson Blvd. in South Lake Tahoe. The trails are 75% beginner and 25% intermediate. No lessons or rentals on site and no fee, but donations are accepted. For information, call the Department of Parks and Recreation, (916) 541-4611.

The U.S. Forest Service maintains trails for beginners at the *Visitor Center/Tallac Historic Site* on the west side of the lake on SH 89, 1 mile north of Camp Richardson and 6.6 miles north of South Lake Tahoe. The site is marked by 3 rustic summer homes built in the early 1900s. Parking is by Sno-Park permit.

A mile or two further north at *Taylor Creek*, an easy, mostly flat trail is marked and leads to Fallen Leaf Lake. No rentals or lessons are available on site. Parking permitted with Sno-Park permit. A 3-mile trail into the *Desolation Wilderness* is for experienced cross-country skiers, and a permit for access must be obtained from the U.S. Forest Service. Call in advance, (916) 573-2600.

Trails at *Trout Creek*, $^3/_4$ mile north of Myers, are intermediate and advanced. About 5 miles of unmarked trails ascend from Oneidas St., off the south side of Pioneer Trail, 1,500 ft to Freel Peak. Advanced trails are also located at *Meiss Meadows*, 5 miles south of US 50 on SH 89.

For additional Nordic trails in the Lake Tahoe area, see Kirkwood, Sierra Ski Ranch, Squaw Valley, and Diamond Peak.

## Snowmobiling

*Zephyr Cove Snowmobile Rentals* at the Zephyr Cove Resort lodge, 760 US 50, Zephyr Cove, offers guided 2- and 3-hour tours with shuttle service from the casino and Park Ave. areas. The lodge has a restaurant, general store, gift shop, restrooms, and suit-up area, (702) 588-3833.

*Lake Tahoe Winter Sports Center*, 3071 US 50, offers track snowmobiling at the Lake Tahoe Country Club and at Sunset Ranch, both on US 50, 1 mile west of the Lake Tahoe Airport. The rate is $22 per ½ hour for a single rider and $44 for a double rider. The center also conducts 2-hour wilderness tours in Hope Valley for $65 single or $90 double rider, (916) 577-2940.

*Tahoe Paradise Sports* offers snowmobiling on a ½ mile track at Tahoe Paradise Golf Course, US 50, 3 miles south of Lake Tahoe Airport. Rates are $20 for 1 person and $30 for 2, (916) 577-2121.

Snowmobile trails are open in winter at the *Taylor Creek* cross-country track on SH 89, 6½ miles north of South Lake Tahoe. Snowmobiles are permitted on the south side of SH 89 only. No rentals on site. Parking by Sno-Park permit.

## Tobogganing, Tubing, and Snow Play

*Hansen's Resort*, 1360 Ski Run Blvd. at the California base, has a 900-ft toboggan hill, as well as a rope tow, snow machine, and rentals. $9.00 for 3 hr. Cabin lodging with fireplaces and kitchens are also available, (916) 544-3361. *Old MacDonald's Enterprise*, 1060 Ski Run Blvd., rents sleds, toboggans, inner tubes, and saucers, for use on a supervised snow-play hill near Heavenly Valley's California base lodge. Moon boots and snow shoes are also available. Rates range from $3 for saucers to $10 for toboggans. Open daily from 9 a.m. to 5 p.m., (916) 544-3663.

*Winter Wonderland*, at 3672 Needle Peak Road, rents saucers for $4 a day, (916) 544-7903.

A bring-your-own equipment play area is also provided at *Taylor Creek* cross-country area on SH 89 adjacent to the Visitors Center, 6½ miles north of South Lake Tahoe. Parking by Sno-park permit only, (916) 573-2600.

## Ice Skating

When weather permits (usually late January to late February), *Lake Tahoe Winter Sports Center* rents skates for use on a small, outdoor pond. Skating is $3 for 2 hours including skates. Open daily from 10 a.m. to 5 p.m., (916) 577-2940. Also see Squaw Valley.

## Sleigh Rides

*Borges Sleigh Rides*, across from Caesars at Lake Parkway East and US 50, offers sleigh rides (snow permitting), (916) 541-2953. *Camp Richardson Corral* also offers 45-minute sleigh rides around Lake Tahoe daily, every hour on the hour. Rates are $10 to $12.

## Dogsled Rides

Half-hour and full-hour rides, parties, and wilderness tours are available through *Husky Express*, South Lake Tahoe, (916) 577-8557.

## Mountaineering

*Sierra Ski Touring* conducts training in mountaineering, including wilderness winter-survival courses, avalanche courses, and mushers course in dogsled handling and basic mountaineering. For dates and fees call (916) 577-8557.

## Winter Hikes

Guided hikes to sites of historic interest. For complete schedule, contact the California Department of Parks and Recreation, (916) 525-7232.

## OTHER ACTIVITIES

**Bowling:** Tahoe Bowl, South Lake Tahoe.
**Cinema:** Stateline Cinema, Tahoe Cinema, and Lakeside.
**Fishing:** Tahoe Sports Fishing, Captain Bruce Hernandez, and Dennis Fishing Charters, South Lake Tahoe.
**Fitness:** Caesars Palace, Harrah's, Harvey's, South Tahoe Fitness, The Muscle Works, and Lakeside Nautilus, all in South Lake Tahoe.
**Gambling:** Harrah's, High Sierra, Caesars Palace, Bill's and Harvey's, all in Stateline, Nevada.
**Indoor Tennis:** South Tahoe Fitness and Caesars, South Lake Tahoe; and the ridge on the Nevada side of Heavenly.
**Racquetball:** Caesars Palace, Lake Tahoe.
**Riding:** The Sunset Ranch, Lake Tahoe.
**Scenic Flights:** Sky Trek Charters, South Lake Tahoe.
**Video Arcades:** Caesars, Harrah's. Harvey's, and High Sierra Casino, Stateline.

## SHOPPING

*Heavenly Sports* ski shops sell Alpine equipment, apparel, and accessories at all 3 base lodges and in South Lake Tahoe at Harrah's, Harvey's, Stateline, Crescent V Center, and Ski Run Blvd.

Ski equipment and apparel, gifts, clothing, jewelry, antiques, art, books, toys, and a host of other products and services are available in and around US 50 at South Lake Tahoe. The major shopping malls include the *South "Y" Center* and *Lampson Plaza* at the junction of US 50 and SH 89, *Swiss Chalet Village* at US 50 and Sierra Blvd., *The Bijou Center* at US 50 and Fairway Ave., and *Crescent V Fashion Center* at US 50 and Park Ave. East of Stateline, the *Round Hill Mall*, 1 1/2 miles from the casinos at US 50 and Elk Point Dr., includes a Safeway Market, 3 art galleries, and several clothing stores.

*Caesars Tahoe Shopping Galleria* at Caesars Palace houses men's and women's boutiques and other shops. Additional shops, restaurants, and services are located in the underground mall that connects Harvey's and Harrah's.

## APRÈS-SKI

The *California Bar* at the California base lodge stays open for skiers until 7 p.m., with live entertainment some weekends. But, given the array of entertainment options at Tahoe's South Shore, Heavenly's après-ski life is somewhat diffused. Some skiers head back to condos or hotels for relaxation, while others take in the lounge shows or wager chips at the casinos along with non-skiing vacationers.

Happy hour comes in all styles. *Bueno Ricos* celebrates fiesta hour with "ricoritas," hand-shaken margaritas, from 4 to 6 p.m. The *Lakeside Cabaret Lounge* is the scene of 2-for-1 drinks, free popcorn, wine tasting, or other happy-hour specials, from 5 to 7 p.m. Live top-40 music is played Sunday through Thursday at *Marie Callendars*, from 9 p.m. to midnight.

Live entertainment is showcased in the *South Shore Room* and the *Stateline Cabaret* at *Harrah's*. Harrah's has 7 bars and a 65,000-sq-ft casino with more than 1,800 slot machines and 170 other gaming tables. *Caesars Tahoe Resort* casino offers games that range from million-dollar progressive slots to race and sports betting. Big-name entertainers perform in the 1,600 seat *Cascade Showroom*. Comedy, music, and revues are also featured in the smaller *Crystal Cabaret*. The cover charge is $8.

*Del Webb's High Sierra Casino* has all the popular games as well. Top performers and musical revues appear in the *Pine Cone Lounge*. *Harvey's* gambling includes a semi-private poker room and a race and sports book, as well as a large variety of slots and tables. *Bill's*, the newest casino at Stateline, boasts "the world's largest slot machine" and "more nickel slots," as well as the first McDonald's to be located in a casino.

The *Emerald Cabaret*, with tiered seating, features live entertainment. 1/4 mile north of Kingsbury Grade, *John's Tahoe Nugget* offers entertainment while gambling. The casino has 250 slot machines, keno, blackjack, and roulette. Combo music at the bar is usually mellow. 1/2 mile east of Stateline, the *Lakeside Inn & Casino* specializes in nickel, dime, and quarter slot machines, but also provides video poker, sports betting, and live entertainment.

For a romantic rendezvous, the *Summit Lounge* at Harrah's is a tranquil retreat, featuring the soft strains of a harp or guitar. Dancing's the thing at glitzy *Turtles Nightclub*, in the Round Hill Mall, west of Stateline. Skiers with leftover energy can dance until 4 a.m. to live and recorded music amid mirrors, brass, and split-level seating. Located 1.5 miles north of Stateline on US 50 in the Round Hill Mall, *Turtles* has 3 dance floors, 3 bars, 9 TV screens, a fireplace, and a game room with pool tables and other sports games. Admission is $6 on Friday and Saturday nights. No cover charge weekdays, (702) 588-7853. Also in Nevada on Kingsbury Grade, *Faces* features dancing and light suppers 7 nights a week.

*Rojo's* on US 50 presents live top-40 and rock-and-roll dance music in an atmosphere of rustic old Tahoe. The action begins at 10 p.m. and ends at 2 a.m. Thursday through Saturday. Live rock-and-roll and top-40 bands also appear nightly from 9 p.m. to 4 a.m. at *Lily's*, a popular dance spot at *Del Webb's High Sierra Hotel and Casino*. Combos at the *Forest Lounge* play top-40, oldies, and big-band favorites for dancing atop *Harrah's*. Jazz is featured on Tuesday and Wednesday evenings at the *89th Street Bar & Grill*, but it's strictly rock-and-roll on Friday and Saturday nights, when the cover charge is $18. Dart tournaments are held on Sunday and Monday nights. At Harvey's *Top of the Wheel*, dancing to live bands begins about 9 p.m.

## RESTAURANTS

**Christiana Inn**  $$$  *(916) 544-7337*
3819 Saddle Road, across from the California base lodge. The small, romantic dining room in the Inn offers steak, lamb, prime rib, and lobster from 10 a.m. to 11 p.m.

**Le Posh**  $$$  *(702) 588-3515*
US 50 in Caesars Tahoe, Stateline. Decorated in a nouveau Victorian motif, Le Posh has earned a reputation for haute cuisine with appetizers such as sautéed duck breast on endive with cherry-vinegar dressing, and entrées like veal medallions with baby scallops and basil.

**Stetson's  $$$**  *(702) 588-6211*
US 50 in the High Sierra Hotel and Casino, Stateline. As the name suggests, the restaurant is decked out in Stetsons. The menu includes a variety of American and continental dishes including pheasant, venison, duck, and salmon.

**The Summit  $$$**  *(702) 588-6611*
US 50, atop Harrah's Hotel at Stateline, this Holiday Award winner offers fine dining in a split-level room with views of Lake Tahoe. The continental menu includes entrées such as chateaubriand and tournedos de boeuf.

**Beacon Restaurant  $$**  *(916) 541-0630*
Off SH 89 at Camp Richardson, S. Lake Tahoe. Diners at this casual restaurant can enjoy a view of the lake while savoring Italian-accented entrées, such as chicken marsala, spinach tortellini, and scalone, a scallop and abalone combination steak sautéed with capers, garlic, butter, and white wine. Open daily for lunch and dinner.

**Bennigan's  $$**  *(702) 588-2996*
Located in Bill's Casino at US 50, Stateline. A variety of dinner selections ranging from western to Italian and Mexican are served in a casual and lively atmosphere.

**Chart House  $$**  *(702) 588-6276*
Kingsbury Grade, 1.5 miles south of US 50, Stateline. The Chart House presents its lavish salad bar, seafood, steaks, and mud pie in a casually elegant atmosphere, with panoramic views of the lake. Open daily for dinner from 5:30 p.m.

**Chicken and Rib House  $$**  *(800) 648-3322 ext. 2452*
SH 50, in Del Webb's High Sierra, Stateline. Families queue up to sample the popular chicken and rib combos.

**Dixie's Cajun and Creole Cuisine  $$**  *(916) 541-0405*
At 681 US 50, S. Lake Tahoe. Dixie's is a modest 1-story bungalow that specializes in tasty creole creations like cajun popcorn, blackened lamb and catfish, and shrimp creole.

**The Dory's Oar  $$**  *(916) 541-6603*
1041 Fremont, S. Lake Tahoe, 2 miles west of Stateline. A New England-style family restaurant offering hearty seafood specials, including Maryland soft-shell crab and live Maine lobster and steak. Open for dinner from 5 p.m. daily.

**El Vaquero  $$**  *(702) 588-2411*
Located in Harvey's in the underpass between Harrah's and Harvey's, Stateline. Hacienda-style decor blends well with Mexican specialties including taco salads, enchiladas, fajitas, and combination plates. Open for lunch except Mondays and Tuesdays, and daily for dinner from 5 p.m.

**Greenhouse  $$**  *(916) 541-5800*
At 4140 Cedar Ave., $1/2$ block from the casinos at Stateline. The Greenhouse is a cozy Tudor-style cottage offering fireside dining amid antique stained glass and lush green plants. Continental entrées include tournedos of lamb, chicken supreme, veal marsala, and roast duckling.

**Petrello's**   $$                                                                      *(916) 541-7868*
900 Emerald Bay Road, 1 mile north of the junction with SH 89, Stateline. Formerly a French restaurant, owner Frank Petrello of Mammoth changed that by bringing his Italian cuisine to South Lake Tahoe. Petrello's features Italian specialties such as calamari, lasagna, and veal scallopini.

**Salmar's**   $$                                                        *(916) 541-8400*
787 Emerald Bay Road, S. Lake Tahoe. Salmar's boasts the largest omelette menu "on earth" for breakfast and lunch, but dinner takes on an Italian personality with pastas, chicken, and prime rib.

**The Swiss Chalet**   $$                                       *(916) 544-3304*
2540 US 50, S. Lake Tahoe. 4 miles from Heavenly. Swiss chalet architecture sets the mood for Alpine favorites such as fondue bourguignonne, cheese fondue, Wiener schnitzel, and sauerbraten. Closed Mondays.

## ACCOMMODATIONS

Some airlines that fly into Reno Cannon International Airport, such as USAir and Delta, offer all-inclusive ski packages to South Lake Tahoe, with round-trip airfare, accommodations, car equipped for skiers, and lift tickets. Rates vary according to the number of nights and lodge selected. Contact a travel agent or the airline for information. Reservations for accommodations at South Lake Tahoe can also be made through the Lake Tahoe Visitors' Authority, (800) 822-5922. A number of realty companies also book hotels, condominiums, and homes in the South Lake Tahoe area. These companies include:

- Alpine Realty Rentals, (916) 544-6978
- Coldwell Banker, (916) 542-0557
- Lucksinger-Yokotake & Associates, (916) 544-7010
- Lake Tahoe Realty & Rentals, (916) 541-5282; (800) 421-5113
- M&M Property Management Vacation Rentals, (916) 542-2777; (800) 542-2100
- Matthews Realty Inc. Vacation Rentals, (916) 541-4842
- Selective Accommodations, (702) 588-8285; (800) 242-5387
- Tahoe Management Co., (702) 588-4504; (800) 624-3887
- Tahoe Valley Motel and Condominiums, (916) 541-0353
- Tamarack Rentals, (916) 541-2595; (800) 232-2123
- Vacation Rental Service of Tahoe, (916) 544-1690
- Vacation Rentals, (916) 544-5300; (800) 962-1489

**Caesars Tahoe**   $$$                          *(702) 588-3515, (800) 648-3353*
Stateline, US 50, 1$^1/_2$ miles from Heavenly Valley. First class, 14-story hotel with more than 400 rooms and suites, some with lake views. Rooms have king-size or

double beds, two TVs, and circular Roman tubs. Facilities include a large casino, showroom with star entertainment, cabaret, 6 restaurants and complete spa with universal gym, saunas, steam rooms, racquetball, Jacuzzi, massage rooms, and indoor swimming pool. Amenities include 24-hr room service, complimentary ski storage, and shuttle bus to Heavenly Valley. Ski packages available in winter.

**Eagle's Nest Inn    $$$**                                      *(702) 588-6492*
At 472 Needle Peak Road, Stateline. The Eagle's Nest Inn has a ski-in, ski-out location adjacent to the Boulder Base lift on the Nevada side of Heavenly. Twenty deluxe suites all have king-size beds, spa tubs, TV, phones, and private decks. Amenities include covered parking, video game room, room service, and a bar and restaurant that serves breakfast, lunch and dinner.

**Harrah's    $$$**                       *(702) 588-6611, (800) 648-3773 West*
US 50 at Stateline, 1½ miles from Heavenly Valley. A Mobil Four Star and AAA Four Diamond winner, Harrah's has 537 stylish rooms decorated in earth tones, some with lake views. Rooms each have TV, phone, mini-bar, and 2 bathrooms (each with its own phone and TV). Butler service is available on the 16th floor. Amenities include an outdoor pool, hot tubs, and health club with suntan center. The hotel also houses a shopping mall, large casino, 4 restaurants and cocktail lounges, 2 showrooms with entertainment, a lounge with dancing, and a children's arcade and ice cream parlor. Concierge service and 24-hr room service. Conference space up to 22,000 sq ft. Free shuttle to Heavenly Valley and Lake Tahoe Airport in South Lake Tahoe. Ski packages with lift tickets available.

**Harvey's    $$$**                            *(702) 588-2411, (800) 548-3361*
US 50 at Stateline. High-rise resort hotel and casino with 2 towers and convention center complex, overlooking the lake. Rooms have phones, TV, marble bathrooms, refrigerators, and honor bars. Other facilities include 7 restaurants, numerous bars, casino, theater lounge entertainment, barber shop and beauty salon, gift shop, and ice cream parlor.

**Heavenly North Condominiums    $$$**           *(702) 588-8258, (800) 242-5387*
On Kingsbury Grade, ½ mile from the Stagecoach Lift, Stateline. 2-, 3-, and 4-bedroom condominiums with light wood accents and good views all have a fireplace, TV, and private Jacuzzi. Kitchens feature Jenn-Air ranges and barbecues and washer/dryer units. Ski packages available.

**Kingsbury of Tahoe Resort    $$$**                              *(702) 588-3553*
335 Tramway, Stateline. Uninspiring from the outside, these fully-appointed, luxury 2-bedroom condominiums and penthouses are attractive and spacious on the inside. Located a few minutes from Heavenly's Stagecoach lift, all units have TVs, VCRs with video-cassette library, 2 or 3 baths, and fully equipped kitchens with dishwashers, microwaves, and washers/dryers. Penthouses include Jacuzzi tub, and TV in the bedroom. A health club has Global exercise machines, tanning booths, sauna, and spa. Also available to guests is a Pub Room with stereo, TV, VCR, wet bar, backgammon table, pool table, and poker table. Racquetball/handball court. Complimentary transportation to the Stage Coach lift.

**Orion Condominiums     $$$**              *(702) 588-8258, (800) 242-5387*
Between Boulder and Stagecoach lifts on the Nevada Side of Heavenly, Stateline. Deluxe 3- and 4-bedroom units, each with 3 baths, have designer interiors, fireplaces, private Jacuzzis, and kitchens with microwaves, conventional ovens, washers/dryers, and private indoor garages.

**Pine Wild     $$$**              *(702) 588-2790, (800) 822-2790*
600 US 50 at Marla Bay. Deluxe lakefront condominiums are 3 miles east of Stateline. Fully equipped 3- and 4-bedroom, 3-bath townhouses, from 1,438 to 2,500 sq ft. Units are equipped with wood-burning fireplaces, TV, telephones, washers/dryers, and some with private hot tubs or Jacuzzi tubs.

**The Ridge Crest     $$$**              *(702) 588-3553, (800) 648-3391*
415 Tramway, Stateline, $1/4$ mile from the Nevada side lifts. Deluxe 1-bedroom units with TV and VCR, kitchens, and fireplaces. Extra charge for maid service.

**The Ridge Tahoe     $$$**              *(702) 588-3553, (800) 648-3391*
400 Ridge Club Dr., 6 miles south of the Stateline casinos via Kingsbury Grade, with private gondola to Heavenly. These posh 1- and 2-bedroom condominiums are decorated in soft shades of mauve and burgundy accented with oak cabinetry and brass details. All units have phones, TV, fireplaces, stereos, and fully equipped kitchens with washer/dryers. The Ridge Club facilities include an indoor-outdoor pool, fitness center, racquetball, indoor tennis, sauna, spa, piano lounge, and gourmet restaurant. Extra charge for maid service. Complimentary hourly shuttle to casinos until 1 a.m.

**Tahoe Seasons     $$$**              *(916) 541-6010,*
*(800) 874-9901 CA, and (800) 874-8770 outside CA*
Saddle Road at Keller, S. Lake Tahoe, 150 yards from the Heavenly Valley Ski Tram at the California base. The Tahoe Seasons has 160 suites and master suites that sleep 4 to 6. Entrance to the small but stylish sitting room in each suite is via the bedroom. An oversized spa tub is the centerpiece of each suite, which includes wet bar and fireplace. Kitchens in 1-bedroom suites have a gas range, microwave, and small refrigerator. Suites are uniformly decorated in rich green, soft rose, and light woods. Facilities include an attractive lobby and bar, elegant dining room with 8 fireplaces, heated pool, spa, gift and sundries shop, room service, conference rooms, underground valet parking, and concierge service. Complimentary 24-hr shuttle to Lake Tahoe Airport and casinos.

**Best Western Station House Inn     $$**              *(916) 542-1101, (800) 822-5953*
901 Park Ave., South Lake Tahoe, 1 mile from Heavenly Valley, 3 blocks from casinos, and a short walk from the Greyhound Station. Tastefully decorated rooms with private baths, TV, phones, and maid service. Facilities include a sauna and hot tub. A restaurant serving breakfast, lunch, and dinner, and a bar are on the premises. Conference rooms available. Complimentary full breakfast buffet, free shuttle to Heavenly Valley, Squaw Valley, Alpine Meadows, Kirkwood, and Sierra Ski Ranch. Package rates available.

**Best Western Timber Cove Lodge**   $$   *(916) 541-6722*
*(800) 528-1234 Nationwide*
On the beach at 3411 US 50 in S. Lake Tahoe, the Timber Cove Lodge has 262 rooms and suites, some with lake views. Rooms have double or king-size beds, or waterbeds. Rooms and mini-suites have sofa beds in the sitting area, and are pleasantly decorated in coordinated colors. All have TV and phones. Suites have refrigerators, vanities, and TV in the bedrooms. Facilities include 2 hot tubs, restaurant, bar, and conference rooms. Shuttle available to Heavenly Valley, Sierra Ski Ranch, Squaw Valley, Alpine Meadows, and Kirkwood, by reservation.

**The Christiana Inn**   $$   *(916) 544-7337, (800) 422-5754*
At 3819 Saddle Road, S. Lake Tahoe, directly across from the Heavenly Valley lifts on the California side, this charming bed-and-breakfast features rooms with sitting areas, individually decorated with careful attention. Suites feature old-fashioned decor, wood-burning fireplaces, and sitting areas with wet bar, steam showers, or private sauna. Facilities include a sauna and whirlpool, a cozy fireside lounge with a bar and large-screen TV, and a dining room.

**Del Webb's High Sierra Casino Hotel**   $$   *(702) 588-6211*
*(800) 648-3322 western states*
*(800) 648-3395 other states including Hawaii*
US 50 at Stateline, 1½ miles from ski lifts. High-rise hotel and casino's 537 first-class rooms and suites are decorated in a western theme. All have TV, phones, and some with lake views. Facilities include hot tubs, room service, 1-acre casino, 4 restaurants, cabaret with live entertainment, and Lily's dance club. Conference rooms available.

**Inn by the Lake**   $$   *(916) 541-7711, (800) 535-0330 CA*
*(800) 822-5922 Nationwide*
At 3300 Lake Tahoe Blvd. (SH 50), S. Lake Tahoe, 2 miles west of Stateline and 1 mile from Heavenly, across the highway from the lake. This first-class motor inn has 98 spacious rooms and suites with kitchens. Units are decorated in light fabrics with a contemporary look, and have phones, TV, and balconies. Some have wet bars. A heated pool, sauna, hot tub, laundry, and ski racks are also available. Conference room for 50 on the premises. Complimentary coffee and pastries. A coffee shop and pizza hut are adjacent. Free shuttle to casinos and lifts.

**Lakeside Inn & Casino**   $$   *(702) 588-7777, (800) 624-7980*
US 50 at Kingsbury Grade, Stateline, ½ mile from the big casinos and 3 miles from the lifts. The 124 rooms and parlor suites vary from budget to moderate. Facilities include 24-hour Timber House Restaurant serving breakfast, lunch, and dinner, a full casino and lounge with live entertainment, dancing, and televised sporting events. Conference rooms.

**Tahoe Beach and Ski Club**   $$   *(916) 541-6220, (800) 822-5962*
3601 US 50, S. Lake Tahoe. ¾ mile from Stateline casinos, near Ski Run Blvd. The Tahoe Beach and Ski Club has 152 first-class rooms, studios, and suites, accented with warm woods and brass. Rooms have phones, TV, and balconies.

Facilities include a heated pool, sauna whirlpool, ski shop, general store, restaurant, lounge, meeting rooms, and a shuttle to the casinos.

**Tahoe Marina Inn**  $$  *(916) 541-2180*
930 Balijou, on the beach off US 50, 1 mile from Heavenly Valley. The Inn has 79 modern motel units, each with 1 or 2 beds, some with kitchens, and 1-bedroom condominium units for 1 to 4 persons. All units have a phone and TV, most with balcony and lake view. Condo units have a fully equipped kitchen, a small living area, loft, fireplace, private balcony, and reserved parking. Facilities include a heated swimming pool, sauna, ski lockers, and meeting room.

**Elm Inn**  $  *(916) 541-7900, (800) 822-5955 CA*
*(800) 822-5922, ext. 223 Nationwide*
4082 SH 50, 1/2 block from Stateline. Two-story motel with king- and queen-size beds in rooms, with TV, phone, and maid service. Hot tub, car rental service, restaurant, and cocktail lounge are on site. Ski packages available. Near shuttle stop.

**Pacifica Lodge**  $  *(916) 544-4131, (800) 822-5922*
931 Park Ave., S. Lake Tahoe, 1 mile from Heavenly Valley lifts and 5 blocks from casinos. A variety of rooms in 2- and 3-story buildings and chalet-style cabins have king-size or double beds or waterbed, TV, and some patios. Suites with sunken tubs and fireplaces available. Two-bedroom apartments have fireplaces and kitchens. Hot tub on premises. Ski shuttle bus across the street.

**Royal Valhalla Motor Lodge**  $  *(916) 544-2233*
Lakeshore and Stateline, off US 50. Plain studios and 1- or 2-bedroom suites, some with kitchens and balconies, include TV and phone. Laundry on premises. Shuttle bus across the street.

**Tahoe West Motor Lodge**  $  *(916) 544-6455, (800) 822-5922*
4082 Pine Blvd., 2 blocks from Stateline casinos and 1 mile to Heavenly Valley. Comfortable rooms with 1 or 2 queen-size beds, TV, and phones. Some kitchenettes and suites. Facilities include a Jacuzzi and sauna. Complimentary coffee and doughnuts. Shuttle bus to casinos. Ski packages available.

# Sierra Ski Ranch

❄

P.O. Box 3501
Twin Bridges, CA 95735
Information: (916) 659-7453
Snowphone: (916) 659-7475

### Driving distances

| | |
|---|---|
| Kings Beach | 52 mi |
| Las Vegas | 477 mi |
| Los Angeles | 469 mi |
| Reno | 72 mi |
| Sacramento | 83 mi |
| San Diego | 572 mi |
| San Francisco | 170 mi |
| San Jose | 200 mi |
| Tahoe City | 42 mi |
| Truckee | 63 mi |

*For road conditions, call*
*(916) 577-3550*

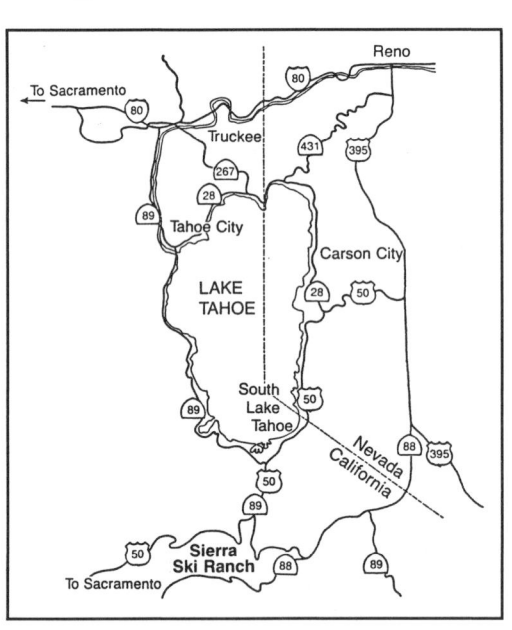

Like the images of fun and adventure conjured up by its name, Huckleberry Mountain at Sierra Ski Ranch lures skiers to frolic away the day on its mostly intermediate, wind-protected slopes. A handful of black-diamond rascals encountered along the way add just enough mischief to make a good tale at the end of the day.

Adding to the fun are special events that range from the zany "Cupid's Capers" on Valentine's Day and Beer Slalom on St. Patrick's Day to the annual battle of the lawmakers, when California congressmen challenge their Nevada counterparts on the slopes for the "cup."

Cut into the El Dorado National Forest, Sierra Ski Ranch has a dual advantage: It's Sacramento's closest ski area, yet only a shuttle-bus ride away from the excitement of South Lake Tahoe.

With reasonable rates, friendly staff, and lodge facilities that include multi-level sun decks, Sierra Ski Ranch projects a lively atmosphere that young, eager skiers find just right.

## LOCATION

Sierra Ski Ranch is in El Dorado County, off US 50 at Twin Bridges, CA, 12 miles southwest of South Lake Tahoe and 83 miles east of Sacramento.

Traveling from San Francisco or Sacramento, US 50 is a 4-lane road to Riverton, where it narrows to 2 lanes and winds its way up to Sierra Ski Ranch at 6,640 ft. Sierra Ski Ranch Road is a right turn off US 50, and 2.2 miles to the base.

From Reno and US 395 or South Lake Tahoe, take US 50 along the South Shore and turn left at the junction of US 50 with SH 89, 8 miles past the town of Meyers.

The Lake Tahoe Airport is 10 miles from Sierra Ski Ranch, with scheduled service direct from San Francisco and San Jose and connections from other California cities. In heavy weather conditions, these flights sometimes bypass the airport and land in Reno instead. Free shuttle transportation operates daily from Stateline to Sierra Ski Ranch.

Cannon International Airport in Reno is the closest major airport to Sierra Ski Ranch, which is also serviced by the Sacramento airport. Four-wheel-drive and cars equipped for skiers are available for rental at all 3 airports.

Amtrak stops in Sacramento, as well as in Truckee and Reno/Sparks. Train service from Los Angeles to Reno runs daily. Autos with chains and racks are available for rent in Truckee at the AAA Auto Rental, adjacent to the Amtrak station. During the peak winter season, 4-wheel-drive vehicles should be reserved a month or more in advance.

Greyhound also operates bus service into South Lake Tahoe 6 to 8 times daily.

## TERRAIN

Although Sierra Ski Ranch contains a surprising 2,000 acres, the runs off Huckleberry Mountain are never more than one chair lift away. Advanced skiers can take the Sensation Lift and rattle down the rougher steeps of *Dynamite* and *Preacher's Passion*, or test their turns on *The Chute*. *Eastbowl* is less steep but amply mogul-loaded.

Wide intermediate runs like *Powderhorn* and *Horsetail* are clustered in the *West Bowl* under the Cougar and Puma lifts and on the back side below the Ranchouse Cafeteria.

The broad, gentle beginner slopes are in front of the base lodge, but beginners will also find their own space on *Sunshine Alley* and *Wagon Wheel* on the back side of the mountain. They can glide all the way from top to bottom on the gentle *Sugar and Spice* trail.

## FACILITIES AT A GLANCE

*Season:* November–April.
*Hours:* 9 a.m.–4:30 p.m. daily.
*Night Skiing:* None.
*Area:* 2,000 acres with 38 runs.
  Beginner: 20%
  Intermediate: 60%
  Advanced: 20%

*Base Elevation:* 6,640 ft
*Summit Elevation:* 8,852 ft
*Vertical Drop:* 2,212 ft
*Longest Run:* 3 1/2 miles.
*Snowmaking:* On problem areas only.
*Snowboarding:* Not permitted.
*Avg. Annual Snowfall:* 450 in.
*Lift Capacity:* 12,600 per hr.

*Lifts:* 9 chair lifts (1 high-speed quad, 6 doubles, 2 triples)

| Name | Length | Vertical |
| --- | --- | --- |
| Blue Jay | 1,170 ft | 113 ft |
| Cougar | 5,019 ft | 1,422 ft |
| Eldorado | 3,490 ft | 728 ft |
| Little Chipmunk | 1,140 ft | 145 ft |
| Nob Hill | 3,604 ft | 860 ft |
| Puma | 5,288 ft | 1,471 ft |
| Rock Garden | 1,500 ft | 322 ft |
| Sensation | 5,170 ft | 1,580 ft |
| Short Stuff | 1,520 ft | 222 ft |

*Lift Passes:*

| | All Day | Afternoon Only |
| --- | --- | --- |
| | 9 a.m. to 4:30 p.m. | 1:15 p.m.–4:30 p.m. |
| Adults | $27 | $20 |
| Children under 12 | $13 | $10 |
| Seniors 54+ | $13 | $10 |

*Group Rates:*   Available by prior arrangement.

*Season Passes:*   Price depends on date of purchase.

|  | Prior to Sep 15 | Sep 16–Oct 31 | After 31 Oct |
|---|---|---|---|
| Adult | $450 | $475 | $500 |
| Child | $200 | $225 | $250 |
| Student 13–18 | $230 | $260 | $290 |
| Midweek* | $325 | $350 | $375 |

*\*The adult midweek pass is valid Monday through Friday except Thanksgiving, Christmas, and Presidents' weekend.*

*Food & Drink:*   In the main lodge, 3 cafeterias with sun decks feature hot entrées, deli foods, and barbecue lunches, weather permitting. The Ranchouse, at the top of Sensation and Eldorado chair lifts, offers snacks, pizza, and barbecue on the upper sun deck. Open 10 a.m. to 4 p.m.

*Parking & Transportation:*   Parking is free at the base. Parking for RVs, daytime only. Complimentary ski shuttle from South Lake Tahoe's casino area 5 times daily, with returns at 2, 3:30, and 5 p.m. For shuttle information call (916) 659-7453 or 659-7535.

*Ski Rentals:*   The base lodge shop is open from 8 a.m. until 5 p.m. weekdays, and 7:30 a.m. to 5 p.m. on weekends and holidays. Includes skis, boots, and poles.

All day: Adult $16. Child $11.
Half day: Adult $12. Child $8.
Demo skis: $18.

*Ski School:*   Phone (916) 659-7475.

*Method:*   ATM.

*Ski School Director:*   Don Greb.

*Class Lessons:*   10:15 a.m. and 1:45 p.m. daily.
$16 (2 hr)
$27 (4 hr)

*Beginner Special:*   $25 includes 4-hr lesson and beginner lifts only: Blue Jay, Little Chipmunk and Rock Garden chair lifts. Must be purchased by 10:30 a.m.

*Superstar Snow School:*   Ages 3–6, Edelweiss Bldg. Includes lessons, lifts, equipment, and supervised ski play.
$40 8:30 a.m.–4 p.m. Includes lunch.
$28 1 p.m.–4 p.m.

*(continued on next page)*

*(continued from previous page)*
  *Private Lessons:*  9:30 a.m. and 12:30 p.m. daily.
    $32 per hr.
    All-day lessons available by prior arrangement.
  *Handicapped:*  By prior arrangement.
  *Telemark Lessons:*  Available upon request.
*Races & Clinics:*  Flying 50: Standard race every Sunday. First run $2, additional run $1.
  *Sierra Tahoe Ski Team:*  Includes season lift pass and weekend coaching all season, $750.
  *Racing Clinics:*  Available upon request from Ski School, with minimum participation required.
*Day Care:*  Day care is available 12 miles northeast in South Lake Tahoe.
*Camper Facilities:*  KOA Kampground, US 50 and Upper Truckee Road in Tahoe Paradise, 6 miles east, has tent sites for $15. RV sites $22. Hookups. (916) 577-3693.
*Medical:*  First aid in the main lodge administered by pro patrol. The closest hospital is Barton Memorial in South Lake Tahoe.
*Other:*  Lockers are available in the main lodge. Ski lock racks can also be rented in the base area.

## SPECIAL EVENTS

- *Mogul Races*—Every other Friday. For advanced skiers on lower Dynamite.
- *Pacific Crest Telemark Race Series*—January.
- *Winter Carnival*—January.
- *Lawmaker's Cup*—January. California legislators vs. Nevada legislators.
- *Cupid's Capers*—Valentine's Day. Skiers can match a number written on half a heart with the half held by a member of the opposite sex.
- *Seniors' Racing and BBQ*—February.
- *Exceptional Children's Ski Adventure*—February.
- *Beer Barrel Slalom*—St. Patrick's Day. Participants use skis made from a beer barrel and ski around obstacles of beer, which they must drink.
- *Preschoolers Snow Play and Picnic Day*—March.
- *All Levels Racing Competition*—March.
- *Bunny Chase*—Easter week.

## WINTER ACTIVITIES

### Cross-Country

*Strawberry Canyon Cross-Country* area is 6 miles west of Sierra Ski Ranch on US 50 at Strawberry Lodge. Due to its low elevation (5,600 ft), the area tends to have a short Nordic ski season. The 11 miles of well-marked beginner and intermediate trails head south and west over 6,800 ft elevations. There are no trail fees or lessons.

Fred Hartmeyer of *Cody's Hut Ski Treks* conducts guided day and overnight treks, for intermediate and advanced skiers, from Strawberry Lodge to Cody's Hut. The hut, which dates back to 1915, is a log cabin dormitory with a pot-bellied stove and indoor and outdoor plumbing. The trail connects to *Kirkwood Cross-Country* between Caples Lake and Kirkwood Ski Area on SH 88. Trails require 6 or 7 hours of skiing. Participants should also be able to traverse downhill.

Beginners can take the Markleeville/Hot Springs Trek. Prices range from $35 to $70 and reservations are required, (916) 626-5097.

*Sierra Ski Ranch on a great powder day!* (Courtesy of Sierra Ski Ranch.)

A restaurant and bar, as well as equipment rentals are available at Strawberry Lodge, which also offers simple economy rooms with old plumbing fixtures, (916) 659-7200.

Five miles west of Sierra Ski Ranch on US 50 at Riverton, Ice House Road leads north 30 miles to the *Loon Lake* cross-country area. Ungroomed trails for all levels range in length from 1$^{1}/_{2}$ to 2 $^{1}/_{2}$ miles. Located just west of Desolation Wilderness, the area is remote and skiers should take extra precautions against weather and avalanches.

The *Echo Lakes* cross-country trail is located 2 miles east off US 50 on Echo Road at Little Norway. Parking is free and there are no trail fees. The intermediate trail goes around the lakes. Entrance into the Desolation Wilderness is by permit only. Permits can be obtained from the U.S. Forest Service. A restaurant, bar, and 2 lodging rooms are available at Little Norway. An unmarked trail is also located across the highway from Little Norway on the south side of US 50 in Ben Meadows. For information, call (916) 573-2600.

See Heavenly Valley for information on snowmobiling, sledding, snow play, sleigh rides, fitness, racquetball, and theater.

## OTHER ACTIVITIES

**Sightseeing:** Historic gold rush town, Placerville; Marshall Gold Discovery Historic State Park, Coloma; Historic 19th century town, Diamond Springs.

**Wine Tasting:** Eldorado Vineyard, Camino; Madrona Vineyards, between Placerville and Camino; Lava Cap Winery and Boeger Winery, Placerville.

## SHOPPING

The *Ski Shop* in the Main Lodge at Sierra Ski Ranch carries a selection of skiwear, accessories, and sundries. The *Pow Wow Ski and Sport*, US 50 at the entrance to the ski area, rents downhill and cross-country skis and saucers for snow play. The shop also sells ski fashions and accessories. West of Sierra Ski Ranch, the *Bennett Sculpture House* is on US 50. A grocery store and deli are located in *Twin Bridges*. Further west in Kyburz, the *Strawberry Market* and a general store are near the Strawberry Lodge. Heading toward South Lake Tahoe, a general store is located adjacent to *Little Norway*, 2 miles east.

Forty-six miles west in Placerville, antique hunters can browse for items such as pot-bellied stoves, brass beds, and painted china. Nearby Diamond Springs and Coloma also offer antique opportunities.

For additional shopping information, see Heavenly Valley.

## APRÈS-SKI

*Little Norway*, on US 50 just 2 miles east of the Sierra Ski Ranch, is the closest watering hole for skiers returning to the South Lake Tahoe area. For those heading west toward Sacramento, the *Strawberry Lodge* offers mountain-lodge ambience, with a large fireplace, overhead TV, and ample bar. The bar closes at 2 a.m. or when everyone goes home. On weekends there's dancing to live country, top-40, or rock music.

For après-ski suggestions in South Lake Tahoe, see Heavenly Valley.

## RESTAURANTS

**Little Norway**  $$ *(916) 659-7181*
On US 50, 2 miles east of Sierra Ski Ranch, Little Norway's restuarant is open from 9 a.m. until midnight and will open earlier for anyone who wants breakfast sooner. Dinner entrées include filet mignon, chicken cordon bleu, and fried shrimp. For smaller appetites, there are burgers, salads, and burritos. Wine, beer, and sodas are also available.

**Strawberry Lodge**  $$ *(916) 659-7200*
On US 50 in Strawberry, 6 miles west of Sierra Ski Ranch, the Strawberry Lodge is open for breakfast, lunch, and dinner. A large stone fireplace adds to the rustic mountain atmosphere. Selections include broiled halibut, trout, scampi, chicken specials, and steak. Wine list.

**St. Paul Inn**  $$ *(916) 293-3384*
US 50 in Pollack Pines, 29 miles west of Sierra Ski Ranch. The Inn is open daily for dinner from 5 p.m. to 9 p.m. and serves sausage, steak, chicken, veal, and BBQ ribs.

For a variety of dining choices available 12 miles northeast in South Lake Tahoe, see Heavenly Valley.

## ACCOMMODATIONS

With no lodging located at the mountain, Sierra Ski Ranch has developed inclusive ski packages with several South Lake Tahoe properties, ranging from rustic lodges to deluxe casino hotels. For information on lodging packages at Sierra Ski Ranch, contact the Lake Tahoe Visitor's Authority, (800) 822-5922. For additional accommodations in South Lake Tahoe, see Heavenly Valley.

**Little Norway**  $ *(916) 659-7181*
On US 50, 2 miles east of Sierra Ski Ranch, Little Norway rents just 2 rooms with queen-size beds, rollaways, and private baths. Rooms sleep up to 2 adults and 2 children. No TV or phones. Maid service, restaurant, and bar.

**Stagecoach Motor Inn** $ *(916) 644-2029*
5940 Pony Express Trail, Pollack Pines, 35 miles west of the mountain. The 2-story Inn with outside balcony has 26 doubles and patio suites, some with king-size beds, all with private baths, 6 with kitchenettes. TV, phone, and air conditioning in rooms. Free coffee and donuts. Conference room.

**Strawberry Lodge** $ *(916) 659-7200*
US 50 in Strawberry. A variety of basic rooms with twin, double, queen-size, or king-size beds, located in the main lodge and in a 1-story annex across US 50. Built in the 1930s, rooms and plumbing are old and worn but clean. Most rooms have toilet and shower. No phones or TV.

# Kirkwood

❄

P.O. Box 1
*Kirkwood, CA 95646.*
*Information: (916) 258-6000*
*Snowphone: (916) 258-3000*

| Driving distances | |
|---|---|
| Las Vegas | 496 mi |
| Los Angeles | 439 mi |
| Reno | 80 mi |
| Sacramento | 114 mi |
| San Diego | 592 mi |
| San Francisco | 201 mi |
| San Jose | 231 mi |
| Stockton | 99 mi |
| Tahoe City | 60 mi |
| Truckee | 81 mi |

*For road conditions, call*
*(209) 223-4455*

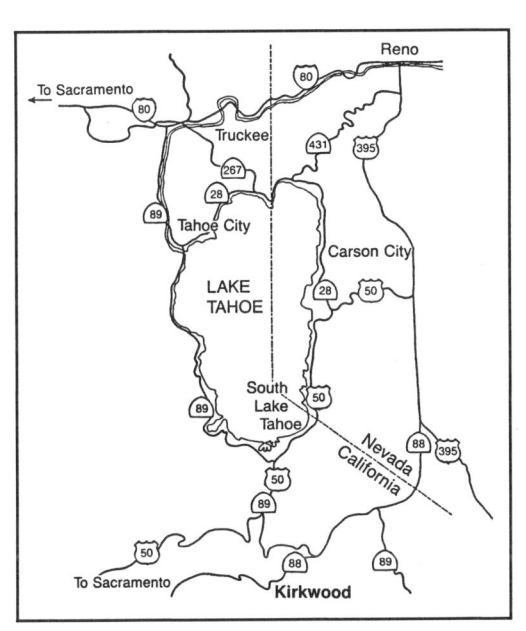

Thirty miles from the neon glitter of South Lake Tahoe, Kirkwood is a self-contained resort with a split personality.

By day, the slopes rock with excitement as skiers pound a path between jagged peaks and whoosh down fast-groomed runs. Even lunch is a spirited affair. Smoky whiffs of barbecued chicken and ribs intermingle with animated conversation on the sunny, outdoor deck. Nearby, sleigh bells and laughter chime in the wind.

By night the rhythm slows as skiers shift into low gear. Bodies recharge in a hot tub, and dinner is enjoyed leisurely at any of the 5 base restaurants. Then, as skiers retreat to condominiums that range from luxury to budget, a calm settles over the village and the night is filled with the quiet of the High Sierra winter. Until morning, that is, when the lifts reopen and, once again, the mountain explodes with the collective exuberance of beginners and experts alike.

## LOCATION

Kirkwood is located on SH 88, 30 miles south of Lake Tahoe, where Alpine, Almador, and El Dorado counties meet. From South Lake Tahoe, follow US 50 south 4 miles to SH 89. Turn left and go 11 miles to SH 88, turn right and go 15 miles, past Carson Pass and Caples Lake, to Kirkwood. From Sacramento, it's a left turn from US 50 to SH 89 and then right on SH 88. From Reno, the SH 88 turnoff is 36 miles south on US 395. Follow SH 88 south then east 44 miles to Kirkwood. Skiers from Stockton can take SH 88 all the way to Kirkwood.

The Lake Tahoe Airport is 28 miles from Kirkwood, with scheduled service direct from San Fransisco and San Jose and connections from other California cities. Depending on weather conditions, these flights sometimes bypass the airport and land in Reno instead. Shuttle transportation operates daily from Stateline and South Lake Tahoe to Kirkwood, (916) 258-6000.

Other airports serving the area are in Reno, Stockton, and Sacramento. Four-wheel-drive and cars equipped for skiers are available for rental at the Lake Tahoe, Reno, and Sacramento airports, but not at Stockton Airport.

Amtrak stops in Stockton and Sacramento, as well as in Truckee and Reno/Sparks. Train service from Los Angeles to Reno is available daily. Autos with chains and racks are available for rent in Truckee at the AAA Auto Rental, adjacent to the Amtrak station. During the busy season, 4-wheel-drive vehicles should be reserved a month or more in advance.

Greyhound also operates bus service into South Lake Tahoe 6 to 8 times daily.

## TERRAIN

Because of its high base elevation at 7,800 ft, Kirkwood's summit is only one chair-ride away from the base. And when unusually warm winter temperatures produce rain at lower elevations in the Tahoe area, chances are it's snowing at Kirkwood, ensuring a season that generally lasts until May. Still, Kirkwood enjoys sunshine about 70% of the time.

Although 50% intermediate, Kirkwood is known more for its advanced slopes that cover 35% of the skiable terrain. Most of the black-diamond runs, like *The Wall*, are off Chair 10, which services expert slopes only. A skull and crossbones marks the entry to the lift line at Chair 10, warning those who are unfamiliar with the mountain. From the top of 10, the skier can turn left to single black-diamond runs like *Wagon Trail*. To the right, along the cornice, under the *The Sisters* and *False Peak*, a half-dozen double diamonds drop into a wide, steep bowl. Less intimidating are the dozen or so single diamond runs and chutes off Chair 6 including *Chamonix*, *Olympic*, and *Look-out-Janek*, a faithful mogul run. The cluster of advanced slopes off Chair 4 also harbor a number of chutes. *Thunder Saddle* holds powder the longest between snows.

Intermediate runs are groomed to be fast. The longest blue trails like *Elevator Shaft* are in the wide bowl, to the left at the top of chair 4. *Buckboard*, under *The Wall*, is another intermediate favorite.

Beginners will find easygoing runs off Chair 1 or Chair 9 where the terrain flattens out. Because there are no steep runs above Chair 9, novices in this area are less likely to be run down by hotshot skiers storming down from the top.

## FACILITIES

Kirkwood has 2 base lodges, each with ski shops, rentals, and eating facilities.

Kirkwood also participates in the Ski Tahoe interchangeable lift ticket with Heavenly Valley, Squaw Valley, Alpine Meadows, and Northstar-at-Tahoe. Ski 5 out of 6 days for $32 per day.

The "Kirkwood Kard" costs $15 and allows the skier to purchase a lift ticket for $28 any day of the season. Skiers also receive discounts when they purchase lessons through various Northern California Safeway markets.

Lodging packages at the mountain include 3-nights' lodging and a 3-day lift ticket for $205 per person midweek or $243 per person weekends, based on double occupancy. Five-night packages with 5-day lift tickets are $342.50 per person, double occupancy.

Kirkwood guarantees that beginners who take 2 lessons will be able to ski the beginner runs or they'll receive free instruction until they do. Kirkwood also promises intermediate and advanced skiers that they'll ski 3,000 vertical ft during a lesson.

Skiers who purchase lift tickets and return them by 12:30 p.m. can receive a half-day credit coupon.

### FACILITIES AT A GLANCE

| | |
|---|---|
| *Season:* | Mid-November–May. |
| *Hours:* | 8:30 a.m.–4:30 p.m. |
| *Night Skiing:* | None. |
| *Area:* | 2,000 acres with 68 runs. |
| | Beginner: 15% |
| | Intermediate: 50% |
| | Advanced: 20% |
| *Base Elevation:* | 7,800 ft |

*(continued on next page)*

*(continued from previous page)*

| | |
|---|---|
| *Summit Elevation:* | 9,876 ft |
| *Vertical Drop:* | 2,000 ft |
| *Longest Run:* | 2.5 miles. |
| *Snowmaking:* | None. |
| *Snowboarding:* | Not permitted. |
| *Avg. Annual Snowfall:* | 425 in. |
| *Lift Capacity:* | 15,000 per hr. |

*Lifts:*   11 lifts (4 triples, 6 doubles, and 1 surface lift)

| Name | Length | Vertical Rise |
|---|---|---|
| 1 Snowkirk | 3,335 ft | 425 ft |
| 2 Caples Crest | 3,000 ft | 600 ft |
| 3 Iron Horse | 2,500 ft | 400 ft |
| 4 Sunrise | 5,500 ft | 1,200 ft |
| 5 Solitude | 3,000 ft | 800 ft |
| 6 Cornice | 4,500 ft | 1,400 ft |
| 7 Hole 'n' Wall | 2,995 ft | 500 ft |
| 8 Puma Lift Tow | 300 ft | 20 ft |
| 9 Bunny | 1,500 ft | 200 ft |
| 10 The Wall | 6,000 ft | 1,700 ft |
| 11 The Reut | 4.000 ft | 900 ft |

*Lift Tickets:*

| | All Day | Half Day |
|---|---|---|
| | 8:30 a.m.–4:30 p.m. | 12:30 p.m.–4:30 p.m. |
| Adults | $33 | $24 |
| Children under 12 | $15 | $10 |
| Seniors 60 + | $15 | $10 |

Adult beginner $20 (Chairs 1 & 9 only)
Child beginner $10 (Chairs 1 & 9 only)

*Multiday Rates:*

| | Adult | Child |
|---|---|---|
| 3 out of 5 days | $93 | $36 |
| 5 out of 6 days | $150 | $50 |

*Season Passes:*   If purchased prior to Nov. 1— adult $525, junior (13–18) $325, child $150, and adult midweek, $325.

If purchased after Nov. 1—adult $625, junior $375, child $200, and adult midweek $425. Family discounts for second adult and dependents.

*Group Rates:* Available by prior arrangement for 20 or more. $28 adult lift pass, $10 child, and 1 free pass per every 20.

*Food & Drink:* A cafeteria, bar, and sun-deck grill are in the Red Cliffs Lodge at the mountain base, along with an Italian deli, croissant shop, and ice cream parlor. La Cocina has tacos and burritos. A cafeteria is also located in Timber Creek Lodge adjacent to lifts 7 and 9, along with Snowshoe Thompson's Bar and Grill, which serves lunch and dinner. The warming hut at Chair 4 offers chili, snacks, and beverages. At the base, The Cornice Cafe and Bar and the Whiskey Creek Bar and Grill are open for lunch and dinner.

*Parking & Transportation:* Free parking at base with shuttle to lifts. Free shuttle also for skiers staying at South Lake Tahoe lodges.

*Ski Rentals:* The base rental shop is open from 8 a.m. to 5 p.m. Includes skis, poles, and boots.
    All day:   Adult $16.   Child $10.
    Half day:   Adult $10.   Child $7.
    High performance skis:
        All day, adult $22.
        Half day, adult $17.
    Cross-country:
        All day, adult $12.   Child $7.
        Half day, adult $9.   Child $4.

*Ski School:* (209) 258-7245.
  *Method:* ATM.
  *Ski School Director:* Peter Curtis.
  *Class Lessons:* 10:15 a.m. and 2 p.m.
    $18 (2 hr)
    $28 (4 hr)

*Beginner Special:* $40 includes 4-hr lesson, use of beginner lift ticket, and equipment rental.

*Skier's Special:* $50 includes 4-hr lesson, all-day lift ticket, and equipment rental.

*Mighty Mountain:* Ages 4–12. 10:30 a.m.–3:30 p.m. at Timber Creek Lodge. Reservations required on weekends.
  $45 includes lessons, lunch, equipment rental, lift ticket, and snacks.
  $22 half-day, 12:45 p.m.–3:30 p.m. No lunch.

*(continued on next page)*

*(continued from previous page)*

    *Private Lessons:* 9 a.m. and 12:30 p.m.
    $40 (1¹/₂ hr) lesson. Additional person $18.
    *Super Lesson:* "The Double Black Diamond Challenge" is designed for expert skiers who can ski any run, under any snow conditions. The lesson shows skiers where to find Kirkwood's best terrain.
    $10 (1¹/₂ hr).
    *Ski Test:* Skiers have an opportunity to test 3 pairs of skis best suited to them during lesson.
    *Handicapped:* Blind skiers' program.
    *Powder and Mogul Lessons:* Upon request, snow conditions permitting.

*Races & Clinics:*
    *Daily Races with Electronic Timer:* Off Chair 5.
    10:30 a.m.–3:30 p.m. 50¢ a race.
    *Clinics:* "Three Days to Better Skiing" camp held each month in winter. The package includes 3-day lift tickets, 5 hours of training, 2 nights' lodging, continental breakfast, wine-and-cheese party, banquet, and video analysis. $330 (per person, double occupancy).
    *Individual Race Coaching:* Offered at same rate as private lessons.

*Day Care:* Ages 3–8. 8:30 a.m.–4:30 p.m. For non-skiing children. Must be toilet trained.
    $5 per hr with 2-hr minimum. Lunch $5 additional.
    $30 all day, including lunch.
    $20 half day, 12 p.m.–5 p.m., including lunch.

*Camper Facilities:* Bear River Lake Resort, 40800 SH 88, 21 miles west of Kirkwood, has 120 camp sites and 75 RV hookups. Fees for the unplowed sites are $14.50–$16.50. Tent sites are $5–10. Facilities include general store, snack bar, laundromat. Additional campgrounds are located at South Lake Tahoe.

*Medical:* A clinic at the mountain is staffed by nurses and doctors on a rotating basis. Closest hospital is Barton Memorial, 30 miles north at South Lake Tahoe.

*Other:* Ski shop, locker and basket rental, gas station.

## SPECIAL EVENTS

- *Santa on Skis*—December 19–25. Strolling carolers, jugglers, magicians.
- *Torchlight Parade and Live Entertainment*—December 31.
- *Family Ski Carnival*—January. Cantina and races.
- *USSA Ballet Competition*—January.
- *USSA Mogul Event*—January.
- *Masters Slalom*—January. USSA members over 25.
- *Kirkwood Mogul Challenge*—January. Speed, technique and aerial maneuvers on 4-ft high moguls.
- *Women's Ski Adventure*—January and February. 4 days of coaching for women by women.
- *Blind Sports International Ski Race*—February.
- *Easter Holiday*—Easter. Children's egg hunt, Easter Bunny.

## WINTER ACTIVITIES

### Cross-Country

*Kirkwood's* 3 connected trail systems spread over 4,200 acres of open bowls and meadows that wind through pine forests. The 29 miles of groomed double tracks and skating lanes are 20% beginner, 60% intermediate, and 20% advanced. A children's Nordic track has child-size obstacles and colorful signs. Facilities include a day lodge and 3 warming huts, 2 parking lots, ski school, and a rental and retail shop. Course rates are $12 for adults and $7 for children ages 7–12, or half day at $9 for adults and $4 for children. Children under 6 ski free. Discounts apply for seniors. Multiday passes, season passes, and twilight passes, beginning at 3 p.m., are also available.

The ski school teaches all ability levels and telemark and biathlon skiing, (209) 258-3000. Class lessons including a trail pass are $22 adult and $16 child. Rental rates are $12 adult and $8 child for all day, and $9 adult and $5 child for half day.

Additional cross-country trails are located 7 miles east of Kirkwood at *Carson Pass Sno-Park*, on SH 88 at Winnemucca Lake. One trail, for intermediate and advanced skiers, circles the lake. The other heads north from SH 88 10 miles to SH 89. Parking is by Sno-Park permit only. No rentals or lessons. Another trail further east runs from SH 88 to Red Lake.

*Hope Valley Cross-Country* at Sorensen's Resort is 14 miles east of Kirkwood on SH 88, $1/2$ mile past the junction with SH 89. Half of the 25 miles of beginner trails are groomed by the Forest Service. No fee, but donations accepted.

230    Skier's Guide to California

*These three Kirkwood skiers are enjoying all the elements of a "classic" ski vacation. (Courtesy of Kirkwood.)*

Sorensen's Resort provides guided day and moonlight tours and rents equipment for $12 a day and $5 for half day. The lodge includes a cafe, which serves beer and wine, breakfast, lunch, and dinner, Thursday to Sunday from 6 p.m. to 8 p.m. Overnight accommodations that sleep from 2 to 8 persons, are available in 23 log cabins and cottages, all with cooking facilities. The lodge also has 3 bed-and-breakfast rooms, (916) 694-2203.

North from SH 88 on SH 89 at the summit of Luther Pass is an unmarked flat trail at *Grass Lake*. The trail runs over a frozen bog and through aspen groves. The *Big Meadow* trails, located 5 miles south of US 50 on SH 89, are unmarked and have an elevation gain of 800 ft. The trails, for advanced skiers, head to Round Lake, Meiss Lake, and Dardanelles Lake.

*Sierra Ski Touring* rents cross-country skis in downtown Markleville and teaches group and private lessons. Rates are $30 per hour with a minimum of 2 skiers. Guided tours include overnight treks to Meiss Hut on the headwaters of the Truckee, with meals included. The cost for the Hut Tour is $95 for 2 nights or $135 for 3 days. Special tours include Hut Cuisine, a back-country gourmet cooking weekend, and a special back-country weekend for women. For dates and reservations, call (916) 577-8557.

For other cross-country courses nearby, see Heavenly Valley and Sierra Ski Ranch.

## Snowmobiling

Snowmobile trails are located in *Hope Valley*, 10 miles north of Kirkwood on SH 88 and at *Bear River*, 14 miles west on SH 88 toward Jackson. See Heavenly Valley for snowmobiling around South Lake Tahoe.

## Tobogganing, Tubing, and Snow Play

A snow-play area for sledding and tubing is available at Carson Pass Sno-Park, 7 miles east on SH 88. Parking by Sno-Park permit.

## Sleigh Rides

The *Lazy K* pack station at Kirkwood offers day and moonlight sleigh rides in a 9-passenger sleigh drawn by Belgian horses. Rides depart from the Kirkwood Inn to Timber Creek Lodge and Red Cliffs Lodge. Rates are $8 for adults and $5 for children, (209) 258-7433.

## Mountaineering

*Sierra Ski Touring* conducts training in mountaineering, including wilderness winter survival courses, avalanche courses, dogsled handling for mushers, and basic mountaineering. For dates and fees, call (916) 577-8557.

**Dogsled Rides**

Wilderness tours via dogsled are conducted through Hope Valley by *Huskey Express*. The rate for 2 persons is $60 for ½ hour and $95 for 1 hour, (916) 577-8557.

## OTHER ACTIVITIES

For other activities available in South Lake Tahoe, see Heavenly Valley.

## APRÈS-SKI

When the lifts close, skiers linger at *Zak's Bar* at the Red Cliffs Lodge to munch appetizers and, on weekends, dance to disco or live bands. The *Cornice Cafe* also has live entertainment on weekends. Locals entertain on Monday nights. The bar is open from 10 a.m. to 11 p.m. and midnight on weekends. See Heavenly Valley for night life at Stateline, 35 miles north.

## RESTAURANTS

**Caples Lake Restaurant   $$**                              *(209) 258-8888*
On SH 88, 1 mile east of Kirkwood on the shores of Caples Lake. Fine dining in an intimate rustic atmosphere. Homemade cuisine includes fresh salmon, mahi mahi, fettucini Alfredo, steak, chicken, and vegetable casserole. Reserve in advance. Selection of fine wines.

**Cornice Cafe Restaurant and Bar   $$**                     *(209) 258-6000*
Across from the Red Cliffs Lodge, the Cornice Cafe Restaurant features California cuisine in an airy dining room. Popular dishes include prawns with roquefort scallion butter, grilled salmon with caviar saffron buerre blanc, and pork tenderloin with fruit chutney. Open for lunch from 11 a.m. to 2:30 p.m. and for dinner from 5:30 p.m. to 10 p.m.

**Snowshoe Thompson's Bar & Restaurant   $$**                *(209) 258-6000*
In the Timber Creek Lodge, Snowshoe Thompson's serves pizza, salad, sandwiches, and pasta.

**Kirkwood Inn   $**                                         *(209) 258-7304*
On SH 88 at the entrance to Kirkwood, the Kirkwood Inn is a rustic log cabin that dates back to 1864. Small and quaint, the room is dominated by the bar. The menu features hamburgers, sandwiches, and soup.

## ACCOMMODATIONS

There are currently 6 condominium complexes at Kirkwood, all within walking distance of the lifts. They range from economy to deluxe and include studios, 1-, 2-, and 3-bedroom units. All have fully equipped kitchens and free firewood. Packages including accommodations and lift tickets are available. For reservations and information, call (209) 258-7000.

**The Meadows    $$$**                                                        *(209) 258-7000*
Kirkwood Village, located midway between Timber Creek Lodge and Red Cliffs Lodge. The Meadows has deluxe rooms, studios, and 1- or 2-bedroom condominiums with smart decor. Studio units each have 1 bathroom, efficiency kitchen, sofa bed, and built-in bunks that sleep up to 4. Units with 1 and 2 bedrooms have 2 baths and full kitchens and sleep from 4 to 6. All units have phones, decks or balconies, and covered parking. TV in most units. A large common room has a fireplace, Jacuzzi, laundry, and game room. Daily maid service.

**Whiskey Run    $$$**                                                        *(209) 258-7000*
Kirkwood Village, adjacent to the Red Cliffs Lodge. Ski-in, ski-out condominiums on the slope. Spacious but spartan units each have 2 bedrooms and mountain views. Phones and TV in most units. Bar and grill on first floor. Daily maid service.

**Edelweiss    $$**                                                           *(209) 258-7000*
Kirkwood Village, across from lifts 7 and 9. Condominiums with 1, 2, and 3 bedrooms with lofts, adjacent to the cross-country trail. Most units have TV and all have phones. Daily maid service.

**Sorensen's Resort    $$**                                                   *(916) 694-2203*
Junction of SH 88 and SH 89, Hope Valley, 15 miles from Kirkwood. Twenty-five country cottages with kitchens, 12 with fireplaces, sleep from 2 to 6. Newer units are the nicest and priced higher. Bunk rooms sleep up to 10. Three bed-and-breakfast rooms share a bath.

**Sun Meadows    $$**                                                         *(209) 258-7000*
Kirkwood Village. Deluxe room studios, and 1-, 2-, and 3-bedroom condominiums with fireplaces in the living rooms and fully equipped kitchens. Most units have TV and all units have phones and views of the mountain and meadows. Daily maid service and covered parking.

**Thimblewood    $$**                                                         *(209) 258-7000*
Kirkwood Village. Moderate 1-bedroom condominiums close to the cross-country ski trails and Timber Creek Lodge. TV in most units. All units have phones and daily maid service.

**Base Camp    $**                                                            *(209) 258-7000*
Kirkwood Village. These 2-bedroom condominiums, the most economical units in Kirkwood, have phones and daily maid service. TV in most units.

# Glossary of Ski Terms

**Alpine Ski Area**—A hill or mountain terrain for skiing downhill.
**Après-ski**—After-skiing social activities and entertainment available at ski areas.
**ATM**—American Teaching Method. A teaching method in which novice skiers are first taught to form a wedge, or "snowplow," to control their skis on a hill before learning to keep their skis parallel.

**Beginner Trail**—Indicates terrain on a downhill slope or cross-country trail suitable for beginner skiers.
**Black Diamond**—A marking on a mountain or trail map indicating difficult terrain, usually suitable for advanced skiers only.
**Blue Square**—A marking on a mountain or trail map indicating a slope that is more difficult than the easier runs, but not as difficult as the advanced. Usually suitable for intermediate skiers.
**Bunny Hill**—A gentle ski slope generally used by beginner skiers.

**Chair Lift**—A motor-driven conveyor consisting of a series of seats suspended from an overhead cable used for transporting skiers uphill to the top of a ski run.
**Chute**—A steep, narrow trail, usually banked on the sides.
**Cornice**—An overhanging ledge of snow or ice.
**Cross-country Skiing**—Movement on skis through the countryside and flatter terrain as opposed to on downhill slopes and runs.
**Cross-country Skis**—Skis used for cross-country skiing, generally lighter and narrower than downhill skis.
**Cruiser**—A smooth run with packed powder and few or no bumps.

**Double Black Diamond**—A marking on the mountain or trail map indicating terrain that is more difficult than the average advanced run, usually for experts only.
**Downhill Race**—A race in which the participants ski straight down a slope with little or no turning, usually at high speeds.
**Downhill Skiing**—Alpine skiing down a mountain, as opposed to on flat terrain as in Nordic/cross-country skiing.

**Freestyle**—Ballet and acrobatics on skis.

**Giant Slalom**—Skiing around widely spaced, upright obstacles or gates set further apart than in slalom skiing, requiring both turning and traversing skills.
**GLM**—Graduated Length Method. A method of teaching beginners to ski by starting them out on short skis and using progressively longer skis as proficiency increases.

# Glossary of Ski Terms

**Green Circle**—Indicates easier runs on a slope or trail map, usually suitable for beginner skiers.

**Half-pipe**—An inclined trail, banked on the sides like a chute, designed for use usually by snowboarders.

**High Speed Detachable Quad**—A chair lift that slows down to let up to four skiers on and off, and then attaches to a faster cable in between.

**Lift Line**—A lineup of skiers waiting for their turn to use the lift.

**Luge**—A small sled that is ridden in a supine position, usually on a specially designed narrow mountain slide with banked sides.

**Mogul**—A bump on a ski run, usually created from the displacement of snow by downhill skiers turning in the same paths.

**NASTAR**—National Standard Race open to the general public, in which participants' times are measured against national pace setters at a given ability level.

**Nordic Skiing**—Also referred to as cross-country skiing, Nordic skiing first evolved as a mode of transportation in the cold, snowbound Nordic and Scandinavian countries. Nordic skiers use lightweight, narrow skis and poles to glide through the countryside.

**Poma Lift**—A surface ski lift consisting of a series of discs hanging from a cable. The cable pulls skiers uphill as they straddle a disc between their legs.

**Powder Skiing**—Skiing on fresh, dry, unpacked snow.

**Rope Tow**—A surface ski lift consisting of a rope that skiers hold on to while being pulled up the hill.

**Schussing**—Skiing fast down a slope.

**Shredders** or **Shred Heads**—Slang for snowboarders.

**Slalom**—Skiing in a zigzag or wavy course between closely set, upright obstacles or gates.

**Skating Lanes**—A track on a cross-country course for skiing on one ski while gliding with the other.

**Snowboard**—A 150cm–200cm plank-like board on which the person stands sidewise, as on a skateboard or surfboard.

**Sno-Park Permit**—A permit purchased from the California Department of Parks and Recreation allowing the purchaser to park his car in designated Sno-Park lots, usually adjacent to public cross-country, snowmobile, or snow-play areas. In California, Sno-Park Permits may be obtained from designated outlets, such as sporting goods stores in the vicinity of the activity, or from the Sno-Park Program Manager, P.O. Box 942896, Sacramento, CA 94296-0001, or by calling (916) 322-8993. Cost is $10 for an annual permit, good from November 1 through May 30, or $2 for a one-day use. A permit does not guarantee the purchaser a place to park, and spaces are available on a first-come, first-served basis. Nevada does not require a permit.

**Snow Play**—Snow-related activities, such as tobogganing, tubing, or sledding, that take place on a snow-covered hill. Designated snow-play areas usually have plowed-out parking spaces and may require a Sno-Park Permit for parking.

**Snowmobile**—A small automotive vehicle with runners for travel on snow.

**Snowplow**—A technique for turning and controlling speed on skis by spreading the skis into a V or wedge position.

**Snowcat**—A tractor used to groom slopes on a mountain.

**Spring Skiing**—A term used to describe snow conditions when they are variable throughout the day. Usually the snow is softened by the warm sun, sometimes to the point of mush, during the day, becoming hard again during the night and early morning. May also imply that snow is thin, granular, or icy, due to a lack of new storms and fresh snow.

**T-bar**—A surface ski lift with a series of T-shaped bars, each of which pulls two skiers up the hill.

**Telemarking**—A turn in cross-country skiing in which the outside ski is advanced considerably ahead of the other ski and then turned inward in a steadily widening angle until the turn is complete. Usually used on a downhill slope.

**Toboggan**—A long, flat-bottomed, light sled made of thin boards curved up at one end, usually with low handrails at the sides.

**Traverse**—Skiing across a slope at a perpendicular angle to the fall line.

**USRSA**—United States Recreational Skiers Association.

**USSA**—United States Ski Association. Formed in 1904, it is the national governing body for the sport of skiing in the United States.

# Index

## A

Alkali Lakes, 7
Almador County, 224
Alpine County, 224
Alpine Meadows, 171–180
Alpine Skills International, 84, 88, 92
Alturas, 3, 5, 7–10
Alturas Ice Rink, 7
Argentine Ridge, 46

## B

Bear Flats, 7
Bear River, 231
Beckwourth, 48
Big Meadow, 231
Bijou Cross-Country Center, 203
Blackwood Canyon Sno-Park, 184, 192
Blairsden, 42, 44, 45, 47–49
Bogard Rest Stop, 38
Boreal, 94, 99–106
Borges Sleigh Rides, 205
Bucks Lake, 46
Bucks Lake Snowmobile Rentals, 46

## C

California Department of Parks and Recreation, 205
Cal-Vada Aircraft, 179, 193
Camp Richardson Corral, 205
Campgrounds, 5, 15, 45, 110, 147, 191, 202, 218, 228
Caples Lake, 219, 224, 232
Carnelian Bay, 126, 127, 128
Carson Pass Sno-Park, 229
Carson Ranger District, 148

Casinos, 138, 206–207
Castle Lake, 16–18
Castle Lake Cross-Country, 16
Castle Peak, 92, 99, 100, 104, 111
Cedar Pass, 3–10
Cedarville, 3, 5, 7–10
Chester, 31–33
Clair Tappan Lodge, 83
Clio, 49
Cody's Hut Ski Treks, 219
Coppervale, 35–41
Cross-Country, 7, 16–17, 27, 38, 46, 83, 91, 104, 111, 124, 136, 137, 148, 160, 184, 192, 202, 219, 229
Crystal Bay, 126, 127, 128, 138, 140, 149, 164

## D

Davis Lake, 47
Day care, 15, 110, 123, 135, 147, 159, 177, 191, 202, 228
Deer Mt. Snowmobile Park, 17
Desolation Wilderness, 203, 220
Diamond Peak, 130–142
Diamond Peak Cross-Country, 136
Dogsled Rides, 205, 232
Donner Lake, 115
Donner Memorial State Park, 84, 111
Donner Ski Ranch, 87–92
Donner Summit, 99
Douglas County, 197

## E

Eagle Lake, 38
Eagle Lake Ranger District, 38

Eagle Lake Summit, 38
Eagle Ridge Outfitters, 105, 112, 125, 161
Echo Lakes Cross-Country, 220
El Dorado County, 197, 215, 224
El Dorado National Forest, 214
Emmigrant Trail Museum, 84, 113

## F

Ft. Bidwell, 7, 8, 10

## G

Gardnerville, Nevada, 137, 149
Glenshire, 113
Graeagle, 42, 43, 44, 46–49
Grass Lake, 231
Granlibakken, 181–185
Gumboat Lake, 20

## H

Hansen's Resort, 204
Heavenly Valley, 196–213
High Sierra Snowmobiling, 126, 161
Heli-skiing, 149
Homewood, 179, 186–195
Hope Valley, 231, 232, 233
Hope Valley Cross-Country, 229
Huckleberry Mountain, 214, 215
Husky Express, 205, 232

## I

Ice fishing, 7, 18
Ice skating, 7, 18, 39, 161, 204
Incline Village, 126, 130–132, 134, 135, 137–142, 150

## J

Jamesville Grade, 38
Johnsville, 43

## K

Kings Beach, 126, 127, 128, 129, 137, 161
Kirkwood, 223–233
Kirkwood Cross-Country, 219, 229
Kyburz, 220

## L

Lake Almanor, 28–30
Lake Davis, 46
Lake Tahoe Visitors Authority, 209, 221
Lake Tahoe Winter Sports Center, 203, 204
Lakes Basin Area, 46
Lamoille, Nevada, 149
Lassen Community College, 35, 37
Lassen County, 35, 38
Lassen National Forest Ranger District, 38
Lassen Park Ski Area, 22–30
Lassen Peak, 22
Lassen Ski Touring Center, 27
Lassen Volcanic National Park, 22–24
Lazy K pack station, 231
Lift ticket, interchangeable,
　Ski Tahoe interchangeable lift ticket, 120, 154, 174, 199, 225
　Ski Tahoe North interchangeable lift ticket, 120, 133, 154, 174, 188
Little Truckee Summit, 110, 112
Loon Lake Cross-Country, 220
Luge, 17

## M

Manzanita Lake, 27
Martis Valley, 126
McCloud, 17–21
Meiss Hut, 231
Meiss Meadows, 203
Mill Creek, 30
Mineral, 23, 27, 29–30
Modoc County, 3
Morgan Summit Snowmobile Park, 27
Mount Rose, 143–150

## Index 239

Mountain Lake Adventures, 161
Mountaineering, 92, 205, 231
Mt. Disney, 78, 80
Mt. Lincoln, 78, 80
Mt. Shasta, 11-12, 15, 17
Mt. Shasta Cross-Country, 16
Mt. Shasta Ranger District, 17-21
Mt. Shasta Ski Park, 11-21
Mumbo Lake, 18

## N

NASTAR, 123, 202
Nevada County, 94, 108
Norden, 77, 78, 84-85, 88, 92, 94
Norpine, 88, 91
North Lake Tahoe, 77-147
Northstar-at-Tahoe, 117-129
Northstar's Cross-Country and Telemark Ski Center, 124
North Tahoe Regional Park, 125, 161

## O

Old Hobart Mill, 105, 125, 161
Old MacDonald's Enterprise, 204

## P

Paige Meadows, 184
Placer County, 78, 88, 95, 100, 118, 152, 172, 181, 187
Plumas County, 31, 42, 45
Plumas Eureka Ski Bowl, 42-50
Plumas Eureka State Park, 42, 43, 46, 47
Plumas Ranger District, 45
Plumas Ski Club, 42, 43
Pollack Pines, 222
Portola, 43, 44, 46-50

## Q

Quincy, 23, 43, 46, 47

## R

Reindeer Lodge, 149
Royal Gorge Cross-Country, 57
Ruby Mountain Heli-Skiing, 149

## S

Scott Camp Creek, 16
Shasta County, 23
Shasta-Trinity National Forest, 16
Sierra Ski Ranch, 214-233
Sierra Ski Teachers Clinics, 103
Sierra Ski Touring, 205, 231, 232
Siskiyou County, 11, 12
Sleigh rides, 84, 87, 113, 125-126, 161, 205, 231
Slide Mountain, 144
Sno-Park permit, 104, 112, 184, 192, 229, 231
Snow Connection, 79, 86, 125, 161
Snow play, 7, 17, 34, 39, 113, 105, 137, 148, 161, 184, 204, 231
Snowboarding, 4, 13, 33, 36, 45, 81, 89, 96, 109, 121, 133, 155, 189, 191, 199
Snowman's Hill, 17
Snowmobiling, 7, 17, 27, 34, 38, 46, 92, 105, 111, 112, 125, 126, 137, 148, 160-161, 184, 192, 204, 231
Snowmobiling Unlimited, 161
Snowshoe Tours, 25
Soda Springs, 94-98
South Lake Tahoe, 196, 176-209, 211-213
Spooner Lake, 202
Spooner Summit, 137
Squaw Valley, 151-170, 171
Squaw Valley Nordic Center, 160
Stateline (South Shore), 197, 202, 206-213
Stover Mountain, 31-34
Strawberry, 221
Strawberry Canyon Cross-Country, 219
Sugar Bowl, 77-86
Sugar Pine Point State Park, 191-193
Susanville, 35, 38-41

## T

Tahoe City, 161, 162, 164–166, 168–170, 179, 180, 185, 195
Tahoe Donner, 106–116
Tahoe Donner Cross-Country, 111, 113
Tahoe Meadows, 148
Tahoe Nordic Cross-Country, 160
Tahoe North Visitors & Convention Bureau, 180, 194
Tahoe Paradise, 218
Tahoe Paradise Sports, 204
Tahoe Queen, 153, 164, 173, 188, 198
Tahoe Ski Bowl, 188
Tahoe Truckee Sports, 125
Tahoe Vista, 126, 127, 128, 132, 134
Tahoma, 194
Taylor Creek, 203
TC Sno Mo's, 160
Tehama County, 23
Toiyabe National Forest, 144
Trail Pass, Ski Tahoe North interchangeable, 111, 125, 137, 203
Trout Creek, 203
Truckee, 84, 92, 105, 113–116, 126, 129, 161
Truckee Chamber of Commerce, 110
Truckee Ranger Station, 112
Twin Bridges, 215, 220

## V

Virginia City, 149
Visitor Center/Tallac Historic Site, 203

## W

Washoe County, 131, 144
Weed, 18, 20
Western America Ski Sport Museum, 56, 92, 99
Westshore Association, 194
Willard Hill, 38
Winter Wonderland, 204

## Z

Zephyr Cove, 204
Zephyr Cove Snowmobile Rentals, 204